FROM BIRTH TO ONE
The year of opportunity

Maria Robinson

OPEN UNIVERSITY PRESS
Buckingham · Philadelphia

Open University Press
Celtic Court
22 Ballmoor
Buckingham
MK18 1XW

email: enquiries@openup.co.uk
world wide web: www.openup.co.uk

and
325 Chestnut Street
Philadelphia, PA 19106, USA

First published 2003

A catalogue record of this book is available from the British Library

ISBN   0 335 20895 9 (pbk)   0 335 20896 7 (hbk)

Library of Congress Cataloging-in-Publication Data
Robinson, Maria.
    From birth to one: the year of opportunity / Maria Robinson.
      p.   cm.
    Includes bibliographical references and index.
    ISBN 0-335-20895-9 (pb) – ISBN 0-335-20896-7 (hb)
      1. Infants–Development.   2. Infants–Care.   3. Parent and infant.
    4. Child care services.   I. Title.
    HQ774 .R614 2002
    305.232—dc21

                                                                2002072513

Typeset by Graphicraft Limited, Hong Kong
Printed in Great Britain by St Edmundsbury Press Ltd,
Bury St Edmunds, Suffolk

CONTENTS

ACKNOWLEDGEMENTS

I would like to thank all those who encouraged me in the writing of this book, especially when I felt I was drowning in a sea of journals, books and papers and the dreaded episodes of self-doubt! The editorial staff at Open University Press were especially patient and constructive in their advice.

Especial thanks to Susan Carter and Stephanie Davydiatis for the time they spent reading the manuscript and for all the help they gave in both a personal and professional capacity. Thanks too to friends who tolerated my lack of sociability and most of all to my husband Stuart who says he will be glad to see me again!

1 INTRODUCTION

The real voyage of discovery consists not in seeking new lands but
in seeing with new eyes.

Marcel Proust (1871–1922)

We must begin again from the very foundations, unless we would
revolve for ever in a circle with mean and contemptible progress.

Francis Bacon (1561–1626)

Life is all about experience – what has happened to us in the past and
what is happening to us now. Experience itself is multi-dimensional
as our lives are affected to a greater or lesser degree by political and
social change, and in this shrinking world the effect of events in distant
countries can influence the circumstances of our day-to-day living.
However, like Russian dolls, where each layer reveals another layer,
when we think about experience we also peel away levels of influence.
The quality of our lives is not only determined by our wider social and
cultural framework but also by our personal, social and professional
relationships. Throughout life our ability to manage life experiences
and our style of living have a qualitative association with our particular
stage of development. We intuitively recognize this and consequently
we label the early years, dividing them into different phases. We refer
to newborns or neonates, infants or babies, toddlers, preschoolers and
schoolchildren.

Of course, this may seem obvious. However, development does not
involve only a physical and cognitive maturation of body and mind but
also an emotional and social distinctiveness that reflects the particular
way in which all of us are able to manage our experiences at a particular
time. In addition, we also have our own particular view, supported by a
shared developmental framework – of which more later.

Once we reach 'adulthood' there is a tendency to consider development
as 'over', when in reality we have the potential to continue developing
cognitively, in particular in the arenas of emotional, social and spiritual
reflection. Wisdom can come with age, but this is not necessarily the case,
especially if these capacities are lost due to an emphasis on, or pursuit
of, 'youth' as the only worthwhile stage of life.

Life stories

Life – and therefore experience – has to have a beginning. One of the great difficulties in our emotionally and morally complex world is that there is no agreed view of when life starts, let alone what life actually *is*. What is true is that as early as 22 weeks into a pregnancy there exists a life that is potentially viable if born. That babies in the womb 'remember' consistent experiences is evidenced by much research as well as the knowledge of mothers themselves, who have long noted that babies will settle when they hear familiar sounds such as household appliances and television programme theme tunes. Time and our chronological life moves on and our individual developmental life story moves along with it, carrying in its wake the accumulation of what happens to us, how we feel and what we know.

CAMEO 1

It is lunchtime in a day nursery. Three babies, all around 8 months of age are hurriedly put into their high chairs. One staff member sits in front of them while another brings the food in bowls together with spoons. The bowls are put down in front of the babies who lean forward eagerly. The staff member begins to feed one baby, the other two look at her and start to bounce and bang on their tables. She tells them to wait. She then stops feeding the first baby and starts with the next; the first baby begins to cry. The third baby still waits. So the process goes on with the babies being fed in this turn-taking way. While she is feeding them, the staff member occasionally talks to them but spends most of the time talking to her colleagues who are sitting with the other children.

CAMEO 2

A health visitor arranges a home visit to carry out a routine 18-month developmental check. She has not seen the child for several months. The mother opens the door and admits the health visitor. As she walks into the sitting room, the boy she has come to see looks up from some toys, stares at her for a moment and then comes towards her and wraps his arms around her knees. His mother laughs and says, 'He always goes up to people like that'.

CAMEO 3

A little girl, about a year old, is brought to a day nursery. It is her first visit and it is Christmas. All around there is noise and activity. She is placed on the floor while her mother goes to see a member of staff. The baby sits quietly, pale, listless. She does not seem to notice her mother's absence nor the presence of the other adults and all the children in the room. A little boy notices her, watches a moment then brings her a teddy and a brick. She looks at the brick, picks it up and smiles at it. Her smile seems joyless. She sits turning the brick slowly in her hands.

In the life stories of each of the participants in these three cameos can be found hints as to what each individual might be thinking and feeling; the quality of their personal experiences. What is so interesting in the case of all children is that their story is influenced by the stories inherent in the adults who care for them. Adults, through their behaviour towards children, provide them with a diversity of experience of both the physical world and the internal world (or 'mental state') of others. We learn about others and ourselves *from* others – we cannot make this discovery alone. However, what we *do* do alone is to make our own meaning from what we experience, because when we come into the world we are already armed with the tools to begin our own storyline. We are born with emotions, with an innate motivation to prefer human faces and an ability to recognize the sounds of our mother's voice and her smell. We already show a temperamental bias towards placidity or activity and our reflexes, such as sucking and rooting, mean that we are already primed to obtain food and, most importantly, to get 'up close and personal'. What happens after this is in the hands of the carers, especially during the first years of life, because it is here more than at any other time that the adult's own story influences the way in which the child's story will unfold. The 'travellers' tales' of parents provide their children with their first reference points. In addition, all human beings share a similar developmental route but each of us sees the routes and the references provided with new eyes.

Human 'oneness'

In science, one of the most telling discoveries has been the 'underlying unity of nature' where apparently diverse forces such as space and time or electro-magnetism and light have been found to be instead examples of a 'unifying oneness' (Stapp 1998). The same principle applies to human beings, because underlying the diversity of human experience and behaviour is a 'unifying oneness': the mechanism by which we all develop. We share our genetic inheritance with all human beings and other creatures – for example, 98.5 per cent is shared with chimpanzees. All humans share a fundamental bodily structure and physiology. Humans stand upright, have two legs and two arms, our mouths are always below our noses and our eyes are placed in line with one another. We all have blood coursing round our bodies and in all the diversity of race, all humans have one of only four blood groups.

The fundamentals of all our natures – the ability to feel, learn and interact – rests in the universal physical, chemical and biological structures of our bodies. However, we not only have shared potential abilities, we also have universal needs (e.g. for social interaction, love and security) and both abilities and needs are united by the one, single unifying mechanism through which all human experience is mediated – the brain. Perry *et al.* (1995) strongly state their belief that all emotional, cognitive, social and psychological functioning takes place in the human brain, and it is therefore within the brain that our minds exist, and therefore our humanity. The brain is hence the great mediator of all experience.

Understanding very early human development is therefore best served by an approach which looks at a wide range of disciplines such as neuroscience, paediatrics, developmental psychology, infant mental health, psychoanalysis and psychiatry. A study of infancy that would fully incorporate all these perspectives is way beyond the scope of this book. However, there is an emphasis throughout on a 'triad' of brain development, experience and internal processes as the fundamental approach taken to thinking about infancy and its place in overall development.

Thinking about infancy

One of the most fascinating aspects of the beginnings of human life is how little we consciously remember about it – and in the case of a forceps delivery perhaps this is a good thing! Infancy is a path we all tread, yet it is almost totally forgotten. However, this 'forgetting' is much more to do with the inability to recall events that are pre-verbal rather than to imagine such memories do not exist. In the first year, what we learn about includes, most importantly, people and first relationships. We also build on what research with babies indicates is an 'abstract' or innate knowledge about, for example, number or gravity. Butterworth (1999) cites some very interesting research about babies and their capacity for noting number changes in presented pictures. Through our concrete experience (i.e. touching, mouthing, tasting, listening, looking) we are able to learn about the reality of the properties of things (objects), motion, space, shape, depth, gravity, colour, light and dark. As we learn the physical reality of what we may innately 'know', we begin to form 'mental representations' of what we have experienced – perceived through our senses. If we did not 'represent' the information we take in, it would not be accessible to recall either consciously or unconsciously. In addition, we begin to learn language, to use social skills, to share meaning and find out what it is to feel emotionally secure. We learn that out of sight does not mean out of mind, we learn what is familiar and what is not, we learn about texture, taste and use all our senses to discover the world around us. We learn about ourselves – and obviously in order to learn, we also remember.

From birth to age 1 is the time when the first map references for any individual's voyage of discovery are put in place. This is not to say that those references cannot be altered – they can – but it may be helpful to compare this first year to our ideas about 'first impressions'. These first 12 months are the individual's 'first impressions' of life and sometimes first impressions can be lasting.

My personal and professional experiences have led me to firmly believe that all those working with children and families, whatever their particular discipline, will find that thinking about, reflecting and learning about development in infancy will further their understanding of both children and their parents. Basically, it is all to do with acknowledging that development is a continuous process with a past as well as a present and a potential future. The behaviour we see and seek to understand, and our own behaviour, changes from moment to moment as we shift our levels of involvement in our current situation, influenced by ongoing bodily sensations (e.g. discomfort, a desire to sneeze, hunger and mood). From the complexity of all this incoming information from external and internal sources, sense is made from what has already gone before. The how and why of each child's own particular way of behaving will help any professional support that child, and furthermore will assist in planning for further care and/or learning opportunities. Knowing the potential impact of inappropriate, troubled or chaotic care in a very young child's life may help support coherent planning for the child's future (resources permitting, which is another issue). In education, children as young as 3 are now eligible for the Foundation Stage curriculum produced by the Qualifications and Curriculum Authority (QCA) for settings that receive nursery grant funding including schools with nursery- and Reception-aged children. Such children are at a very early stage in their developmental history and much of their early development has been involved with learning about relationships, emotions, managing their emotions and building up a picture of who they are in a very basic way. They have only just reached the stage where they fully understand that people and things still exist when separated by time and place, and have learned that people can be the same person even if they have different moods. These two concepts are termed 'object permanence' and 'object constancy' respectively. The teacher and their assistants must be aware of how a child of 3 views the world and whether it is different from a year ago, both from a cognitive and emotional perspective. Understanding a child's cognitive perspective will help us to understand how well they might comprehend what is being asked of them, and the emotional perspective helps clarify how the child might respond. Teachers and other professionals will also be aware of the sheer vulnerability of the concepts such young children have been learning to acquire and how their 'knowledge' can be threatened by new situations and/or distress. The qualitative difference between children will be their own history.

Other professionals such as nursery nurses are coming into contact with infants at younger and younger ages – in some settings from as young as 8 weeks, and in some circumstances babies and very young children are in day care for long periods of time. The importance of staff stability, knowledge and insight into the needs of these babies and the way these needs may change as they develop is paramount.

Adults, children, attitudes – making links and finding reasons

To give an example of the diversity of children and adult responses, we can think about the cameos given on pages 2–3. Dependent on the situation, the general questions we could ask might include:

- Regarding the child(ren):
  What has the child learned about being with their carers, e.g. are adults trustworthy or not?
  What experiences might the child have of being in previously unknown places and/or meeting new people?
  What do we know about the potential stage of development and most usual behaviour at the child's particular age?
  What particular strategies for coping with new situations might the child already have learned?
- Regarding the adults:
  What might be the attitude of the adults towards their work?
  What do they understand about the children they meet?
  What may motivate the responses of the adults to the child?
  What are their beliefs and values about the care and development of children?
  How far do they consider their actions affect the child?

The answers to all these questions (and others of course) help us to understand the relationship dynamics between the adults and the children, and between the adults themselves. Adult responses define their belief system about themselves, about other adults and of course about children. To take a further example, a crying, hysterical child can be seen as requiring comfort and support or as being 'naughty' or 'spoilt'. A child who leaves a parent in a new setting without distress may be thought of as 'confident', and this may indeed be the case. However, the child's response or strategy may also be a 'learned' indifference to the leaving of their carer – including suppression of their possible distress. The labelling of the child as 'confident' may mean that they do not receive the attention that they crave. Only careful observation of a child and the way they respond to the adults caring for them will give a clue as to whether such a response is due to confidence or lack of trust in adults.

Some adults working with children can find 'distress' behaviour such as crying and clinging very disturbing and may adopt a distant or even punitive attitude (e.g. 'You can stay sitting on that chair until you've calmed down'). Others deal with their own feelings by using strategies such as sarcasm (e.g. 'Don't you think you're a bit old for that now?'), pleading (e.g. *'Please* don't cry, come and play') and brisk kindness (e.g. 'Come on, there, there, stop crying and come and see what we can do').

The helplessness that is often felt by professionals in the face of the distressed child can also lead to a variety of advice to the leaving carer, such as leaving quietly when the child is occupied. One can only imagine how the child might feel when they look up to find their carer has gone and they don't know where or when! Parents of course are equally diverse, with some being able to tolerate the child's response and others showing anger, frustration, indifference and so on. Staff in care settings have just as much work coping with parental responses as with those of the children – plus their own responses to both!

It seems surprising that we adults expect (or perhaps more truthfully, *want*) very small children to undergo new experiences without turning a proverbial hair – because of course if children do this, it saves our feelings. However, we adults in comparable situations know that we can feel a whole gamut of emotions! Very few adults find situations such as going to a party where they know only the host, attending an interview, a first day at a new job or college completely anxiety-free. We have learned not to cry or rage when we can't even find the entrance to a building or when no one will speak to us at a party, but we may still feel like it! The only difference is that we have learned to manage our emotions in a particular way.

Very young children, who are only just beginning to learn the social niceties of what emotions you can express in public, simply let you know how they are feeling. These raw expressions of emotion, particularly distress or rage, are frequently painful for adults who often don't want to fully acknowledge or identify with what the child is experiencing. We therefore adopt our defence strategies and this in turn can lead to us behaving in ways that on reflection we wish we did not. This is crucial, because although children are much less skilled as 'emotion managers' they, like us, behave in response to feelings.

All children need to feel secure and that emotional security is learned from the ongoing relationships of a child with their adult carer(s), based on the patterns of behaviour laid down in the first year. Changes in internal perspectives can occur throughout the life cycle, but initially the potential for alleviating negative experiences, reinforcing positive ones or (most dangerously for the child) reinforcing negative ones, lies in the hands of the adults who come into contact with the child.

New births, new beginnings

Emde (1985: 325) movingly describes the powerful emotions that are commonly evoked in adults by infants. The birth of a new baby represents a 'new beginning; it is a time of promise when there are, as yet, few disappointments'. He goes on to say that in many families, and in society in general, a new baby can represent hopes that unfulfilled wishes, dreams and desires may come to fruition. Thus babies enter the world carrying not only their parents' genetic inheritance, their particular innate temperament and a predisposition to form relationships with their carers, but also the hopes and fantasies of their future life which their parents might harbour. However, it must be stressed that personal beliefs, attitudes, experience and personal parenting history affect how all of us respond to babies, young children and their families.

In order to work positively and effectively with children, it seems a cliché to say that we need to recognize the individuality of each child and to put the needs of that child first. However, in practice, to work towards achieving this ideal it is important to start at the beginning and to acknowledge our own attitudes and beliefs about babies and their development in general and about each baby we work with in particular. Some important questions are:

- What do I usually see when I look at babies? What do I see when I look at this baby? (Is it the same?)
- What do I usually feel when I look at babies? What do I feel when I look at this baby?
- What is my knowledge and understanding about what babies in general can do and what do I know about what this baby can do?
- What is my understanding of how babies learn about themselves and others? How does this baby react to me, parents and other adults?
- What is my understanding of the impact of experience on development? What is this baby's history?

The circumstances of your role and interventions will circumscribe the depth to which you will need to answer each question and the availability and/or appropriateness of the information, but these questions represent a yardstick for thinking about those with whom you have contact.

Thinking about needs

Babies essentially need love from their carers, but what does this actually mean? The answer to the question 'What is love?' has exercised the mind of poets, philosophers and playwrights throughout history. Montagu (1994) says: 'Love is the ability to communicate to others your profound involvement in their welfare, that you will never commit the supreme treason of letting them down whenever they most stand in need of you, and that you will minister to and encourage the growth and development of their potentialities. That's love'. Put like this, it is easy to see that the simple statement 'Babies need love from their carers' brings with it a huge packet of responsibility. Loving a baby essentially means being:

- sensitive to methods of communication (body language, eye contact, facial expression, crying and later smiling);
- emotionally 'available' for the baby (simply being physically present is a long way from the whole picture);
- able to spend time attending to physical needs and providing additional stimulation through play and playful experiences;
- sensitive to the need for rest and quiet times, for safety and routine, for warmth – both physical and emotional.

A daunting list! It demonstrates very clearly that 'loving' a baby means very much more than an idealized, romantic version that can be seen as essentially passive. To carry out 'love in action' is a much more dynamic and demanding process. A further aspect is that this giving of love in such a context by a parent to a baby is a 'one-way system'. The baby needs to learn to 'love' – that is, form a strong bond between themselves and the parents – but the parents have to do it first!

A great deal of research on babies and young children has indicated that the experiences outlined above help the baby to learn about emotional security. It is a complex process that combines a consistent, stable, caring environment, including physical comfort and warmth, with an emotional environment of warmth, caring and acceptance. Over time, the dual effect of combined external and internal sensations begins to form part of the baby's psychological development. In turn, feelings of emotional safety or the lack of it influence the baby's view of the world and lay the foundations for future relationships. To put it very simply, 'It's not what you do, it's the way that you do it'.

The very apparent need of babies for physical care and attention can encourage an emphasis on these needs with the result that less attention is paid to the dramatic and fantastic explosion of development in the realms of social, emotional and cognitive understanding. This situation may be a reason for the perpetuation of the sad myth that anyone

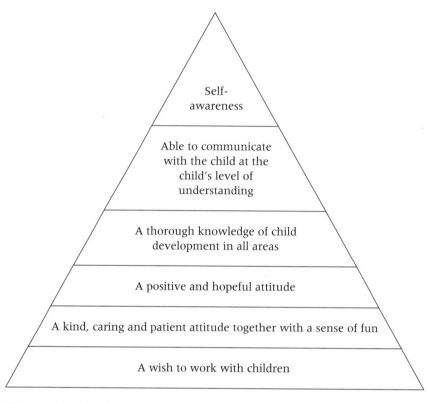

Figure 1.1   Ideal attributes for early years professionals (format based on Maslow's hierarchy of needs)

(especially if female) can look after babies. This means that, in some circumstances, people without training and/or experience can be employed to look after infants at a sensitive period of development. A quick overview of advertisements for 'nannies' or 'mother's helps' will provide a graphic illustration of this point. The unhappy paradox is that in the first year of life babies need the most sensitive and skilled care adults are capable of giving.

Figure 1.1 reflects my views on the fundamental requirements for anyone working with infants and very young children.

About the organization of this book

There are two parts to the book. The first deals with the main topic of developmental progression in the first year and the intimate links between development and baby/adult interaction. Chapters 4, 5 and 6 deal with development from birth to 3 months, from 3 to 7 months and from 8 to 12 months. These 'blocks' very broadly correspond with the 'peaks' in brain activity that accompany increasingly complex modes of emotional expression, cognition and behaviour. Of course, development in individual children is not so clearly defined and varies both within individual children and within domains. For example, a child may achieve mobility 'quickly' but may be less rapid in their ability to grasp or make sounds. Readers are encouraged to think about links between all aspects of development, and the thought-provoking direct links between actual experience and brain development during this period.

The importance of social and emotional development underpins Part 1. One of the most powerful theoretical approaches to social and emotional interaction – attachment theory – is discussed in Chapter 6. However, the process of forming attachments is also an integral part of the preceding chapters. Attachment theory has been given prominence because it provides an extremely powerful and well-researched approach (in both humans and primates) for understanding individual variance in social interaction and behaviour. Anecdotal evidence from colleagues in psychology and social work testifies to the effective use of this approach in thinking about children and their parents. However, the widely disseminated teaching of attachment theory brings an inherent danger, as there can be a temptation for professionals to categorize the perceived quality of children's attachments to their carers. For example, children can be loosely described as 'insecure', 'avoidant' and so on without the requisite, formal assessment having taken place. In these instances, judgements may have been made on the basis of relatively brief and/or short-term observation in varying contexts and with little opportunity for the practitioner to 'check out' their own objectivity. The best one can and should do in these circumstances is to report that the child's *observed behaviour* may indicate a particular type of attachment relationship because . . . followed by clear examples. Another danger is that only attachment relationships to the mother may be considered without reflection on the actual relationship the child may have with the father and/or other male or female carers. Nevertheless, these dangers aside, this theoretical approach to understanding how we humans acquire emotional security and develop relationships with others does provide rich and meaningful opportunities for insight and reflection.

The responsibility of parenthood and, by default, the responsibilities of those who come into contact with babies and young children providing care and/or interventions/assessment is very great. Chapter 3 sets out to reflect on what being a parent can mean to individuals, the reasons for becoming a parent in the first place and how these issues combine together to influence the way parents behave towards their new infant. While considering the parent during the pregnancy, we need to consider the concurrent development of the baby within the womb. Professionals who are parents themselves may find that some of their own attitudes to parenting and experiences of being parented influence their day-to-day work. It is sometimes very difficult for professionals to recognize that their own parenting style may be reflected in the parents they work with – negatively as well as positively.

The final chapter in Part 1 is entitled 'Unhappy babies'. Although we may prefer not to think of babies in this way, nevertheless babies will respond to their surroundings emotionally. The potential source of un-happiness is the same for babies as it is for adults: the quality of relation-ships, the interactions we have with those around us and the overall environment in which we live. A baby, of course, cannot define 'happi-ness' or 'unhappiness', but it is able to present a 'feeling response' to its experiences.

What all those who come into contact with babies and their families need to fully acknowledge is the importance of themselves in the deliv-ery of quality care and interventions. Part 2 provides an opportunity to think about professional and personal issues that may cause difficulty and/or distress while working with babies and their families. It reflects my very strong belief about the vital role of the individual as a person when working professionally in the early years – and indeed in any of the 'caring' professions. Work with infants and their families is demand-ing, in no small part due to the emotional impact that such work can have, such as the realities of becoming 'attached' to the babies in our care, and the mixed emotions that arise from working with their fami-lies, both positive and negative. For example, feeling a sense of rivalry or judgement about the parents' attitudes and approach to their child.

Professionals might also face personal and professional difficulties in their practice when dealing with painful situations such as neglect and other forms of abuse, disability, separation and loss. What is so interest-ing is that, while situations are always difficult, any one situation may present particular difficulties to individual workers because of their own unique personalities and psychological histories. Identifying and dealing with the realities of personal defences against professional and personal anxieties demands great courage on the part of the professional.

Using the information

Readers can consult different chapters in isolation as time and need permit. The format also enables those who wish only to reflect on their working practice (Part 2) to do so without needing to read the develop-mental section. It is also possible to read Chapter 2 in isolation as this gives a general overview of certain aspects of early development, in particular the important role that social and emotional development plays in the overall life of an individual. The chapter also provides a broader framework for thinking about infancy, acknowledging that infancy is literally only the first part of a lifelong developmental journey.

There is one final practical issue and that is the use of terminology. It is one of the drawbacks of psychology that terminology is often obscure, interchangeable or has different terms, dependent on the theoretical 'school', for approximately the same concept! For example, emotions. Any reader familiar with psychoanalytical literature will find that 'emotions' are frequently described as 'affects', and the two terms can be used interchangeably. Another example, which has relevance when thinking about how a baby learns about the world around them is the use of the word 'object' – which in psychoanalytical terms refers to mental representations of people together with an amalgam of associated perceptions, feelings and so on with emotions as the centre. In contrast, in the terminology of cognitive developmental psychologists such as Piaget, the term 'object' (helpfully clarified by Perlow 1995) refers to a 'toy' or rather, a 'thing'. 'Representations' or mental objects, from this standpoint, refer to 'cognitive representations of reality'. Usage of similar terms for widely divergent concepts and approaches can cause confusion as we struggle to understand how an infant 'gets to grips' with day-to-day experience. Nevertheless, thinking about what is going on inside the 'mind' of the infant is an important part of being able to support the holistic health of that child.

Potential barriers to reflection on developmental influences

Finally, there are a few 'ground rules' to guide your thinking and reflecting on the ideas, issues and concepts discussed in this book, because of their emphasis on the power of the emotional context of interactions between adults and infants/children. First, let me offer a note of caution to all of you who work with and/or study children, their development and the adults around them. No human adult is 'perfect' and we can all behave towards others – family, friends, colleagues and clients/patients – in ways we regret from time to time. It is also impossible because of the stresses and strains in our own lives to be endlessly patient, kind and sensitively aware of the needs of others, both in our personal and professional lives. We get angry, impatient, frustrated and sometimes it is us – you and I – who are in need of the kindness, patience and tolerance of others, including our client group – whether they be children or adults.

Following on from the unreality of 'perfection' we come to 'blame'. Blame, or rather *blaming*, implies a simple cause and effect scenario that is unhelpful. We human beings are more complex than that and even the worst of human behaviour has a logic of sorts. On the other hand a desire *not* to blame can also mean that issues such as the early impact of parents on children, the influence of lifestyle and the quality of day care may not be discussed fully for fear of being accused of 'mother blaming'. However, just as blame is unhelpful, so is burying our heads in the sand and trying to pretend that what we adults do to children doesn't really affect them – after all, we have been affected by our early experiences! Parents are responsible for their own actions towards their children and their actions have reasons. In each parent there exists an internal, personal logic based on the baggage of their own parenting and life experiences, and what these mean to them. Of course, the same is true for any adult working with infants and young children. That is why when, as a society, we think about the reasons for unwanted behaviour in children and the negative attitudes and beliefs that their parents may demonstrate, we need to perform a difficult balancing act. We need to look at the adult's present behaviour and past experiences with an honest and compassionate eye *and* keep the needs of the child paramount with a full and frank acknowledgement of how the adult may be affecting the child.

A note of hope: a baby is not going to be affected by a carer's transitory moods and behaviour unless this leads to experiences that are frightening or disturbing to the baby who will then, like anyone else, need time to recover confidence. What is important is the *general ethos* of the family or care framework in which the baby spends most of its time. If the baby is loved, appreciated and respected then it is far better able to tolerate the adult's 'failings'. Nevertheless, the potential power of early experiences cannot, and should not, be underestimated.

I must add that topics or thoughts within this book may activate memories of your own childhood or circumstances in the lives of your own children, or bring a particular case history to mind which may be difficult or rather painful. All I can say is that if this happens – and work or study concerning children always runs this risk – there is a choice. We may feel regret or sadness or self-blame but we can also take a deep breath and think about how we can reflect on our past differently – with compassion and understanding of past selves and/or the past selves of others – and move on.

We must also acknowledge and celebrate the fact that most human beings (including ourselves!) are essentially balanced, caring people who function well within their particular society/culture, are understanding of others and show kindness and compassion – all thanks to sensitive and loving parent families and other carers/educators.

Part 1
DEVELOPMENT IN THE FIRST YEAR

2 MAKING CONNECTIONS: A PERSPECTIVE ON DEVELOPMENT

One of the most obvious facts about grown-ups to a child is that they have forgotten what it is like to be a child.

Randall Jarrell (1914–65)

Children have never been very good at listening to their elders, but they have never failed to imitate them. They must, they have no other models.

James Baldwin (1924–87)

We humans are inextricably linked to time. Our lifespan is marked out in years and our daily lives by hours, minutes and seconds. We are linked to the timely rhythms of our planet and our process of development is also linked to an internal biological clock, which while presenting a broad range between individuals and affected by cultural practices, nevertheless establishes a framework common to all human beings. We move from one developmental framework in each separate but intimately connected domain to the next, building on the past as we go. Perry (2001) states that 'time pushes us through life, from one developmental stage to another. The brain develops, changing its organization and function from infancy to early childhood, through adolescence and into adulthood. We have little choice in this matter'.

Time also is involved with the simultaneous way that the different inputs from our bodies and the external environment are 'put together' in the brain, a synchronised orchestration which produces the apparently immediate thoughts and actions which emerge as a continuous conscious stream – a result of the constant shifts of environmental input.

Development is also all about transitions. All our lives are a series of transitions: conception to birth, birth to toddlerhood, toddler to pre-schooler, school-age child to adolescent, adolescent to adult, adult to our final transition – when we die. Throughout this time we have the capacity for change and adaptation, but we all need a starting point. Our universal starting point is when we emerge from our mothers into the world as a bundle of raw, unregulated emotion. From that first moment through our primary experiences of need and response comes the formation of the first feelings of emotional security and safety. In the life of an infant the minute by minute, hour by hour experiences serve to provide a mass of information which the child 'learns from', gradually becoming acquainted with what is familiar. We gradually build, adapt, review and/or consolidate our sense of self from these humble beginnings.

As Perry (2001) says, growth and development in the brain are also affected by and dependent on experience. What the child experiences on a daily basis will affect all aspects of their being, including their ability to learn – in their personal, social, formal and informal educational environments. Although it is not always possible, for a variety of reasons, for those working with children to have access to even limited knowledge of the varying relationships within a specific child's family, it is vitally important that professionals have regard for the importance of the social and emotional context in which any child lives out their day-to-day existence.

The importance, therefore, of the quality of early interactions provides the link between the different elements discussed here which address the broad key areas of development in early childhood. These are: emotions and emotional regulation/management (which includes communication, meaning and understanding); learning and memory; making relationships; and the forming of an idea of self and behaviour. The organ where thinking, feeling and learning takes place is of course the brain, so aspects of brain development will be discussed throughout.

Understanding development: why, what and how

Why?

The why of development is a philosophical question that includes what 'makes' a human being and what is our purpose. We could say that development, especially in the early years from birth to adolescence, is a preparatory time for 'adulthood'. As adults we are, in general, expected to be able to self-motivate, carry out actions independently, have a view of who we are, have a sense of morality and behave in accordance with the social and legal 'rules' of our society and culture. We are also expected to be able to care for and protect those who are young and/or vulnerable, form lasting relationships and (usually) have children of our own. As we get older we continue to react to changing events and our particular perspective will affect the way in which we carry out our adult 'tasks'. As adults we may gain increasing understanding of our own motivations and behaviour, and build on or gain (and even regain) positive feelings of self-esteem/self-worth. We may, however, be stuck in an emotional 'time warp' where every frustration appears to be personally directed towards us; when our understanding of others remains at a basic level achieved by a 5- or 6-year-old. Just as reading levels can be different in adults, with some never reaching (or even wanting to reach) beyond a basic stage, so can emotional and/or social development remain at basic levels, not necessarily related to cognitive or language development. For example, someone can be highly intelligent but still prone to throw things, 'lash out' verbally or physically or sulk when frustrated. How we live our lives depends on the way we understand and give meaning to our experiences, but we all learn about the same skills – supported and promoted by the adults around us. It is the depth, type and quality of our learning in all developmental domains that differentiates people – our sense of self and our ability to take our place in the world.

What?

Development from birth to 1 is obviously only a part of a lifetime's story of change and development. What therefore do we mean by 'development'? Does this have the same meaning for a baby, a toddler, an adolescent, an adult or someone approaching their final years? The answer is both yes and no. The domains of development remain the same throughout life – i.e. emotional (including spiritual), social, cognitive, language and physical – but the focus and emphasis, both physiologically and psychologically, change. Physical development, for example, is extremely important from birth to adolescence with a strong, innate physiological/biological time frame. However, other domains of development can modify and change throughout the lifespan. This brings us to another question: whether development has distinct 'stages' or whether it is part of a more fluid, dynamic process. Again, the possible answer is both. Human development appears to have distinct 'shifts' which seem to be universal, but each shift depends on the previous aspects of development being in place and on the nature of the current experiences afforded to the child. To take a simple physical example, a baby develops head control before being able to develop upper body posture. A baby left for hours and days in their cot has the potential capacity for head control, sitting and moving but the *rate and quality* of this development will be adversely affected. Differences in the quality of development in each domain may therefore be influenced by either a genetic/biological positive or negative predisposition and/or by influences within each human's environmental experiences.

There is also considerable evidence that although we humans develop at our own individual pace, nevertheless we follow a common underpinning, temporal pattern of development which includes times when 'learning from experience' is at its optimum – sometimes termed 'sensitive periods'. The classic example that first indicated the existence of sensitive periods was the discovery that the functioning of the visual cortex in cats was irreversibly affected with deprivation of experience 2–3 months after birth and did not repair on subsequent introduction of 'normal experience'.

In order to support children's development and ensure parental/educational/social experiences are appropriate, we need to acknowledge that sometimes opportunities lost or inappropriate experiences during these 'sensitive periods' may mean difficulties (although not necessarily impossibilities) in the future. These sensitive periods also have some links with noted surges in brain activity. These surges in turn seem to occur after a plateau or even a decrease in brain activity. This process suggests that a shift or 'discontinuity' in a particular domain of development follows a period of consolidation of the integration between innate processes and experience. For example, the period between 6–12 months of age is when babies lose their ability to recognize sounds not used in their own particular language. Instead, they 'tune in' to the sounds of their native language. Hence, a Japanese baby can hear the difference between the sounds of 'r' and 'l' but can no longer do this when a year old. Thai babies can hear three 'steps' between the sounds 'p' and 'b' and so can English babies – but not for long! The particular brain connections which are 'unused' consistently appear to be 'pruned'. As adults it is certainly possible for us to learn new languages, but we are best at this before the age of 11. After this it becomes very difficult to learn languages fluently as the ability to differentiate between subtle sounds has gone. A further example is children who, for some reason, have restricted opportunities to walk until around the age of 4, and will learn to walk later, but never quite as smoothly as their unrestricted peers.

Sensitive periods also apply to emotional development. Children who have previously been raised in very emotionally deprived environments will still be able to form attachments to new carers beyond 3 years, but there is evidence that the quality of these attachments may be vulnerable. Several researchers point out that while experience is important for healthy development in all areas, additional 'enrichment' of the child's environment beyond what is 'normal' for most children seems to have little effect. The picture that seems to be emerging is that it is impoverished environments – whether emotional, cognitive, social or physical – that appear to make the difference, not enriched ones. Greenough and Black (1992) differentiate between what they term 'experience expectant' and 'experience dependent' learning in the brain. Experience expectant implies the type of learning that all humans would encounter – for example, the visual system 'expects' exposure to light. However, experience dependent brain development responds to the individual experiences of human beings.

It is important to remember that as 'external' time marches on and the child develops greater skills, their understanding will still be framed by their own specific knowledge as well as their cognitive (learning) ability – their own internal 'developmental clock'. Children with Down's syndrome, for example, may not recognise themselves in a mirror until nearly 3 years, and sometimes later than this – i.e. until they have reached that particular stage of cognitive understanding which unimpaired children usually achieve around 18 months. Conversely, it is only when children are able to understand what others might be thinking and feeling ('mental states') that an adult's behaviour towards the child can be more accurately assessed by the child – i.e. the child can begin to ascribe motives to what adults do.

A further point is that for each child, their particular skills or capacities will vary not only across developmental areas but also within them. For example, a child may be excellent at running and jumping but find threading beads hard. Both are aspects of physical/motor development but are at different stages of development within the child, although overall the child may well be developing satisfactorily in more 'global' parameters of age-appropriate physical development. They can thread beads, but not as skilfully as they can run and jump. The other factor to consider is that all aspects of development link together and this is true for the different aspects of physical/physiological development as well. For example, children normally achieve adult visual levels of perception and sensitivity at around 4–6 years, whereas peripheral vision and contrast sensitivity are not reached until 6–7 years. Similarly it is between the ages of 3–6 years that the 'fine detail' of development in motor movement and language begins to take place as the left side of the brain continues its surge in activity. Both vision and motor development combine together to enable children 'refine' their skills.

Educators therefore need to think carefully about a child's general development and their individual developmental characteristics when attempting to assess progress or teach a new skill as well as other issues such as timing in a global sense – i.e. does the teacher think the child is ready for this next step? Children are not able to perform tasks for which they are not developmentally ready. This principle applies equally to babies and their carers. Babies need to have carers who are in tune with the various stages of development so that they can support and promote the infant in forming relationships and listening to language, at the same time ensuring that they do not overstimulate, exhaust or make unreasonable demands. For example, expecting an 8-month-old baby not to feel and play with their food.

How?

The way that development occurs is a complex interaction between nature and nurture, brought together by a ceaseless learning process. As will be seen in Chapters 3 and 4, we enter the world with a wide array of skills ready to meet our environment. Initially, that environment is provided solely by our immediate carers. Learning takes place through the synthesizing of all the information received from experience (Fox *et al.* 1994; Schwarz and Perry 1994; Perry *et al.* 1995; Panksepp 1998; Perry 1998; Perry and Pollard 1998). This information initially arrives at different parts of the brain (e.g. visual information arrives mainly, although not exclusively, at the visual cortex). However, the synthesis and ultimate meaning of the information mainly takes place in the prefrontal cortex, situated behind our foreheads.[1] This, the 'newest' part of our brain, is a large deep layer of neurons which covers the two hemispheres of the brain, and is the area where we process sensations, movements and thoughts. Each hemisphere is further divided into four areas or lobes: the frontal, parietal, temporal and occipital. Each of these areas is associated with different functions, although the brain works essentially by parallel processing of the information received and so we appear to 'respond' immediately to sensory input.

Ultimately, learning from our experiences takes place through patterns of similarity and the introduction of difference or novelty. In order that we can understand differences, we have first to have discovered similarities. In turn, we learn about similarities through a process of familiarization or 'habituation'. Through repeated experiences we then form patterns or templates of understanding through an association between the various stimuli we have received, including our internal/emotional responses as well as stimuli such as pain, pressure, temperature, joint position, muscle sense, movement, touch, smell, sound, taste and vision. Through this process, we can learn to 'ignore' familiar background sensation (e.g. the touch of our clothes, the feel of the floor) so that we can concentrate on people or objects that interest us. This habituation or familiarity also means that we can make 'predictions' about what might happen. To take a simple example, if you or I drop something, we know that it will fall to the floor. Those physicists among you will also know that an object falls at a particular rate. We know that objects don't roll uphill. If something did roll uphill (as was apparently the case on the 'magic road' on Craggy Island in the Channel 4 television comedy *Father Ted*), this experience would bring in the other dimension of how we learn – novelty. When something happens which is different to what we anticipate, our brains try to make sense of the new information, causing a shift in our previous knowledge base. This can apply to any type of learning and the subsequent strength of the cognitive, emotional and behavioural associations we make will influence how far this new experience will build on or revise our previous 'knowledge'.

For example, abstract concepts such as insight fundamentally arise from the physical processes within the brain – a result of the simultaneous exquisite connections of thousands of neurons[2] forming a new pattern in the micro-universe of our brains in response to some stimuli which could be as prosaic as watching steam rising from a kettle or an apple falling to the ground. The new patterns formed by the brain's response to both internal (physical or emotional) and external stimuli are built out of the connections laid down in response to similar stimuli in the past. The 'new thought' or skill occurs when the organization of the stimuli achieves a particular coherence brought about by the addition of a stimuli which of itself may be 'ordinary' but provides the final link in that particular chain. Einstein, for example, began to develop his famous theory of relativity when he imagined what it might be like to ride a beam of light. The stimulus here was the idea of riding the beam of light, but all the information he needed was already there – as possibly was the theory – just waiting for the right connection!

This emphasis on repetition and familiarity has another dimension for those who wish to support children's learning. We learn about people and things by forming 'representations' of both. This is a form of patterning whereby, through a mix of sensory and emotional experience, we build up a 'picture' or representation of living and inanimate objects. For example, a child forms a 'representation' of four-legged creatures and then, over time, can differentiate between, for example, dogs, cows and horses. What actual form this representation takes in our brains is still unknown (i.e. whether it is a chemical or formed from signal patterns composed of light and/or sound). However, somehow experiences are collected together, transformed into packets of information, memorized, embedded in emotion, shaped by meaning and then filed away by the brain – available for recall by either conscious thought or other stimuli such as sight, sound, touch, smell or taste. If we think of how a smell can evoke a long-forgotten memory or a taste can remind us of an experience, or how a touch can bring comfort or fear, we can begin to comprehend the complexity of our brain coding, memory and 'filing' systems. What this also demonstrates, as Damasio (1994) points out, is that whatever the mechanism our 'representations' are real to us and over time we know that others can make similar 'images' which are remarkably consistent.

What we can safely assume is that there will be a logical formation of events within the brain as there is evidence of pattern and number throughout the universe. For example, music is closely linked to mathematics and the diversity of physical and chemical manifestations rest on just a few fundamental laws. A glimpse of the underlying logic of the processes or systems of our brains can be shown in many ways and seems to follow the innate 'guidelines' for development. For example, once the fertilized human egg starts to divide, the genetic blueprint provides the destination of each of those dividing cells – liver, brain, blood, heart, hormonal system, reproductive system – and this truly amazing process proceeds in an orderly and highly structured way. Development outside the womb seems to me to proceed in the same coherent way with each stage or phase the culmination of both experience and unfolding physical maturation in the body and brain. I was very happy to discover that what I had intuitively felt was supported by research that indicates that 'learning' is 'interleaved' and also takes place slowly, so that previously learned information is not 'undone' by the new information coming in.

To highlight this, the development of the relatively new (in evolutionary terms) cerebral cortex of our brains seems to follow an overall pattern of growth from the back to the front and there are differences in emphasis in the growth of different parts of the brain. For example, between the ages of 17 and 21, this growth seems particularly focused on the frontal cortex which deals with 'executive' (i.e. rational and logical) processes. When we consider that this is about the age when many teenagers stop 'grunting' or taking degrees in flouncing and start speaking again, it makes sense!

In addition, actual brain growth also follows a sequence, although different brain areas are involved in varying degrees depending on what is going on at the time, both in terms of specific and more generalized development. Overall, there appears to be a period of rapid growth followed by a deceleration and then a plateau. If we consider walking as an example we can see how this sequence works. First, babies move unsteadily, with little coordination and much effort. Then walking in a straight line becomes easier, then they can negotiate obstacles and eventually they are able to walk smoothly and easily without 'noticing'. The various brain areas required are firing away at a great rate once mobility begins. Once the required connections are established, activity decreases and then stabilizes.

The extent that basic skills are 'hard wired' is demonstrated when, for example, we might be asked to go to another room or area. We all walk forwards and generally adopt a direct route to where we want to go, moving around obstacles which may be in our path.

A further example is learning to ride a bicycle. This involves a coordinated set of movements which have had to be practised in order to establish a pattern between brain, nerves and muscle. However, a child must be able to walk and balance before learning to ride a bike so the new skills learnt are built on pre-existing skills. Great neuronal activity would resume again for running, hopping, dancing or riding your bike with your feet on the handlebars until that too became 'easy'. A study of adults by Fletcher *et al.* (2001) demonstrated that brain activity in the frontal cortex decreases and disappears as tasks become well learned and automatic but that activity in a part of the prefrontal cortex is activated by unpredictability or novelty.

This patterning of learning stretches across all aspects of development. A baby learns that opening the fingers means an object held 'drops', and keeps repeating the action. Educators talk of 'schemas' – when children find the different associations between, for example, up and down, side to side and inside and outside by repeating patterns of behaviour such as constantly hiding and retrieving objects, 'posting' objects and wrapping anything that does not move (Nutbrown 1999)!

We need familiarity and repetition to help us learn. The evidence for this is supported by interesting research with primates. Merzenich *et al.* (1988) showed, for example, that monkeys given a food acquisition task where they could use only three fingers illustrated that not only did the repetition of the task produce strengthening of the neural connections involved but also affected the shape of the particular region (presumably because of the actual increased density of connections between the neurons). Learning through repetition therefore strengthens the 'memory' for that task and also has a neuroanatomical outcome in that the actual shape of the brain can be altered.

We can see that babies and children (and therefore you and I) build on the concepts we already know and those working with babies and young children will often be in the situation of helping a child develop a new skill or widen their knowledge/experience. The adult's skill is demonstrated by their ability to recognize when the child may be ready to learn something new and build on what the child can do. Their response to the child's efforts will then influence how the child might learn how to persist and try again. For example, if a child is asked to do something that is beyond their particular capacity and receives a negative response from the adult, leading to upset and frustration, this may, if repeated over time, lead to a fear of failure and a reluctance to try anything new. This can be illustrated by considering the potential difficulties of a 4-year-old child with poorly developed fine motor skills when asked to write his name 'neatly'. The 'neat' part is actually beyond the child's abilities and failure to achieve this goal can lead to problems. As we saw above, the child's fine motor development is only in its early stages. In addition, the degree of 'neatness' required by individual educators may vary, adding to the child's burden of trying to work out and do what the adult wants.

There are two other important factors in the 'how' of development.

First, the particular 'dominance' of one or other side of the brain, and second the chemical processes within the brain. The cortex of our brains is divided into two main hemispheres with the older parts of the brain straddling underneath both areas. The two hemispheres are joined by a body known as the 'corpus callosum'. In the first three years of life, the right side of the brain is the most active developmentally. This side has been shown to be strongly associated with emotions and also with the ability to take the 'overall view' both visually and later metaphorically. We need our right brains to provide us with the range of options which our left brain then reduces down into our (hopefully) logical choices. What is fascinating is that this dominant right hemisphere is more 'tuned in' to low auditory tones, to outline, to general shape and size, facial recognition and space perception. As Ornstein (1997) puts it, the right hemisphere is 'much quicker and more accurate at detecting very large waves of visual information whereas the left is much better at detecting the very short waves'. The right hemisphere overall provides babies with the wherewithal to 'get a handle' on their experience. The left hemisphere begins to overtake the right at around 18 months and is very active between 3–6 years when the importance of grammatical structure in language becomes vital as young children learn the vagaries of their own language. It is also around this time that the symptoms of autism begin to be more apparent. (I say more apparent as parents are often aware that something may not be 'right' beforehand.)

What is very clear from research studies on people who have suffered right or left hemispheric brain damage is that while in many people the left hemisphere is the most 'dominant' – possibly due to our emphasis on spoken language and our need for logical thought – loss of function in the right hemisphere means that people are no longer able to gain a comprehensive view of their world. The hemispheres are in many ways 'mirror' images of each other but the function of each hemisphere is focused on different aspects of the same stimuli. To again use speech as an example, both hemispheres are involved with speech but process different aspects. This 'mirroring' seems to affect handedness (we all have a preferred hand while needing both) and the way we move. Research shows that even frogs and toads have a preferred 'paw' and males and females when simply moving around will naturally turn mainly in one direction – males to the right and females to the left! The left hemisphere appears to be responsible for the fine detail, such as the individual details of vision and fine motor movements, which explains why in non-musicians, the right hemisphere is more involved when thinking about melodies while musicians seem to use the left hemisphere more as they are more skilled at identifying the finer details of the melody while a non-musician (like myself) would be more focused on the overall 'tune'. Thinking about when the left hemisphere becomes the centre of the developmental stage may indicate why it may be potentially counterproductive to introduce formal 'writing' exercises to preschool children while their fine motor capacity is still developing, and illustrates how knowledge about our brain development should be taken into account when considering the implementation of educational ideals.

In the first years of life, we need to know the general information about what and who we encounter, we need to be able to process the major emotions and to understand where we are in space in relation to our environment. We need to get the 'broad view' and this skill remains the domain of the right hemisphere throughout life.

Second, we need to think about the influence of chemicals in the brain. As stated in Note 2, messages are passed between the dendrites of neurons by chemical messengers (neurotransmitters) which provide the one-way communication channels. So the workings of the brain are both electrical and chemical and it is the chemicals that 'decide' the messages. Panksepp (1998: 84) describes this thus:

At the synapse, the frequency-coded language of action potentials is converted to graded signals in the postsynaptic neuron. This is a consequence of the convergence of a variety of chemical transmitters. Each transmitter or neuromodulator constitutes a synaptic language conveying specific types of electrical messages.

In other words, it is the chemicals that 'tell the story' to the different neurons in various areas of the brain. If we think of the effects of alcohol and other drugs or hormone treatment on mood, for example, we can see how the chemical effects of these mimic, enhance or alter the 'natural' effects of the chemicals naturally present in the brain, including substances known as peptides which provide control over such functions as appetite, stress and some emotions.

To summarize: development is learning. We talk about learning to walk, to speak, learning about ourselves – putting together what we know in its broadest sense with what we feel. Over time this knowledge is combined so that it becomes part of who we are. The way this is achieved can be equated with learning a recipe. Imagine that you want to try a new Delia Smith or Jamie Oliver dish. It is one you are completely unfamiliar with but sounds good! First, you would carefully read all the ingredients, checking and rechecking the list. You would then carefully follow the instructions, stopping to read them again as you go, perhaps making mistakes. Over time, as you make this dish again and again, you no longer need to check the recipe quite so often and in the end you don't need to look at all. You have memorised or 'internalized' the recipe. You may even feel confident enough to make changes, to add or subtract items, so that in the end the dish becomes yours rather than theirs. However, what does remain is the fundamental recipe that led to the whole process. Developing skills and knowledge builds on the fundamental list of ingredients (genetic inheritance) and the basic recipe – nature and nurture mixed together. As these elements combine in more complex ways, you become you. You have internalized the basic elements.

Now we move on to thinking in a little more detail about memory.

Learning and memory

The 'seat' of learning and memory, emotion and language is, of course, the brain. This somewhat unprepossessing organ – greyish, wrinkled, not particularly large and with the consistency of an over-ripe peach – belies the amazing capabilities within, which are far greater than the fastest computers. Crittenden (2000) considers how the brain makes sense of information received and this process of 'making sense' is linked with two particular influences. First, learning or cognition (and the quality of learning in any context) is affected by what, how and when the information occurs. Second, emotion (and the quality or intensity of emotion linked to the experience) influences the 'meaning' and finally the process whereby the brain files away the information for future use – memory.

The systems for learning, memory and making sense are, of necessity, present from birth – if organizational patterns were not laid down, then the infant would remain in a state of disordered confusion. (Think about how you feel when you don't really understand what is going on around you and about what helps you – any landmark such as a familiar face which helps the rest click into place.) Crittenden presents her interpretation of memory systems as follows:

- *Procedural memory* which codes information about things that are happening in time and space and only requires primitive cerebellar and brainstem processing.
- *Imaged* or *perceptual memory* which is processed in the limbic system and is therefore strongly linked with emotional content. Both procedural and imaged memory are pre-verbal and it is not until the child is about 3 that memory systems more dependent on verbal recall are brought into this process. These are the remaining three methods of 'making sense', as follows.
- *Semantic memory* represents verbal procedural information (i.e. the 'if/then rules' that can be used to guide behaviour).
- *Episodic memory* which represents events in the past which are a mixture of the cognitive procedural and the affective imaging in a verbal form.

- *Working memory* which is an integrative process finalized in the prefrontal cortex which allows comparison (I feel this but I think that), weighing up of outcomes (I could do this but I may do that), planning and change (I have responded like this in the past but this time . . .).

This of course, as Crittenden points out, is a (relatively) slow process and is managed consciously. In children, it depends on their particular level of cognitive skill.

It is important to remember that procedural and imaged memory are processed within the brain extremely quickly. All the verbal forms of memory/learning take longer, which again adds weight to why we often act first and think later, and why very young children almost invariably 'act first'. As we know, patterns of thinking based on experience enable us not only to 'learn' about things but also about people, emotions and abstract concepts. However, the very processes which help us formulate and develop patterns and new ways of thinking can also work against us in that chronic neglect or abuse in the early years can also lay down patterns of response which impair brain development (Green *et al.* 1981; Ito *et al.* 1993; Courchesne *et al.* 1994; van der Kolk 1994; Perry 1999).

The actual way that memories are 'laid down' is also complex. Only since the 1960s has it been recognized that we 'file away' different memories in different ways. Over the past ten years many researchers such as Crittenden have come to believe that there is a range of memory systems of which two (emotional memory and contextual memory) depend particularly on the workings of two structures in the brain's limbic system – the amygdala and the hippocampus.[3] Studies of people with damage to either of these areas have helped researchers realise that one system can work separately from the other and that different experiences can alter the way each functions.

There is one further intriguing facet of memory which is raising some interesting questions: whether memory is laid down only in the brain or whether all the cells in our body retain some information about who we are. The question has arisen because of the ethical considerations surrounding organ donation and transplants. The case of a heart transplant patient who found themselves developing a liking for foods previously not eaten and which were then discovered to have been a favourite of the donor has added to this intriguing hypothesis. What is known is that there are very strong connections between regions of the brain and the heart – the heart not only sends nutrients to all parts of the body, but also patterns of energy (Schwartz *et al.* 1997). The heart is certainly a most interesting organ: while on the one hand it could be termed merely a 'pump' (although obviously a very vital pump), on the other it has for millennia been referred to as the 'seat' of emotion. Just consider the language we use when speaking of love and grief. We also speak of 'learn-ing by heart' and 'knowing by heart'. We may instinctively know the truth without knowing why or how and perhaps brain and heart are closely entwined in both memory, learning and our next topic – emotions.

Emotions and 'emotional regulation'

Much of our sense of satisfaction or dissatisfaction about our daily lives is underpinned by three factors:

- how we feel and think about ourselves (self-esteem/self-worth) and what we believe others feel and think about us;
- our relationships, both personal and professional;
- our ability to make sense of our experiences and the behaviours of those around us.

In the first instance, we have to find out who we are before we can think about ourselves; we have to achieve a sense of 'me' and 'mine' before we can understand 'you and yours'; and we have to learn how to become 'independent' both physically and psychologically. We need to be able to adapt to circumstances, manage our emotions and consider our actions. Essentially, these 'tasks' are a lifelong process (and some may never be fully achieved), but in the early years of childhood we learn the fundamentals. In school and especially in adolescence, our friends become powerful influences, but in the early years it is mainly adults whom we imitate, from whom we learn and who define the particular world we inhabit.

The 'powerhouse' for shaping and determining our mental well-being and framing the way we behave, interact and live alongside others is our emotions. Izard *et al.* (1984) specify a 'differential emotion theory' which states that the emotions system is the primary motivational system for human beings. Emotions and their accompanying bodily feelings influ-ence all aspects of our daily life, directly or indirectly. The belief system of a parent based about competitiveness may influence, for example, the degree of physical activity permitted or promoted within the family culture, which in turn may influence positively or negatively a child's own self-belief/self-esteem and behaviour, dependent on the child's own inherent inclinations. The parent's attitude in the first place may be rooted in remembered feelings of shame at always coming last in races, or frustration at not being as athletically able as some of their peers.

Another question that could be asked is why do we have emotions at all. Of course, as any *Star Trek* enthusiast would know, Mr Spock would consider emotions as considerable barriers to the use of logic, which nicely illustrates how feelings can certainly override thought. This is understandable, however, as feelings are present from birth and thought as a 'conscious stream' of internal dialogue certainly is not – although whether thought occurs in another dimension of personal expressiveness in the early months of life is another matter. After all, 'communication', which implies conscious activity and intent, does not require language as babies communicate well with their carers and indicate a self-initiated response to experience. This is a form of non-verbal 'thinking' – just as animals can 'converse' together and act jointly to achieve a goal. Captain Kirk would tell Mr Spock that emotions and the bodily sensations/feelings that accompany them are what makes us human, but what purpose do they serve?

Emotions certainly help with survival. If we think about the social signalling of the baby (crying and later smiling), these manifestations of distress and pleasure help bring the carers to the baby and maintain their contact through the mutual pleasure of their interactions. Feeling pleasure, joy and delight in another's presence means that we maintain social friendships and groups allowing mutual care and nurture. Of course, there is a price to pay as loss through separation or death brings grief and great distress with feelings of longing and symptoms of pining. Other emotions such as shame and guilt also allow us to curb feelings which otherwise might cause harm, such as anger and hate, but even these can be positive as we can 'hate' cruelty and feel anger at injustice. Without anger at some level we may lack motivation for change when we are emotionally hurt, and may be too passive for our own emotional health. If we did not feel fear we would not recognize danger, which is a prime safeguard for survival.

As we grow older, more complex emotions arise such as jealousy, feelings of revenge or retribution. We can also have emotions that we sometimes label as 'spiritual' and which tend to be uplifting and supportive. All these form part of our social world, both interpersonal and within social groups, communities and societies.

There is also perhaps a deeper purpose to emotions. Damasio (1994) describes a patient of his who suffered extensive damage to particular areas of the frontal cortex. She would 'lie in bed with her eyes open but with a blank facial expression'. On recovery, it transpired that she recollected little 'real thinking or reasoning'. It appeared in Damasio's view that her blank face was an appropriate reflection of her 'lack of mental animation'. This suggests that without emotional expression, without feeling, we lack something more than 'motivation'; something connected with the life force that enables us to reach out towards others. A comparison might also be with those who are depressed and the frequently associated dampening of emotions and concurrent lack of energy. Other patients that Damasio has studied also indicated that damage to the areas of the brain associated with emotions brought about a qualitative negative change in the personality and functioning of individuals unrelated to their continuing pre-injury intellectual language or social functioning. What seems to make the essential difference is that emotions help us orientate to our environment, to attend to what is around us and most importantly, the people who are with us.

The life force we possess may be a mixture of attention and curiosity brought about by the emotions engendered in us when something 'catches our eye', without which we would not be 'involved'. If we felt nothing, we would have no motivation to take further interest. Laevers (1996) too links his definition of involvement as an active process, 'characterised by motivation, interest and fascination', and emotional well-being and sees it as paramount for positive learning outcomes.

Without emotions, Captain Kirk is right – we would lose an essential part of what it is to be human and certainly we would not belong to the great family of animals who in varying degrees share with us some of the basic emotions (although some scientists still feel the jury is out on this). However, anyone who has animal companions or who raises animals in farming will testify to their emotional expressiveness – even if we assume they do not know what it is they are feeling, nevertheless they *are* feeling – rather like babies!

When thinking about the influence of emotions, there are three topics we can address:

- What is an emotion?
- How do we learn to organize or 'manage' our emotions?
- How do feelings affect behaviour?

What is an emotion?

Stroufe (1997) gives a masterly overview of the conceptual issues and theoretical approaches towards understanding emotions. He also makes the very salient point that, overall, very few researchers consider emotions only as an experienced, subjective 'feeling'. Rather, they are regarded as part of a *very* complex process which includes 'mechanisms such as perception, recognition, appraisal, judgement or meaning analysis' (Stroufe 1997: 12) – concepts which are part of almost every theory. In other words, we experience feelings but our interpretation of these feelings depends on the meaning these feelings have for us. An example that might illustrate this is thinking about two people standing and looking at a roller-coaster ride. Both might experience similar sensations (feelings) of 'butterflies in the stomach', flutterings in the chest, tightening of muscles but one person, 'A', may interpret this as excitement while the other, 'B', ascribes a fear label. The emotion they would talk about refers to their understanding of their feelings.

The way we label emotions has to do with a complex mix of how adults have labelled them for us – i.e. the actual semantics and the associated physiological sensations and experience, particularly the emotional context of how others have reacted and our responses. To use the example of the roller-coaster ride, the initial response of A as a 'first timer' may have been curious and maybe a little anxious, but a supportive person went with the child (or adult!), acknowledged the anxiety, emphasized the fun aspect, showed pleasure and excitement, admitted to their own fears or apprehension, comforted and soothed, and also perhaps waited until A indicated a willingness to 'have a go'. Person B may have been told 'not to be silly' that there is 'nothing to be scared of' and their fears ridiculed or minimized with no comfort or encouragement. What others do with our feelings actively influences how we express them and in the early years, when we have not acquired the capacity to think about the motives of others, self-soothe or otherwise defend against those responses, their affect is very powerful.

In Chapter 6, the concept of 'social referencing' is introduced. This is when babies watch the reactions of the adults around them which indicate 'how to feel' (is this person safe or not?) and even 'how much to feel' (i.e. what is the level of the adult's own emotional response?). If the adult shows great fear at seeing a dog or a wasp then it is highly likely that the child, once it has reached this stage of development, will pattern the adult's responses. It is noteworthy that in times of uncertainty, even adults will follow the main emotion shown by someone who seems to be 'in charge'. Think about a panic-inducing event such as a traffic accident. If someone is able to take control and remain calm, this seems to influence most of those around that person. In babies and young children this need to 'use' adults to make sense of novel happenings is very strong. Adults are the main 'markers' available to children after all. It is also useful to remind ourselves that emotions vary enormously between individuals, with similar events evoking different responses and behaviours – as in the roller-coaster example. A useful observation to make is when you are next at a railway station: watch the different reactions to a missed train! The responses you might see will be governed by:

- how important catching that particular train was – context;
- the way in which that individual is able to control their feelings – managing emotions;
- the type of emotion they feel;
- the personal meaning to them, which is not the same as the importance, because the meaning might be evidence of how the world is 'against' the individual.

Managing emotions

Our ability to understand and express our emotions is closely linked to our cognitive development. There has been an explosion of research in this area in the last ten years and work on memory, trauma and brain physiology has led many neurologists to believe that early experience 'hardwires' the brain, determining which particular neural pathways are highly influential. The importance and implications of this research may not have been fully taken on board by professionals or society as a whole in thinking about the overall care of very young children but, on the other hand, a dangerous paradox would be if differences in brain development were interpreted in a strictly causal way – that is as being the sole reason for behaviour problems.

What is still unclear is whether the anatomical and/or physiological differences observed in both form and function of the brain are caused by genetics, early experience, during the process of foetal development or through pre-birth experience via stressors within and without the foetal environment. In many cases a mixture of all of these may have some part to play. However, that experience influences the fundamental patterns of development both within and between different developmental domains seems to be beyond doubt. Of course, emotions/feelings and how we interpret these (and subsequently how we behave) form a significant part of our whole development towards ultimate maturity, and in the early years feelings and behaviour have a much more direct route between them because thought processes which allow us to label, reflect and rationalize our emotions are still literally (as well as metaphorically) in their infancy.

Stroufe (1997) identifies a straightforward chain of events illustrating the process by which experience and emotions lead to outward behaviour. Each step in the chain does of course mask many levels of complexity. The chain is as follows:

Stimulus-in-context → cognitive process → experienced feeling → behaviour

My own view regarding Stroufe's chain of events is that 'experienced feeling' comes before 'cognitive processes'. For example, we may react fearfully to a sudden sound before we bring to our conscious attention an interpretation of what the sound might be. The work of LeDoux (1998) and Panksepp (1998) discusses these particular processes in depth. Stroufe points out that variations in theoretical approaches appear to concentrate around emphasis of the importance of a particular part of the emotional/behavioural sequence (e.g. facial change concurrent with a feeling or as a cognitive interpretation). What most theorists appear to be agreed on is that emotions generally involve simultaneous internal (physiological) and external bodily changes such as facial expression, body posture (or movement), or eye movements. This potentially explains why communication via 'body language' can be so telling and in adults frequently more truly linked with what a person is actually feeling compared with what they might be saying. For example, we might say to a friend before an important presentation at a meeting, 'I feel perfectly confident' and even, to a degree, consciously believe this, knowing that we have prepared well for the meeting. Simultaneously, however, our heart might be beating rapidly, our palms sweating and we may give the game away by frequent visits to the toilet, pallor or flushing, fidgeting, constant fiddling with our hair or presentation notes and so on. These responses tie in with a fear response and the fear in this instance could be a deep-seated dread of failure or of making a fool of oneself in public. Our physiological response to our emotional state rather than our expressed thoughts is not surprising when we remember that the 'emotional' area of our brains is in an older part than the logical, rational frontal cortex.

To summarize, the carer's responses promote the physiological connections to the appropriate centres in the brain, resulting in a combined psychological and biological response. This process, over time, allows a developing sense of equilibrium. This emotional balance – similar to the way in which our body stays in balance for good health – ultimately influences our particular approach to life. Emotions are at the heart of this process because of the gradual predominance of a certain type of feeling. Over time and based on what constitutes the major part of a particular baby's day-to-day experiences, the baby will feel generally content or anxious, fearful or distressed, and this will become that particular baby's state of equilibrium – or the general sensation that is most familiar to that infant. To understand this further, consider your own prevailing view of life. Are you generally optimistic or pessimistic? Do you embrace change or shun it? Do you feel loveable? Are you beset by anxiety? You will discover that you have a state of being that is familiar to you and this has often – but not exclusively – arisen out of the type of response to your own emotions you experienced in your early years.

The parallel intertwining and separateness of emotion and cognition are clearly demonstrated in times of severe stress when the depth of emotion can prevent logical thought or when we find ourselves 'reacting' to a look, gesture or word. As older children and adults, we can choose to suppress, rationalize or act on an emotional 'reaction' and we now turn to how we learn to do this.

How do you respond when someone 'lets you down', jumps a queue, shouts at you or shuns you? How do you display anger, appreciation, love and sadness? The displays of emotion that we permit ourselves are not only culturally based (compare an argument in a café in Italy and one in England), but also reflect the culture within a particular family. In some families, a specific emotion such as anger or jealousy is seen as undesirable and any outward manifestation of that particular emotion involved is quickly suppressed, but of course the emotion remains within the person's psyche, bubbling away below the surface. The way each family interprets emotion and the use they put it to will also depend on the particular family culture. In some families displays of affection are welcomed, and in others they are to be avoided.

Family culture and the individual temperament of the carer will all work towards the way babies and young children learn about how they can express what they feel and what meaning, positive or negative, the emotions generate. One of the differences in managing emotions as we get older is that we have more choice in regulating our environment and therefore actively influencing those circumstances which may raise or lower our feelings of pleasure or unease/fear. An adult strategy in managing emotions is to regulate as far as possible our environment. Babies and young children do not have this luxury. They are flung into situations by the adults around them with little or no opportunity to withdraw if they want to, other than by showing their distress.

Fonagy (2000: 4) states that: 'None of us is born with the capacity to regulate our own emotional reactions', and he emphasizes strongly how babies are helped to regulate their reactions through the meaning given to their behaviour and the response of the caregiver. If a baby shows distress by crying, it is the caregiver's role to soothe and help the baby's mind and body return to a state of equilibrium – i.e. hopefully, a sensation of calm and contentment.

Bion quoted by Marrone (1998) postulated a concept which he termed 'containment' to describe how the carer is able to 'tolerate' and respond positively to the baby's expressions of emotion and need. This ability to tolerate the needs and demands of an infant may in its turn be affected by a carer's own capacity to separate out their own needs from those of the baby. However, all of the above depends on and implies an accurate interpretation by the caregiver of the infant's cues or signals, as the caregiver will also have their own attitudes, wishes, beliefs and desires (often termed 'mental states') which will be about the baby, together with their role and responsibilities, motivation, temperament and their own capacity to give care and love. This will then influence the degree to which they can sensitively and appropriately respond to the child's emotional displays/behaviour. The response the baby receives in turn provides the context in which the infant can begin to organize, or make links between, feelings and experience. This linking between emotions and responses provides the brain with the materials to sense a pattern which over time the child 'follows' until a new experience moderates the pattern (Zafrana 2000). These specific yet malleable patterns provide the building blocks for the child's 'internal working model'[4] a phrase, coined by Bowlby ([1969] 1991) to describe a child's mental or cognitive map[5] about their bodily and psychological experiences. The concept of an internal working model has also been varyingly described and with slight differences in emphasis as a 'script', 'schema' or 'template'. However, all are an attempt to name the process by which we acquire a persistent internal 'state' which in turn shapes our responses to others and our attitude to ourselves.

What might influence the parent's/carer's own individual state of mind? Fonagy (Fonagy *et al.* 1991; Fonagy 2000) puts forward a very interesting concept which he calls the 'self-reflective function'. This function is any individual's capacity to understand the mental states of another person. Fonagy believes that this ability is an essential part of emotional development and without it people are unable to make sense of the world around them and those within it. He states that our understanding of the world around us is tied up with our everyday understanding of each other. In other words, our relationships and dealings with others only make sense if we believe and understand that they have wishes, beliefs, values and assumptions, as we do. They may not be the same as ours, but they exist. For example, Wordsworth's famous poem about 'a host of golden daffodils' evokes a picture which, in most people's minds, will have various features in common: the colour of the flowers; the fact there are very many of them and, most likely, that they are beautiful. Thus a simple phrase contains elements which produce a joint understanding of colour, form and feeling.

What must be borne in mind is that the capacity to understand different mental states only begins in a very simple form at around 18 months to 2 years. This is when a bemused child understands that someone may actually prefer broccoli to chips (Gopnik *et al.* 1999)! At 3 years children shown that a chocolate box is full of pencils will say that their friend, who has not seen the open box, will think there are pencils in it too. It is only by four years that most children can understand that their friend will think there are chocolates in the box. However, this mainly refers to fairly 'concrete' information, as the capacity for abstract thinking is not developed for some years.

However, the ability to 'self-reflect' is not necessarily fully developed in all adults either. Those with so-called 'personality disorder' are described as having primitive modes of thought with 'concrete thinking'.[6] A lack of self-reflection seems to be linked to having a poor understanding of the mental states of others that can thereby lead to an absence of care and concern. The capacity for reflective function has close links with what we might term 'self-awareness' or 'insight'. A parent's ability to self-reflect is affected not only by their own particular potential ability to do so, but also by their own mental state. For example, if a parent already has mental health problems, is addicted to drugs and/or alcohol, is depressed or does not have a positive view of themselves or their own abilities. All these factors could influence the ability to sensitively assess a baby's needs and be tuned into their baby's cues. This is particularly relevant for mothers who are often the principal carers in the early part of a child's life. There are also considerable implications for day-care workers, nannies and childminders who may be looking after infants for considerable parts of each day.

We also have to remember that a parent or carer's ability to self-reflect will not only depend on overall mental states. Our emotional antennae towards others are affected by everyday experiences as well as innate tendencies which themselves are built on our own personal histories. Consider how our own ability to understand and appreciate someone else's point of view (whether in our personal or professional life) is affected by our own mood, preoccupation with a personal problem or determination to do something 'our way'.

Another perspective comes from Marrone (1998: 43, emphasis added) who talks of 'sensitive responsiveness' which he differentiates from 'empathy':

> The notion of *sensitive responsiveness* is similar to that of *empathy*. However, the word *empathy* implies identification with the other's mental state. Sensitive responsiveness, instead, involves some internal negotiation between the momentary state of feeling like the other and the ability to react as a separate being.

Our mothers, because they are frequently our first contact and most often the person who provides daily care, become the primary mediators of a baby's day-to-day experiences. In other words, the adults (especially the one(s) in most contact) surrounding the baby are the ultimate resource. It is through them that the baby will experience positive or negative responses to their demands and needs, and they will also provide the physical environment of warmth or cold, soft or hard, etc. As the adults mediate the type of experience the baby has, the baby's brain acts as the mediator of all these experiences in a similar fashion. The 'internal working model' is the product of an ongoing process of a 'sorting out' of experiences. It is this linking, this forming of patterns from the very beginning through daily care processes such as feeding and sleeping, through the carer's responses to crying, signs of pleasure and need for comfort that we slowly begin to self-soothe and thereby self-regulate. A baby can begin to tolerate a wait for a feed because it has learned that food *will* come. The baby has been soothed and comforted sufficiently to be able to be brave enough to explore their world and lie or sit playing with hands or toes, or a mobile, without distress and with active interest. The baby has learned that for much of the time crying brings comfort and smiles bring answering smiles. Shouts of joy are met with a joyous response and the baby, through this initial sensory security, starts to build a secure base on which to explore and widen its experience. It has learned that if it is tired, the adults around it are peaceful and that someone is close by most of the time. Through the carer's ability to think about the baby's moods, talk about them and label them the baby receives responses which usually 'match up'. As the child gets older, the same sequence applies. Adults help children to identify and learn about their feelings and begin to express these feelings in positive ways. A toddler in the middle of a full-blown tantrum needs an adult who can think about what might be the cause of the tantrum and can respond by acknowledging the real distress and frustration, and helping the child see that the adult is neither terrified nor overwhelmed by the strength of its rage.

However, verbal and physical interaction between parent and baby is not a one-way process but a transactional one, as identified by Sameroff (2000) who wrote a very clear account of his transactional model for The Open University which indicates that the infant is not only 'acted on' but also 'acts upon' their environment (which includes caregivers), which in turn provokes a further response. The baby's joyful vocalization may be met with equal joy and expressive vocalizing from the parent, as above, or the baby may be 'hushed' or even receive an angry response from a parent who does not share the baby's mood. The baby's joy therefore may be enhanced or brutally diminished. Dependent on the consistency of response, the baby's experiences of the adult will shape the strength of particular neural pathways, laying their mark on the child's psychology. We can only learn to experience ourselves through the response of others to our signals – adults truly 'mirror' the child back to them. Each adult's mirror is affected by their own history and experience and will therefore influence the type of 'reflection of itself' that the baby will receive. However, what Sameroff does not elucidate is what might be the forces that influence particular responses. In both infant and adult there is not only a transactional process at work but also an intrapersonal process in each participant that reflects Stroufe's (1997) chain of events (see p. 34).

How do feelings affect behaviour?

The roots of our adult behaviour can be seen to lie in infancy, and one of the key factors we are learning in understanding behaviour and the shape of our particular internal world is the power of emotion and the emotional response to our experiences. Sound knowledge of common developmental pathways provides a baseline from which the child's individual capacities, strengths and areas requiring help can be assessed. As we progress through life, from infancy to adulthood, we continually develop and/or refine particular strategies. The manner in which this occurs is influenced by the extent to which we can formulate reasons for the actions of others and for our own behaviour. A 2-year-old, for example, may understand that someone is feeling sad and needs comforting. However, they are most likely to offer the adult comfort in the form that they themselves find comforting (e.g. offering their teddy or their 'comforter' such as a woolly blanket). The young child is essentially 'egocentric', a term that is sometimes wrongly described as 'selfishness'. Such a child is not being selfish in the derogatory adult understanding of the word but is looking at the world from, literally, their point of view. What we have to remember is that at this particular stage in the child's development, the egocentric view is the only one the child has at their disposal.

Such knowledge about the cognitive capacity of children is vital for all those working with them, as we must see the world from their perspective, not from our own relatively sophisticated standpoint with its greater intellectual depth and breadth, ability to reason or attribute motives and understanding of cause and effect. We do not think that the sun shines to keep 'me' warm, but a child of 4 might. A preschool child believes that even inanimate objects like a teddy bear can feel and be genuinely upset if treated roughly. Once we have made every effort to see the world from the child's perspective we can begin to understand their behaviour. From infancy, we develop strategies that strive to fulfil our need to be loved and feel worthwhile. Through the responses to our needs and demands we may begin to learn to self-soothe, to wait a little, to tolerate change, to explore, to express ourselves. We learn whether we feel mainly happy or sad or anxious, even if we can't label these emotions, and we learn what gets the attention we so want from our carers. We may learn that our signals do not bring rapid, soothing responses but rough handling and/or angry voices. Alternatively, the adult may be erratic in their behaviour, sometimes soothing, sometimes shouting, or we may be left for hours, alone and miserable. If we are picked up, we may not be spoken to, comforted or played with. In all these circumstances, if the adult does not teach us emotional comfort, we as babies will learn a response to limit the degree of distress we feel or will become increasingly fractious – as erratic as the carer.

Our experience frames our behaviour – it is as simple and as complex as that.

Making relationships

Making relationships, attachments or affectional bonds to primary carers is a fundamental part of how an internal working model (or inner world view if you prefer) is formed. It is the foundation of self-esteem/self-worth, of positive mental well-being, of feeling loved and worthwhile. For many of us the relationships we have with partners, family, friends and work colleagues directly and profoundly influence our levels of personal contentment. I have used 'contentment' here, as to me this word carries with it connotations of a more permanent state (e.g. someone may feel 'happy' when they are with their friends, but bored and frustrated when by themselves). Contentment implies a stage where someone is able to have a realistic view of the world accompanied by a deep sense of hope about the inherent goodness in others and faith in eventual positive outcomes. This can only come about if the child or adult feels emotionally secure.

Becoming secure is closely linked with the attachments made by the baby to their primary carer, who is able to respond to the baby with love, affection and acceptance. What arises from this process are feelings of confidence and trust. However, babies – partly because they have no choice – will make attachments to their carers even if those carers are not responsive, loving or accepting. If you imagine a baby being flung out into the ocean, the adults around it are the lifebelt that will help it to survive. The baby will cling to the lifebelt even if the lifebelt is damaged – there is no other support. Without even minimal help, the baby will die, and so making these close relationships is inherently about survival. The baby's initial crying and then smiling are all innate weapons to ensure that carers take care and respond with warmth. It is this powerful need for security, both physical and emotional, that explains why babies will make relationships with indifferent or abusive carers.

Researchers seem to feel that this survival/motivational push to make relationships helps the baby in two particular ways. First, the carer can reduce the fearfulness of new situations and manage stress (in its broadest sense): they can give confidence. Second, this confidence, provided by an emotionally secure relationship, is closely linked to feelings of self-worth and self-esteem. In other words, the child who is loved, encouraged, respected and comforted is able to learn about the world in a context of emotional safety, and about themselves as fundamentally loveable. Children demonstrate clear preferences for their carers well before their first birthday, and once they become mobile will actively seek out their company. Also, at around 7–8 months, the child becomes more distressed at separations and more anxious with unknown people. Attachment theory and classifications are discussed in more depth in Chapter 6, which deals with development from approximately 8 months to a year, but suffice to say here that the affectional bonds formed in the first year of life are powerful indicators of the potential self-image and the quality of internal world view the child will have.

Incidentally, the formation of these bonds also highlights the co-dependency of emotional experience, internal (brain) organization, cognitive development (memory, perception, language) and physical development. A key factor in the development of positive relationships is a mutual sense of happiness and joy in the presence of the other, and laughter is one facet of the way in which we express this. Humans often use humour to 'manage' different situations, and so we will now turn briefly to think about this particular aspect of human expressiveness.

Laughter and humour

Perhaps one of the most delightful sights is that of a baby laughing and chortling as an adult pulls faces or tickles them or the baby is chortling with delight at some new and novel event. I am quite sure that few adults could resist smiling back at a laughing baby and going further – trying to add to and sustain these moments of mutual joy. Laughter of course serves many functions. It indicates happiness and fun, and can also be a great reliever of tension – as a well-timed joke in a difficult meeting can illustrate. It also has a darker side in that often we laugh at another's embarrassment and we are also able to laugh 'sarcastically' and without any accompanying feelings of real mirth or happiness. However, at its best, laughter is a joyous ability and is innate: blind and deaf children laugh too, showing that imitation is not the source. Laughter seems to develop later than crying – as can be witnessed in the signalling of babies. Panksepp (1998) presents us with intriguing information as to the evolutionary usefulness and original source of crying and laughter. As he says, social distress may be the required precursor to allow social bonding to take place and laughter certainly helps to bind people together.

The brain is involved in processing stimuli and it would appear that laughing is an innate response to playful approaches, including physical ones such as tickling. In fact, while we humans tend to believe that laughter is unique to our species, some research demonstrates that gorillas pant and grunt rhythmically when tickled and laboratory rats produce a melodic chirruping when they are tickled. Babies learn to smile early on in their development (around 4–6 weeks) and this 'pleasure smiling' develops into chuckles and chortles. Laughter in young children is spontaneous and infectious and children will often start giggling helplessly together when playing. Laughter, as with most of our activities, appears to involve different parts of the brain including those relating to mouth movements, pleasure areas and areas associated with speech. It may well be that as well as being the precursor to seeing the 'funny side of life', the chuckles and delighted squeals of a baby are also as much a part of learning language as babbling and cooing. This again emphasizes the importance of play, fun and laughter for balancing out feelings of anxiety, fear and negativity, and promoting and enhancing development across domains.

Who am I? Thinking about me and you

As an adult, being able to self-reflect implies a knowledge about who I am and who you are, and how we might be the same and how different. As with all aspects of development there is a starting point and we all have to learn about 'me' from a combination of how others treat and react to us and how we feel inside. We also need to know that we have a body and that we experience the world through our own eyes. Our first experiences are sensory and through these we learn about bodily sensations that include our emotional as well as our physiological feelings. One of the great leaps of understanding occurs at about 18 months, when most children recognize that it is themselves they see in a mirror or in a photograph.

Somehow, babies have put together all the myriad sensations and experiences that allow us to recognize our own faces, even as a mirror image. We know that our face is different from other faces we know, and can reliably identify 'me'. A sense of self is therefore linked with self-experience and self-knowledge, and these are in turn linked to concurrent internal processes involving emotional and cognitive development. The change in self-perception which occurs over time can be demonstrated by how young children frequently use 'descriptors' to talk about themselves such as 'I am 5, I have brown hair', while adolescents will use more interpersonal language and describe inner thoughts and feelings. Over time our sense of who we are develops in complexity and potential abstractness to the stage when we can reflect on our own behaviour, think about our own thinking and question our own beliefs. The way in which we categorize, think and talk about 'me' has a developmental dimension which varies from individual to individual.

The philosophical issue regarding the existence of the self has taxed minds down the centuries. The influence of genetics or environment – the nature versus nurture debate – continues as heatedly as ever with issues such as temperament/personality being acquired or 'innate' being continually revisited. Graham (1999), in an article about self-awareness, describes how some philosophers feel that the 'self' is a 'fiction' rather than a reality. Another perspective comes from the 'new' science of evolutionary psychology (EP) which maintains that most human behaviour is mapped out in our genes which, through evolution, have reached this particular stage in human history. Increasingly, human genes are decoded and specific genes identified as being the 'cause' of various human ills or attributes including the formation of the 'self'. As organization and interpretation of stimuli arises in the brain, proponents of EP such as Pinker (1998) radically insist that there is no unified self and compare the workings of the brain to a collection of computers, each performing a highly specialized function. In their view, natural selection acting over millions of years may account for the existence of these 'computers'. This rather extreme view has implications when one considers the potential of raising a child's self-awareness and self-esteem. What might be our attitude, for example, if we take the view that our personality, and hence behaviour, is already predetermined in a particular genetic make-up? Fortunately, the jury is still out and this book takes the perspective that an individual unique self *does* exist and the phrase 'self-awareness' has meaning. However, whether our understanding of our sense of self is a perception rather than some kind of existential reality, this in no way diminishes the task that we as babies have to perform in learning about who we are and from there understanding others.

Kihlstrom refers to his own definition of self from one of his previous publications as follows: 'We define the self as one's mental representation of oneself, no different in principle from mental representations that person has concerning other ideas, objects and events and their attributes and implications'. And then he states:

> The self may be construed as a person's mental representations of his or her own personality . . . Formed through both experience and thought, it is encoded in memory alongside mental representations of other objects, real and imagined, in the physical and social world. The mental representation of the self includes both abstract information about the person's attributes (semantic knowledge) and concrete information about the person's experiences, thoughts and actions (episodic knowledge).
>
> (Kihlstrom *et al.* 1997: 146)

We also have a self that is perceived by others. Both perceptions can alter through the life cycle because of growing insight/understanding as to the motivations of one's own behaviour or because of an increased awareness of how we appear to others, or a mix of the two. This in turn means that we may change the way we behave, but the 'why' could depend on a hoped-for outcome which may or may not mean an alternation in the underlying emotions which formerly powered the original behaviours. For example, a child might stop crying when they fall down and hurt themselves if they get hit for crying, but this won't stop the feeling of distress at the fall. Similarly, someone may act kindly to someone else in the hope of some financial gain rather than because they feel real empathy.

The difficulty in catching hold of our identity or sense of self is partly due to the self's fluidity. As human beings our mood can change from hour to hour. Our behaviour may alter, for example, if someone enters the room or another person joins a group. These outward, transitory changes produce an adaptation both consciously and unconsciously in behaviour, leading to pleasure or vigilance or anxiety, depending on the meaning of the new person to the individual. It can be seen that within this fluidity of daily adaptation to circumstance there usually remains a consistency of response over time to particular groups and personality types as well as individuals themselves. Consider how you may generally react to a traffic warden, a doctor, a street person or to someone who is a 'party animal' or quiet and shy – irrespective of them as individual human beings.

One aspect that you might recognize is that your response is influenced by your emotions, although you would probably have some kind of rationale which would be based on such things as previous experience, your belief system about authority or a moral stance. This reasoning would be part of a process of 'within mind' organization of such past experiences which over time and in parallel with all the other aspects of your development have led to you responding at that particular moment in that particular way. In other words, the capacity for change or adaptation is embedded in a consistent framework of behaviour that has been formed through the organization and synthesis of our experiences since birth.

Magnusson (1999) describes 'self-organization' as 'a process by which new structures and "patterns" emerge from existing ones'. It can be seen how such an idea helps to untangle how we become who we are, as it emphasizes the patterning process by which we learn our responses and behaviour. We do not, as adults, respond to day-to-day occurrences in radically dissimilar ways from the previous day and if any 'extra'-ordinary experiences occur, our brain attempts to link these with what we already know. Truly shocking experiences, whether positive or negative, can lead to a state of feeling helpless and out of control as we seek to 'frame' the experience in terms that we can deal. Ultimately, we may 'reframe' our understanding. This is reminiscent of the pattern-sensing, pattern-making and pattern-following type of learning referred to earlier (see p. 37).

The importance for professionals lies in the fact that in much of the training literature a great deal of emphasis is placed on supporting and promoting a child's positive self-concept and/or self-esteem/self-worth.

This widespread emphasis suggests a general recognition that how we feel about ourselves (our sense of self) can influence how we learn, relate to others and behave, and that adults influence a child's self-belief.

Although the manifestation of the meaning of self can vary between cultures – for example, Asian and Japanese cultures consider that it is most important for the individual to fit in within the group and further its goals, while European and American traditions value self-sufficiency and independence – a human being could not function without any idea about who they are, no matter how expressed (Neisser and Jopling 1997). I cannot imagine any human being who does not experience a range of intrapersonal feelings as responses to cultural and social experiences, and who in the privacy of their own heart and mind does not have a 'picture' or representation of who they are, what they are like and what meaning life has for them – no matter how their picture differs from that of those around them.

In essence we believe that we are loveable or we are not. From this simple premise arises behaviour, the application of defensive strategies, the quality of our relationships and the demands we make on family, friends and children. If we are emotionally confident in ourselves, we can more successfully cope with adversity and reach out to others. If we are emotionally needy, we will endlessly seek the approval that will make us 'feel better', although the strategies we adopt will depend on what life has taught us.

Summary

One of the greatest gifts we are given at birth is potential. Each of us comes into the world armed with our own unique DNA 'list of ingredients' which not only includes our familial characteristics but also carries within every cell of our bodies the echoes of our evolutionary history. We also possess innate temporal, maturational processes (e.g. puberty occurs within a similar age range in early adolescence) and the literally millions of neurons we possess at birth hold untold possibilities for the type of connections to be made between them waiting for the 'starting handle' of experience. We move from largely uncoordinated responses to stimuli in the early weeks after birth to increasingly more regulated responses, eventually reaching the highly coordinated and proactive behaviours seen in adults (Yufik 1998). As we get older however, as Yufik points out, the potentiality of our choices diminishes as we base our responses increasingly on our past experiences and the quality and type of those experiences will shape, both literally and metaphorically, our brains and behaviour.

When we consider development, we also have to take into account the fact that we too are products of millennia of adaptation. One of the adaptations is the unique ability to make novel connections between experiences (think of the examples given earlier on p. 23). Animals and birds have a much more limited capacity to extrapolate learning into different situations. We also have mechanisms which ensure we are able to socialize and interact with others and the groundwork for empathy, kindness and understanding, for love and the ability to play, and also for loneliness, grief, fear and anger.

Experience is the blind sculptor that shapes the brain, and as the brain is the mediator of experience, experience also shapes the individual. The ancient metaphor of humans being formed of clay illustrates an intuitive understanding of the inherent malleability of human personality, based as it is on the 'clay' of genetic inheritance, innate ability and unknown potential. Babies are at the threshold of their experiences – what we do to them counts.

Notes

1 The human brain is very approximately divided into three parts, termed the 'triune brain' by Paul MacLean (1990). These parts constitute the innermost reptilian core, which influences instinctive behaviours such as rooting, sucking, seeking, feeding and sexuality. The old mammalian brain incorporates the limbic system which specifically 'mediates the social emotions, such as separation, distress/social bonding, playfulness and maternal nurturance' and the cortex which generates reasoning, logical thought, evaluations and beliefs (Panksepp 1998).

2 Neurons are the cells in the brain. They connect to one another by means of axons and dendrites via an electrical charge which passes down the axon and which is activated by external or internal stimuli. There is a minute space between the dendrites of one neuron and those of another. Chemical transmitters (neurotransmitters) 'carry' the impulse across the space where it reconverts into an electrical charge. The *strength* of the stimuli is the source of the neuron 'firing' or not firing. A single neuron can receive messages from thousands of synapses but the flow of information is always in one direction and so there is an essential 'organized and orderly flow' of information within the various brain circuits.

3 Both the amygdala and the hippocampus are located deep inside the medial part of the temporal lobe which itself is at the 'sides' of the brain. The amygdala is closely associated with emotions and the hippocampus is associated with memory. The amygdala is fairly mature at birth and appears to be *fully mature* by a child's first birthday.

4 See Karen (1998) Chapter 15 for a detailed explanation of Bowlby's hypothesis of the internal working model, and links with Piaget's concepts of representations.

5 Cognitive 'maps' can also be termed 'representations' or 'schemas'.

6 This term is used by cognitive psychologists and is based on Jean Piaget's stages of cognitive development (please note that ages are approximate): sensorimotor stage (birth–2 years); pre-operational period (2–7 years); concrete operational period (7–11 years); formal operational period (11–15 years), which includes the ability to consider abstract ideas.

3 SETTING THE SCENE: PARENTS AND PARENTING

The reasons why someone wants to be, or becomes, a parent are multiple and complex, involving both conscious and unconscious processes. Even before a baby is born, the parent(s) have formed some kind of attitude or belief about this baby and may already have expectations, dreams and fantasies about who this baby might be and what they may become. The baby in the womb during the prenatal period is, of course, not entirely passive. They are growing at a tremendous rate and in the later stages of pregnancy are able to hear, move spontaneously and respond to stimuli. What is happening to the mother affects the unborn child. It is for this reason that this chapter considers parenthood and the development of the child in the womb as a precursor to thinking about development in the first three months of life.

The young of most species (except perhaps snakes, alligators and spiders!) tend to produce the 'Aaah' factor in many of us, and babies do this beautifully. The instinctive reaction of many humans, children as well as adults, is to feel warmth and protectiveness towards a newborn infant. However, while this is true, it is perhaps more difficult to take on board the fact that although we humans may be biologically 'programmed' to nurture and protect babies, it may not be the case that we are equally programmed to be *parents* to the babies who will become the next generation's adults. The paediatrician and psychoanalyst Donald Winnicott (1965) talked of the 'good enough' mother – not in a derogatory sense but with the meaning that no parent had to be perfect and that an overall atmosphere of love and sensitivity towards an individual infant ensured the emotional and physical well-being of the growing child.

However, our capacity to be a 'good enough' parent seems to be very much linked with our attitudes, beliefs, individual experience and recall of being parented. This principle of experience informing attitude applies equally to professionals who come into close contact with babies in their day-to-day work – for example, nursery nurses, nannies, foster carers, childminders and a whole host of allied health and social work practitioners.

The approach and attitudes of professionals working in the early years towards the individual baby and the advice that is given to the parents is not wholly governed by professional training. Our own inner worlds influence our professional practice irrespective of whether we are parents ourselves. In this chapter, I am going to consider the requirements for a baby's optimal development – i.e. what parents and other carers need to *do*. This is obviously essential for those who are giving alternative care to babies, making assessments or supporting parents in their role. It is also important for professionals to acknowledge that when working with a child in whatever capacity, the encounter crosses the child's developmental 'stream'. There already exists a multifaceted history, intimately connected with the interactions between parent and child. Once the professional moves on, so does the child, with their 'stream' altered – no matter how subtly – by the impact of the professional's input.

Becoming a parent

An interesting initial question to ask is why does someone want to be a parent in the first place? This question is not usually given in these terms, but is more commonly phrased as why does someone want to 'have a baby'? The myriad possible answers will already give a clue to the type of emotional context which the new baby will encounter.

To 'have a baby' can be perceived as the automatic 'follow on' activity for a heterosexual couple who in turn can be the recipients of great pressure from their parents as to when the grandchild is going to appear. In recent years, there has been debate on the possibility of single-sex couples also 'having a baby' through *in-vitro* fertilization or donor insemination. This issue, surrogacy and the 'rights' of women past menopausal age to have a child bring important ethical issues to the fore with implications in terms of not only adult 'rights' to have children but also the rationale for the importance of 'a baby' and what this baby means to the adults concerned, as well as potential outcomes.

However, it is possible to contend that 'having a baby' and being a parent are essentially two different perspectives. The first implies that to 'have' a baby is the end product, whereas being a parent brings with it all the responsibilities associated with the care and protection of a new, vulnerable human being who, when born, is at the threshold of his or her life. The experiences a child receives after birth are those that will help shape its future. Every woman who 'carries' and gives birth to a child is a 'mother' and every man who has fertilized an ovum is a 'father', but these people's ability to 'mother' or 'father' in the sense of 'parenting' is not necessarily an automatic consequence of the biological process. A quote attributed to Pope John XXIII by an Italian churchman named Angelo Roncalli says: 'It is easier for a father to have children than for children to have a real father'. An even more challenging view is that of the playwright, Jo Orton in *Entertaining Mr Sloane*: 'It's all any reasonable child can expect if the dad is present at the conception'. However, in these days of artificial insemination, even Orton's expectations may seem unrealistic!

The qualitative difference between 'having a baby' and being a parent is highlighted in a study by Langridge *et al.* (2000) which specifically explored the reasons for having a child. They interviewed 10 couples expecting their first baby and a further 14 couples who were undergoing fertility treatment. All participants were interviewed individually, thereby including the views of potential fathers as well as mothers. Interestingly, no obvious gender differences in motivation were identified. While there were some differences between the groups, the primary reasons given were centred on a desire to give and receive love, to experience the enjoyment of a child and to create something that was part of both members of the couple, creating a 'family'. Few social pressures were mentioned as being influential in the decision, although as the authors point out those interviewed could have been reluctant to mention this, even if such pressures had played a part. Many studies have highlighted the tendency for people to give 'internal' reasons for positive events, rarely feeling the need to provide further explanations, while for more negative events an external cause is often cited (or blamed).

The findings of wishing to give and receive love as a reason for wanting a child take on a different perspective when considering them in the light of 'being a parent' – moving from an abstract concept to the interpretation of 'giving love' in a very real sense. The reason of wanting to 'receive love' is interesting because it hints at the psychological processes that are at work. The choice of infertility treatment rather than choosing to adopt a child potentially indicates that the giving and receiving of love is not the whole picture but that the presence of a child 'of their own' is what will be fulfilling – not just the opportunity to love, care and be responsible for another individual. Issues surrounding surrogacy are even more complex to contemplate and are outside the range of the discussion at this point.

The reasons for wanting to have a baby are many and complex and an individual's approach can be as varied as the number of potential parents in any population. The couples in the study cited above had all planned their pregnancy, but pregnancy can also be a 'mistake', an 'accident', a 'disaster' caused by too much alcohol and too good a time, and a woman can become pregnant because of rape. Social and/or emotional pressures from partner and/or family, or cultural expectations, can also encourage or coerce a woman to become pregnant. A couple or an individual can keep wanting the woman to get pregnant in order to achieve a desired number of children, a balance of males and females, to obtain a desired son or daughter, or even (as a female client of a health visitor colleague of mine said) 'I want a girl now as you can dress them up so nicely'. More covert reasons may be linked to issues such as an adult's 'need to be needed' which can lead to a possessiveness regarding the child which is not uncommon. Some parents are reluctant to allow a child, even as an adult, any emotional or physical 'space'. They remain wanting to be the central focus of their child's life and resent their friends and partners.

The reasons for having a baby, for the pregnancy being planned or unplanned, represents the *psychological context* of conception. Wrapped up in all the reasons given above are the attitudes and fantasies already being formed about the child who, at this stage, is not even born. When in the womb, the child may already have been given a personality, even the sex decided: 'The baby kicks all the time – must be a boy'. Siddiqui *et al.* (2000) demonstrated that pregnant women's thoughts and feelings about their baby were linked with their own memories of parenting, closeness and/or acknowledged feelings of rejection. In addition, experiences of loss/bereavement, such as the loss of a previous baby, can impact on the way the mother relates to her baby, even pre-birth, dependent on how she has resolved her feelings of grief and the support she has had.

What being pregnant means to a particular woman (or girl) will, therefore, already begin to affect the way she will look after herself, think about and reflect on the unborn child and consider its future. In some tragic situations, the pregnancy can be utterly denied or hidden until the inevitable birth occurs. It is important to point out however that an 'unplanned' baby can be, and often is, a very welcome baby and a 'planned' baby may only be planned within the family or social context rather than as a result of the inner wishes of the woman concerned (and her partner).

Another facet to be considered is when, in the life of the adult, is this baby to be born? We do not stop our developmental process once we have reached adolescence. Each human being faces their own 'life tasks' which influence the particular adaptability of each parent towards a child. An example is the adolescent mother (and father) who are having to make a huge transition into the adult care of another human being when they are still locked in their own strivings for independence, self-awareness and a role in society.

The actual birth of a child is also surrounded by convention, myth and ideology and there is often a balance to be struck between the wants and wishes of the mother (and sometimes father gets a look in!) versus the needs of the child. Childbirth is deemed a 'natural' occurrence but is not without danger both to the mother and to the child, and emergencies can and do happen. The degree to which the birth matches, meets or disappoints the mother's plans and expectations can potentially influence her feelings and attitudes towards the newborn child – for example, if the mother had hoped for a 'natural' birth but instrumental help was needed to deliver the baby. A study by Maclean *et al.* (2000) of just such a circumstance demonstrated that the women reported their feelings about the birth, six weeks later, as being 'very' or 'extremely' distressed. This is not to imply that this experience automatically affected their attitudes towards their baby, but it is not inconceivable to suggest that those early weeks might have been more problematic for mother, child and partner (or family). This is not meant to imply – and this is *very* important – that any such difficulties would necessarily have long-term consequences. However, it can be seen how such a circumstance *combined with other adverse factors* could result in a mother who is less than sensitive to her baby's cues.

Not every woman, even with a relatively 'straightforward' pregnancy and birth, feels an immediate rush of love for their child. The possible accompanying guilt at not feeling how she is 'supposed' to may get in the way of the important business of learning about her child – the process of 'getting to know you', or rather 'getting to know each other'. For some women it can take a long time before they feel real love and affection for their child, and sometimes it is other carers who provide the emotional warmth as opposed to the physical warmth and care. When I was a health visitor I was fortunate to have several clients who felt able to discuss their feelings regarding their babies. While some were immediately besotted, others confessed that it was only when the baby had started to become more physically active that they felt any real enjoyment. One woman was riddled with guilt because she really did not want to breast-feed her baby (for all sorts of reasons), but felt that she should and so she and the baby underwent a couple of weeks of misery before accepting that physical closeness, cuddles and contact can be achieved when giving a bottle feed too.

In summary, while the baby is developing in the womb, the pregnant woman is already constructing the emotional scaffolding for the future relationship between herself and the baby. How she feels about the pregnancy will also affect the way she thinks about herself, takes care of herself (or not) and her responses to her changing shape and mood. These in turn will be affected by how she *is* perceived by others – partner, family, friends, social and cultural group – and even how she *thinks* she is perceived by others, which might not be the same. For example, she may feel her changed shape is 'ugly' while her husband/partner may find great beauty in her and reassure her accordingly.

The role of the father must not be forgotten. They too carry with them a parenting history and experience and also, as Lis and Zinnaro (1997) point out, have their own imaginings, hopes and fears about the baby. Interestingly, Lis and Zennaro quote studies which indicate that fathers-to-be have more difficulty imagining the new child as a 'baby' and find it easier to think about the child as more 'grown up'. This may explain why a proud new father bought his baby a train set! On a serious note, and I realize that this view may be contentious, the father's 'imaging' of the baby may reflect the evolutionary 'preparedness' for when the male input becomes more mutually in tune with the developing needs of the baby – i.e. as playmate (particularly rough and tumble play), protector and role model for the infant once mobile. I liken it to the different rates of hemispheric brain development in early life, where different functions are primary at different stages before the overall picture is obtained.

It can be seen how the pregnant woman's own life experiences and the circumstances of the pregnancy will influence the way in which she meets her new bodily and emotional changes and the transition from her existing role(s) (whatever they may be) to that of also becoming a 'mother'. In UK society, the transition from a current role to this new one can be difficult, as preparedness for adulthood seems to encompass much more of a preparedness for work rather than parenthood.

In 1963, Morris Wessel described how societal changes meant that traditional forms of support for both parents were diminishing, and it would seem little has changed. The competence (and perhaps status) that an adult might display in their work role often does little to prepare them for the unpredictability and non-stop demands of a new baby. Parenting, however, is still often seen as something that comes 'naturally' and requires little or no additional knowledge, understanding or practice.

This belief that the ability to parent is 'natural', or rather requires no specific preparation or knowledge, applies to both parents, although the father can be on the periphery of the care and services offered to the pregnant woman. Of course, a partner is not always present, or if present may not be supportive. The reality of this does not diminish the fact that most men who have pregnant partners are, or wish to be, involved and carry just as many hopes and fears about the baby as the mother. A supportive partner has to deal with the increasing preoccupation and introspection of the mother to be, and may find that they play a supportive but lonely role with many demands for their understanding but little patience or acknowledgement from society in general about their own needs and difficulties in coming to terms with the new state of affairs. In fact, even when they are acknowledged it is often in negative terms implying a lack of 'maturity' in the man. Fathers too bring with them their own parenting 'baggage' and their wife's or partner's pregnancy may reawaken feelings long since set aside. Men can also experience 'sympathetic' discomfort, suffering from nausea and abdominal pains during their partner's pregnancy that again Wessel would consider to be part of the psychological process that men also go through in meeting the new challenge of being a father. In other societies it is recognized that these psychosomatic symptoms are a demonstration of a wish to care for and protect both mother and child, and they are fully accepted and acknowledged. It seems that it is in our more supposedly sophisticated western societies that any such demonstrations of empathic sensations are dismissed at best and derided at worst.

Schonkoff and Philips (2000: 245) describe the ability to 'parent' the new baby as being 'able to interpret and adjust their own behaviour and respond appropriately to their [the baby's] bids for attention, moods and states, expressions of interest and efforts to communicate their needs'. One aspect which must be stressed is that a parent's expectations, beliefs and attitudes towards their unborn child, bounded as they are by the parents' own histories and current understanding, are also unique for each child. Time is continuous and as we live each day we may modify our own ways of thinking and our dependency on our life experiences. A child entering a family comes at a specific time in the lives of its parents and so previous experience and current thinking may radically affect how a new child is perceived – positively or negatively. As each child is unique, so is the particular set of circumstances surrounding its conception, prenatal development and birth, as well as its life experiences after that time. Professionals must try not to make the mistake of assuming that a parent will think about, or treat, each of their children in the same way.

Understanding human behaviour involves understanding nature and nurture. We have considered the circumstances that may affect the potential nurturing context for the new baby; we now need to turn to the developing foetus and think about the baby before he or she enters centre stage as a new human being.

Summary for professionals

- Professionals need to take note that the mother (and the father if present) will have brought to the pregnancy of each of their children their expectations, hopes and fears together with the influence of their own past history, which may or may not be revised or reviewed in the light of any subsequent or previous pregnancies.

- Assessment of an infant or a child should include as far as possible consideration of the attitude of each parent towards the child, together with the circumstances of the birth.
- The influence of the adult's own parenting history should not be underestimated and if time and circumstances permit efforts should be made to ascertain aspects of that history

The complexity of reasons for wanting a child are also reflected in the complexity of emotions embedded in the rationales for adoption and fostering, and I would suspect influence the choice of career in working with very young children. Awareness of human 'need' in either the self or others is important in facilitating understanding and may be vital when making assessments.

Waiting in the wings: from a cell to a baby

Prenatal development is astonishing and almost overwhelming when we stop to think about the process from fertilization to birth.[1] The meeting of ovum and sperm with their genetic blueprint from the parents and the coding from our evolutionary history, setting out which of the rapidly dividing cells go where and the formation of bone, muscle, skin, blood, internal organs, senses, gender and the colour of our hair, skin and eyes is the beginning of a process that is truly miraculous in its highly specific organization and complexity. For example, nerves that relay touch perceptions appear on the skin of the foetus by about the tenth week and by 28 weeks a foetus will respond to loud noises. A sense of smell is present by week 24 when a foetus can apparently absorb odours in the amniotic fluid.[2] The ears first appear in week 3 of gestation and become functional by week 16. The foetus begins active listening by week 20 (although some sources cite week 24). Shahidullah and Hepper (1992) contend from their studies of ultrasound observations that the foetus hears and responds to a sound pulse from 16 weeks, even before ear construction is complete. It is not surprising therefore that the sense of hearing is probably the most developed of all the senses before birth. The intuitive talking and singing to the foetus that many mothers do may serve to encourage the development of this wonderful sense.

The pre-birth infant is also not without vision. In the womb, the eyelids remain closed until about week 26, but the foetus is sensitive to light, responding with heart-rate accelerations to projections of light on the mother's abdomen. Babies also have vision when born, which we will discuss later, and it is surprising how many people still believe that newborn babies are unable to see. Researchers have discovered that babies are dreaming as early as 23 weeks, when rapid eye movement (REM) sleep is first observed (Birnholz 1981). Studies of premature babies have revealed intense dreaming activity, occupying 100 per cent of sleep time at 30 weeks gestational age and gradually diminishing to around 50 per cent by term, which fits the pattern of dream sleep in 'normal' newborns. As sleep and dreaming activity are important for development, this too will be discussed later.

During prenatal development, the developing baby is far from passive. Foetal movements start around 7 weeks and reach a peak at 15–17 weeks, although when observed via ultrasound imaging the foetus is displaying highly active and surprisingly synchronized movements by about 12 weeks. Many mothers start to feel movement around 16–18 weeks, when the foetus is getting big enough to make his or her presence felt! It is around this time that the 'wiring' of the regions that control movement begins to take place and continues for up to two years after birth. This area is in the cerebellum which controls posture and movement and it is around 18 months to 2 years that most children are able to climb furniture, creep up stairs and walk confidently without having to 'focus'.

DeMause (1982: 254) describes the reactions of the baby in the latter part of pregnancy as follows:

> The fetus during the second trimester, while the amniotic sac is still rather roomy, now floats peacefully, now kicks vigorously, turns somersaults, hiccoughs, sighs, urinates, swallows and breathes amniotic fluid and urine, sucks its thumb, fingers and toes, grabs its umbilicus, gets excited at sudden noises, calms down when the mother talks quietly, and gets rocked back to sleep as she walks about.

It is interesting to consider that movements within the womb are supported by the amniotic fluid (rather like people floating in the Dead Sea). Once born, the baby has to learn to coordinate movement without this support and with the influence of gravity. It is no wonder it takes time and much repetition of apparently 'aimless' movements to build up the necessary combination of brain activity and muscle to coordinate movement 'in space'. These supported foetal movements may also explain how innate 'reflex' actions such as the 'stepping reflex' of the newborn (which disappears by around 2 months) are formed.

The amniotic fluid supports the vulnerable and still developing foetus allowing the basic neural connections to be formed which are the template for initial survival: grasping, rooting, sucking and startle, together with the foundations for future mobility. Another very important occurrence is taking place too – the gender of the baby. Although there has been some interpretation of the emergence of gender as indicating that the foetus is 'female' to start with, current thinking is tending towards the foetus in early development being 'neutral' with gender-specific attributes being consolidated later in the pregnancy and relevant hormones influencing the physiological characteristics of gender-specific brain development. For example, it is the presence of testosterone in the third part of the pregnancy that influences the hypothalamus for males so that the release of hormones governing male sexuality and reproduction do not follow a cyclic pattern, as in females.

Once the cells in the various developing organs have reached their destinations they become neurons and begin to grow axons that are the connecting 'tubes' between the neurons. Genes determine where the axons will go to connect but chemical neurotransmitters refine the process so that the axons reach their particular targets and don't get lost! After birth, it is experience, rather than genes, that sends the axons wending their way to different destinations. Before birth it is the genetic blueprint that dictates how foetal development takes place. Brain development itself begins with the formation and closure of the 'neural tube'. The tube forms the 'neural plate' which begins to form about 16 days after conception. This plate lengthens and starts folding up, front to back, forming a groove at around 18 days and then closing up at around 22 days. If this groove fails to close at the top end then a tragically fatal condition known as 'anencephaly' occurs. This means that the baby is born without a cerebral cortex and does not survive. If the groove does not close at the lower end, then the condition of 'spina bifida' occurs which, dependent on the degree of non-closure, can range from symptomless to a high level of physical disability.

Babies in the womb move, kick, suck their thumbs, respond to light and sound and the emotional state of the mother. The abilities of breathing, sucking and swallowing are controlled by the brain stem which sits above the spinal cord but below the cerebral cortex. This is almost mature by the end of 6 months' gestation, which is when babies can begin to survive outside the womb. The last to develop is the cerebral cortex, which only just begins to function at the end of gestation. Research shows that premature babies have very basic electrical activity in the primary sensory regions of the cerebral cortex (i.e. those that detect touch, vision, hearing and basic 'motor' regions). In other words, when we are born we are primed for survival but not yet for living.

It is the sensitive duality of organization and complexity which means that the developing foetus is susceptible to adversity through disease, substance misuse, violence, maternal physical or psychological illness or prescribed drugs. The thalidomide tragedy some years ago highlighted in a devastating way how a drug (albeit prescribed with the best of intentions) led to severe physical deformities through its effect on the rapidly dividing and migrating cells. Of course, as is well known, a 'mistake' in the genetic blueprint can also lead to physical malformations and learning disabilities.

What about mum – and dad?

While in the UK a birth is usually celebrated, once mother and baby are at home and a few days have passed, the new mother is left to 'get on with things' with hopefully sound professional advice from midwives and health visitors for support. Family support however, will depend on the personal circumstances for the mother concerned and if the birth has been problem free, more intensive support might not occur. Although there are changes to paternal leave and many partners, new grandparents, friends and neighbours can and do give much-needed support, it is not unknown for the new mother to be alone with the baby for much of the time.

In non-industrialized countries, it is interesting to note that many cultures have a period of time after the birth that is seen as a 'rite of passage' and can involve not eating certain foods, preclude any sexual activity and provide instructions for behaviour. Such practices can vary in length from a month to a year. Rites, rituals and traditional practices such as this, whether or not individually welcomed by a new mother, nevertheless give time and space for the physical and emotional changes to settle down. Close contact with the new mother also means that any adverse signs are noticed, and other carers are willing and able to 'step in' to care for both mother and baby.

The gradual erosion of traditions which served to highlight the importance of a new birth means that the reality of what a baby can mean to a particular family also becomes eroded. Maternal and parental leave, while welcome, nevertheless carries with it an implication, in my view, that this is merely a gap in the process of outside work rather than a true recognition of the impact on the role and function of the woman and her partner.

The first few days of a baby's life will be influenced by the type of birth – for example, if the baby needs additional care, it may mean that mother and baby are not able to be in close contact. It is reassuring that the importance of contact is now recognized and parents are encouraged to touch and stroke even the tiniest, most vulnerable babies. It is also reassuring to remember what was said in Chapter 2. The 'bonding' and 'attachment' processes is a dynamic one and not suddenly 'formed' within the first few days, although obviously more contact means more opportunity for the sensitive 'dialogue' between baby and carer to begin.

Home with baby

The American journal *Zero to Three* outlines some requirements for the optimal mental health for young children:

- healthy attachment between the child and the caregivers, parents, and guardians;
- emerging self-confidence;
- competency in human relationships; and
- behaviour appropriate to developmental age.

This process begins once the baby is born and at home.

In Chapter 1, an outline of 'love' and care for a baby indicated the need to be:

- sensitive to the baby's methods of communication (body language, eye contact, facial expression, crying and later smiling);
- emotionally (as well as physically) 'available' for the baby;
- able to spend time, attending to his/her physical needs and providing additional stimulation through play and playful experiences;
- sensitive to the baby's need for rest and quiet times, for safety and routine and for warmth, both physical and emotional.

In Chapter 2 I discussed in generalized terms the importance of sensitive interaction and responsiveness of the adult. Now we can examine these issues from the point of view of the parents of a new baby. The first two 'ingredients' are closely intertwined and so will be dealt with together.

The real business of loving: sensitivity and emotional availability

The degree of understanding and perception that the adults surrounding a child have about the needs of that child is vital to the future well-being of that child. Studies of troubled families point out more and more that what differentiates non-abusing from abusing families is the degree of social cognition – i.e. the ability to separate out the child's needs from the adults', and to see the child as a unique individual. As Pianta *et al.* (1989: 307) point out:

> Women who have not resolved interpersonal issues of trust, dependency and autonomy are likely to be considerably stressed when faced with the demands of a highly dependent child. With respect to meeting the needs of a child, these women will have difficulty

viewing the child's behaviour from the perspective of an independent, mature adult.

Unlike the hoped for equal loving partnership between two adults, where each hopes to be able to depend on the other, a parent cannot 'depend' on a child but, instead, has to deal with a vulnerable and highly dependent being. The issue of separating out our own feelings and emotions from those of the baby reintroduces the concept of the 'self-reflective function' referred to in Chapter 2. Fonagy (2000) quotes one of his own research studies from 1994 where findings indicated that mothers with troubled backgrounds were nevertheless able to provide loving and sensitive care and their children were assessed as 'securely attached'. These mothers differed from others with similar backgrounds in that they were able to productively consider their own feelings, attitudes, thoughts and past experiences. This finding ties in with those of Fraiberg *et al.* (1975) in their seminal paper entitled 'Ghosts in the Nursery'. Therapeutic work with apparently distant and uncaring mothers showed that it was only when these mothers were able to acknowledge and accept the distress of their own past histories that they were able to finally recognize the reality of the distress in their baby's cries and respond to it. The capacity of these mothers to eventually be able to 'self-reflect' echoes Fonagy's findings with the cohort of mothers able to sensitively care for their children.

A further perspective comes from the findings of research using the Adult Attachment Interview (AAI). The AAI is an assessment tool devised by Main and Kaplan (1991) to discover whether the types of attachment demonstrated by adults regarding their relationships with their parents demonstrated similar patterns to those displayed in childhood, and further whether the adult's ratings corresponded with the type of relationship demonstrated by their children. The AAI produced four categories identified as follows:

- *Autonomous* – individuals who value relationships and are able to remember their past in emotionally realistic terms and with some insight/understanding as to the possible motives of their carers for the behaviours encountered.
- *Dismissing* – adults who deny, devalue or idealize early relationships.
- *Insecure/preoccupied* – individuals who find the memory of the experience difficult to link with meaning. They may still be highly involved with the emotions and memories of past experiences, and are often still confused or angry.
- *Unresolved* – speech and thought patterns about attachment relationships are often confused or contradictory, especially when discussing trauma or loss.

Main and Kaplan's research on adults' current assessments of their relationships with their parents and their childhood demonstrated a correlation between these ratings and the attachment ratings of their children.
Adults who were identified as being autonomous were much more likely
to have their children assessed as 'securely attached'. Those adults who
were identified as dismissing, anxious or preoccupied had their capacity
for self-reflection impaired by the sheer mental effort involved in coping
with their own day-to-day emotional responses. To illustrate this, I will
give an example that has nothing to do with babies!

A colleague, who I shall call Rita, in a new job, was having enormous
problems with two members of her team who seemed to resent everything she was brought in to do. Rita eventually decided to talk to each of
these people individually and it dawned on her that while she did speak
to one, she had been avoiding talking to the other. On discussion, it
transpired that she was intimidated by this particular woman and on
further discussion, Rita suddenly realized that this woman strongly re-
minded her of her own mother with whom she had had a difficult
relationship. Rita's mother had been a highly critical woman who had
constantly belittled her. This insight helped Rita realize that she had
been reacting to the woman *as if* she was her mother and therefore all
her skills, knowledge and experience were as nothing. In this woman's
presence, Rita felt helpless, small and incompetent.

In this example, it can be seen that Rita's emotional response to the
woman created a barrier to her being able to think clearly about the
work situation. Parents can react to their children in a similar way. If a
mother (or father) is caught up in particular ways of responding and
behaving because of their own lack of emotional security, seeing the
baby as the source of *their* comfort or seeing in the baby some characteristic that is disliked, or conversely idealizing the baby, then their ability
to think clearly about the actual baby and respond to its needs will
be imparied. Another very interesting study by Crandell *et al.* (1997),
although very carefully hedged with 'maybes', again showed some
very salient links between the way in which the mothers studied had
mentally organized and integrated their childhood experiences and the
way in which they interacted with their children. The mothers who
had experienced loving and secure relationships with their parents, or
alternatively had come to terms with unloving and painful relationships seemed able to show more warmth, less intrusiveness and more
encouraging behaviour towards their children in the research situation.
The researchers also made a very salient point that the mothers who
had been classified as 'insecure' may not (and probably did not) commit
gross acts of abuse towards their children but might transmit 'low
level, chronic and pervasive messages that convey negative attitudes
to and about the child, intrude upon and or dismiss crucial affective

experiences and thus distort the interactive picture' (Crandell *et al.* 1997: 262).

Below is an example which highlights how a parent's perceptions have distorted the child's perception of themselves as an individual.

> Joe and Jack are identical twins aged 5. Their parents refer to them as 'Joe and Jack' as if they were one person and encourage relatives and friends to do the same. Their mother became quite upset one day when a teacher referred to them as 'Jack and Joe'. 'It is Joe and Jack' she said. One day the teacher asked the children in her class to draw a picture of themselves. Joe drew a figure with two heads and Jack drew a circle.

Around the ages of 5 and 6, children are capable of drawing a representation of themselves which has distinct head and body segments as opposed to the earlier 'tadpole' stage which most children seem to go through, no matter how briefly (Cox and Howarth 1989). In other words, the representations are identifiable as people and usually they have a smiley mouth, eyes and hair. In the above scenario, the twin who had been identified and treated by the parents as the 'first' seems to have internalized the perceptions of the mother in that he was not one person but two. The other twin is developmentally at a much earlier stage of 'drawing', but by drawing a circle also demonstrates a possible internalization of his 'invisibility'. We can only speculate as to why the mother had adopted this particular view of her twins – of being one person, rather than two. It is not inconceivable that she feels overwhelmed by the needs of two babies and was perhaps post-natally depressed (see Chapter 7 for a discussion on maternal depression). Her attitudes towards her babies may not have been 'picked up' until they reached school age. She also demonstrates a clear example of not being able to 'self-reflect' as she has no obvious insight or awareness of the consequences of her attitudes and beliefs about and towards her boys.

Such situations raise very difficult and potentially painful issues when thinking about the responsibility of being a parent and the need for sensitive interaction with babies and children. Of course no one is perfect and no one is the ideal parent. All parents get cross and tired, irritable and downhearted to varying degrees at different times. We catch colds, we get sick, we have headaches, money problems, rows with partners or families – all are grist to the daily mill of life. In the middle of all this is a new baby or very young child. I cannot repeat often enough that it is the *consistency of reaction* that makes the difference. But, and it is a very big but, what we as human beings cannot escape is the fact that what our caregivers did when we were young affected us, often in a manner that is chronic and low key. In other words, not devastating, not rendering us calmly confident or psychotic or neurotic but simply providing us with fundamental responses which manifest themselves particularly when we are under stress or faced with a totally dependent human being.

Caring for a baby is hard work, both physically and psychologically. 'Loving' a baby helps the process and nature helps enormously through a finely balanced production of hormones which increase mothers' desire to care for their children. This may be where the 'natural' bit comes in! Studies of rat populations have identified several neurochemical processes which assist the mother rat to care for her young, which are supported and enhanced by social learning – i.e. experience also affects maternal behaviour. The role of oxytocin in human mothers in supporting the 'let down' reflex for breast milk is well known and it would seem feasible that hormonal fine-tuning in the days before, during and after the birth 'sets the stage' for the optimum care of the infant.

Dr Cort Pederson at the University of North Carolina outlined his studies on oxytocin's role in maternal behaviour in a posting for a psychoanalytical discussion group website (Pederson 2001). One of his findings was that in rodents and primates the amount of nurturing received in infancy is strongly related to the amount of nurturing exhibited as an adult, mediated by oxytocin. Before we humans get agitated at being compared to monkeys or rats, we have to remember how many of our emotional brain and chemical transmitters are shared with them. Studies of troubled and abusive mothers often indicate a history of a lack of actual physical and emotional nurturing care, so the processes which may imprint for future nurturing for animals may also imprint for humans, thereby playing a part in understanding the reasons for the neglectful care of some infants.

In animal studies, this brain/chemical process diminishes as the actual 'doing' of the nursing and care becomes established, so again, nature would seem to 'kick-start' the process of nurturing. As with animals, humans are susceptible to the results of their experiences and individual temperament, and so within this 'natural' sequence the actual outcome for mother and baby will vary because of the mother's own personal history and lifestyle, including their own emotional needs, experience, use of drugs/alcohol, temperament and life choices. Any or all of these may overcome the 'natural' effect of pregnancy and birth resulting in a mother who may not be emotionally available for their baby.

Communication

In babies, the quality of physical care is linked closely with a total mind/body experience which includes the emotional as well as environmental context of that experience. By this I mean the mood or attitude towards the baby will influence how the experience is felt subjectively by the baby. We are not able, as babies, to label our emotions or describe them – it is up to the adults around us to do this, but we certainly do feel and each of our experiences produces a 'subjective' inner response that includes physiological processes. The helplessness of a baby emphasizes the power of the way both baby and adult communicate with each other. Due to the very obvious physical limitations of the baby, communication is limited to facial expression, some hand/body movements, eye contact and vocal signals. These all play an important part in the cues that the baby can give to the carer to indicate their 'mood' or feeling.

The importance of non-verbal communication is demonstrated in the study by Brozgold *et al.* (1998) which examined social functioning and facial expression in a group of people with depression, right-sided brain damage and schizophrenia. The overall finding was that difficulties in social interaction seemed to lie in impairments related to giving out and receiving (i.e. processing) emotional information, with consequent implications for the formation and retention of relationships at all levels. These include relationships with children, because carers can also have depression, schizophrenia, brain disabilities or be under the influence of drugs when 'in charge' of an infant. The significance of this and similar studies for babies is that the mood or emotion of their carers affects the 'how' of their response to the baby. For example, mothers with depression who look and behave in a depressed manner tend to have an effect on the behaviour of their babies. A study by Murray *et al.* (1996) showed that depressed mothers were less sensitively attuned to their infants and were 'less affirming and more negating of infant experience'.

A recent study by Kamel and Dockrell (2000) on caregivers' and observers' interpretation of infant expression and behaviour illustrates the importance of how behaviour is perceived and interpreted. They pointed out that the carers' (in this case the mothers') interpretations tended to be more meaningful than those of the observers, and that the interpretation of the infants' facial expressions and emotional states by the mothers was also more influenced by the situational context. There are two important points here. First, from the point of view of the baby, it is the mothers' interpretation that matters – i.e. how they perceive the expressions and actions of their babies and how this influences their responses. The issue for the baby is what is going on inside the mother and how positively or negatively, sensitively or insensitively, she is in tune with the infant. Second, the differences between the observers' and the mothers' interpretations can help to identify how in tune or 'out of touch' a mother might be in her actual responses to her baby, rather than relying on her own reporting of her responses and interactions – a very important point for all those working with children and families. Professionals must take the opportunity as far as possible to actually observe over time interactions between child and parent and share information regarding their own interpretations.

A very powerful example of out of tune interpretation at work was at a recent workshop on 'Infant Brains' led by Janet Dean, director of the Community Infant Programme in Colorado and Mary Sue Moore, a child and adolescent psychotherapist, also based in Colorado. They showed videos of interactions between infants and carers and in particular a video of the parents of an infant who was losing weight rapidly without obvious cause. The mother was able to describe clearly and accurately the signals of a hungry baby (mouthing, fist in mouth, crying, rooting) but interpreted these same behaviours in her baby as 'tiredness', 'boredom' and 'maybe unhappy'. Thankfully the therapists were able to help her and her husband to respond to the baby more appropriately but this powerfully demonstrated how a parent can totally 'misread' what may seem obvious to someone else – to the desperation of the baby. Of course, this is as true for professionals working with babies and children as for their primary carers, especially where professionals *are* the primary carers – for example, when an infant or child is in day care for many hours a day. The childminder or the nursery nurse also need to be in tune.

Another way that carers show how they are interpreting infant behaviour is the way they label it. For example, 'Whose a happy boy then?', 'Are you laughing? Are you happy?', 'Oh, you're feeling sad', 'What are you so angry about?', 'Are you in pain?' All these 'labels' demonstrate that what the baby is doing has meaning for them. The validity or not of the interpretation of the baby's behaviour will depend on the attitude of the carer and the emotional and/or practical context of the interaction which will, in turn, influence the way in which the interaction is experienced by the child.

Language

The word 'language' covers a wide range of meanings and including body language, sign language, the written word and the spoken word. We have to learn not only the words and the symbols which represent them, but also meaning (semantics), the order in which our particular language groups words (syntax), the appropriate social use of language (pragmatics) together with the physiological and bodily processes which allow us to speak, including voice and articulation. A hefty task!

Parents and other carers have a powerful role in the development of this primary form of communication and parents should be encouraged to talk to their babies as much as possible. Fortunately, most parents instinctively do this by the 'labelling' of emotions, as mentioned above, or by simply telling the baby what they are doing, describing something, soothing, playing and so on. Research on language development illustrates time and again that babies who are spoken to frequently are generally more fluent speakers. Parents and carers should also ensure that they talk to their baby boys as much as they do to their baby girls. Magnetic resonance imaging (MRI) has demonstrated that males have far more localized brain activity (left hemisphere) when undergoing tasks requiring speech than females. Females tend to demonstrate a more diffuse activity across both hemispheres and, interestingly, female children demonstrate far fewer language problems in early childhood than male children. It should be noted, however, that some of the main speech areas in the brain are localized in the left hemisphere, but what this research demonstrates is that speech carries with it a whole range of emotional, social and cognitive implications and consequent brain activity. So – talk to those boys is the advice professionals need to give!

Attention to physical needs and additional stimulation

For babies, there are hundreds of 'new' experiences involving bodily movements, sensations and reactions. As the baby gets used to, for example, nappy changing, he or she will gradually become less distressed, or continue to be glad when it is over – some babies hate being 'undressed' while others seem to want to be naked as much as possible. Whatever their particular response, the underlying process of nappy changing itself becomes a predictable procedure. This is sometimes referred to as 'habituation' – i.e. the baby 'understands' the experience. It must be emphasized that the baby's experience is a whole body one, with internal and external sensations linked to movement. In the case of very young babies, movement is passive and generally in the control of the adult carers, except for eye movement and head control. Hence we need to remember how we feel in situations when our own ability to be proactive is diminished either physically or psychologically. Babies are permanently helpless until they become mobile. The implication for carers is, of course, their own degree of sensitivity to what the baby may be experiencing. Some babies enjoy active games while others prefer a quieter and slower approach. Alternatively, a parent or carer may be more aware of their own needs – for example wanting a 'happy' baby – and consequently be over-intrusive or over-stimulating in their approach to the baby. The baby has a very limited repetoire of behaviours to adjust the level of stimulation input and therefore the onus is on the carers to adjust their behaviour to suit that of the baby. During day-to-day care activities and when ordinarily playing with and talking to the baby, carers must tread a fine line between providing the baby with novel and interesting experiences and allowing time for the baby to assimilate those experiences and not be overwhelmed. Babies also need the opportunity to simply 'stop and stare'.

Parents and babies together

As outlined in Chapter 4, babies are individuals with their own particular temperament or behavioural style. What is important is the degree of understanding that the parents have about the child and their feelings both about and towards that child. Levine *et al.* (1999) have produced a 'goodness of fit' model which is based on the matching of temperament styles in parent and child or at least the tolerance and patience of the adult if their style is different to that of their baby. We all have a particular temperament which, according to ongoing studies, does have a biological source. However, environmental experiences influence and shape how this temperamental predisposition will manifest itself over time. There are nine categories of temperamental characteristic, all of which are important to the quality of our social interactions – either as babies, children or adults. These are:

- *Activity levels* – in babies these can range from sleep/wake cycles to the level of activity when being bathed, changed, etc.
- *Rhythmicity* (regularity) – this relates to predictability or unpredictability (e.g. sleep/wake cycles, feeding and so on).
- *Approach or withdrawal* – the baby's interest (or otherwise) in new stimuli, which can be anything from a new toy to a new food or a new person.
- *Adaptability* – the ease with which, for example, a fearful response can be soothed and settled.
- *Threshold of responsiveness* – this links with approach or withdrawal and illustrates how 'sensitive' the baby might be. Some babies startle to the slightest sound while others appear to be unfazed by even fairly loud noise levels. A baby who is 'sensitive' to stimuli may also be reserved in their approach to novelty.
- *Intensity of reaction* – the degree of responsiveness to a stimuli, whether positive or negative.
- *Quality of mood* – this refers to the amount of pleasant or unfriendly behaviour exhibited by the baby.
- *Distractability* – this refers to how easily or otherwise the baby shifts its attention from one thing to another.
- *Attention span and persistence* – how long a child will pursue an activity and how far they will progress with it in spite of obstacles.

The interaction between temperament and experience was demonstrated by Sameroff (2000), who cites a 1982 study by Crockenberg and Smith which found that alert infants had mothers who spent more time in contact with them – although we cannot assume that the attention given to these alert infants was automatically positive. They also found that 'mothers of irritable females responded more quickly to their fussing and crying than the mothers of irritable males'. This difference in response means that similar behaviours received different responses. Over time, and if consistent, this will affect the babies' individual experiences of outcomes to their distress.

Temperament characteristics apply across the lifespan. What makes the difference is how we and other people deal with our own temperamental proclivities. For children, what is especially important is how adults help them deal with their particular characteristics. The parents' own attitudes, beliefs, styles of behaviour and levels of understanding will all influence the degree to which the baby's own style is accepted.

Of course, it is not only the parents or carers whose individual way of coping is important for the baby. The behavioural style of the professionals looking after it or making assessments of it is also important. To what extent, for example, might a professional's own temperament affect their judgement of a child who cries at strangers or is hesitant about new experiences? If the professional is an outgoing, adventurous person they may see the child's temperamental style as a potential problem or as simply 'irritating' and respond accordingly!

Sensitivity to the baby's need for rest, routine and warmth

The final part of the requirements for parents and carers when 'loving' their babies ties in with the others. I have already spoken of the need for parents to be sensitive to their baby's cues and of the need for all babies not to be overwhelmed by experience but for parents to follow the needs of the child and take into account the baby's behavioural style or temperament. As many parents who have had to suffer disturbed nights may recognize, many babies are upset following a busy day. Although there is no research evidence for such a thing, I would consider it perfectly feasible that babies can suffer the infant equivalent of 'tension headaches' and can feel real distress if handed round to too many people, subjected to constant changes in routine or to no routine and haphazard care.

I have also spoken of the importance of the 'how' babies are cared for. Babies learn to love through being loved by their carers. Human babies who have a primal need for affection and emotional security will soon learn if their primary carers do not care about them and will react accordingly. The attachment theory approach helps to provide a framework for the necessity of 'loving'. As I have often said, fortunately the vast majority of parents do love their children and provide them with safety and some kind of routine. However, there are loving parents who, because of their own lifestyle and inclinations, may not realize the importance of providing some consistency and routine for their baby and professionals who offer advice should help parents to see the reasoning for this and help them formulate some way of helping their babies while being sensitive to their individual rights and lifestyles.

Summary of points for professionals

Professionals need to:

- help parents have realistic expectations of their baby;
- remind parents to trust their own instincts towards their baby;
- help parents accept that they will have a range of feelings about and towards the baby;
- help parents realize that their baby is entirely dependent on them for emotional and physical safety and security, and give support;
- remind parents that babies need to 'learn' the rhythms of night and day, feeding, being awake and being comforted;
- remind parents that not all babies respond in the same way, even within the same family;
- tell parents that no one can predict the future for any child, but each parent can help the child have a positive start;
- reassure parents that support is available;
- build a relationship with the parents, with the child as the central focus;
- remind parents that their own history will influence how they react;
- act quickly if parents are unable or unwilling to care for their child.

Notes

1 There are many excellent texts which give detailed accounts of the month by month progression of foetal development for those who wish to study this further.
2 The amniotic fluid is the substance which surrounds the baby in the womb, which helps to absorb maternal movements and keeps the baby gently 'suspended'. The 'water's breaking' is a well-known term used to describe when this amniotic fluid is released prior to birth and is a precursor to the birthing process.

4 STARTING OUT (BIRTH TO 3 MONTHS)

Infants do not cry without some legitimate cause.

Ferrarius (sixteenth century)

Our own birth is the time of one of our greatest transitions – from life in the womb to life outside. It is therefore a time of fundamentals, when first experiences in the world build on the templates laid down in pre-natal development. This is the time when babies start to get used to their own particular environment and begin, most importantly, to build the foundations of emotional security – i.e. that through generally consistent care their basic needs for safety, comfort, warmth and food will hopefully be met.

During these first few weeks, babies work extremely hard at finding out about and making sense of their immediate environment. They are at the mercy of their carers and the only methods available to them of controlling interactions between themselves and their carer are the use of eye contact and (later) head turning. They can also, of course, sleep, which is not only the time when experience can be consolidated in the brain but also a respite from external stimulation. As sleeping, feeding and crying, and their role in the primary 'organization' of experiences are so important at this time, these will be discussed individually before moving on to the relationships between infant and carer.

Although this chapter considers development in the period from birth to 3 months I want to emphasize that whenever we talk about development we have to remember that each baby is an individual and will develop at its own pace within the human biological framework. At the same time, however, there are aspects of development that are usually achieved by most babies (in all cultures) at approximately the same time.

Thinking about experiences

CAMEO

Two babies are hungry and crying. They each provide clues as to the cause of their distress by mouth opening, head turning, and fists in the mouth, accompanied by sucking noises, in between their cries. The expression on their faces provides further cues that they are not content. Each of their respective carers responds to these cues but in very different ways. Baby A is soothed and talked to while the carer waits for the bottle to heat. Baby B cries on alone. Eventually both babies are fed. Baby A is cuddled and soothed and given time to feed. The carer only ceases the feed when the baby sends signals that indicate 'that's enough, thanks', such as head turning, relaxing, mouth closing and general hand movements. There is plenty of eye contact with the carer, smiles and that wonderful descriptive monologue that many mothers instinctively engage in: 'My, you are hungry today, don't go so fast, there there' and so on. Baby A relaxes and feels comfortably full. This sensation is a whole-body experience which is pleasurable. That the baby is engaged in this sensory experience is observed through body language such as slow eye closing, gentle coos and gurgles and a relaxed body posture. The carer interprets this as indicating 'fullness' and sensory satisfaction/contentment through their own understanding of what these bodily movements might represent.

Baby B is also fed but the bottle is propped up and Baby B receives little or no human stimulation or contact. Any verbal interaction may be weary, dismissing or even hostile.

In this cameo, both babies receive a similar response to their cries, which have been interpreted by their respective carers as a need for food, and both babies are fed. However, there is a world of difference between the qualities of their actual experience. If this manner of feeding Baby B is only a 'now and then' occurrence, and at other times feeding and other care is similar to Baby A, then the positive experiences will outweigh the negative. However, if this type of contact is Baby B's usual experience then his view of his world will reflect his experiences and is likely to result in his being lonely and/or fearful. This interpretation of the type of feeling Baby B might experience is only a pale shadow of the actual experience, because Baby B has no understanding of the reasons which might predispose his carer to treat him in such a way. He can make no excuses, he cannot rationalize – he can only feel his needs and give his responses in their purest form. Even if there has been no verbal interaction, the way in which he has been handled (the bottle propped up within his reach and his general physical environment) will be the emotional currency for his 'piggy bank' of experience.

Baby B will need to learn strategies to cope with the poverty of experience and negative sensations as a form of emotional 'self-protection'. His primary reactions to novel experiences will be based on, or affected by, this template and the quality of his continuing experiences will reenforce or alleviate what he has already begun to learn.

Graham Greene, is his book *The Power and the Glory* says: 'There is always one moment in childhood when the door opens and lets the future in'. In the cameo, a potential future for these two babies is already knocking at the door. I will refer to the cameo again to illustrate the importance of non-verbal communication and the development of a baby's first understanding of their environment.

The first thing to stress is that babies are remarkably resilient. Throughout the world and through the centuries they have survived times of plenty and hardship, wars, famines, flood and disease. Human beings, or rather human babies, have also survived (and continue to do so) in spite of diverse and often diametrically opposing advice and guidance on parental practice from 'experts', grandparents, friends, the media, magazines and the internet. However, the very adaptability of human babies, which leads to our own unique style of behaviour and personality in the context of our particular culture, has its roots in the commonality of our shared psychological and physiological systems.

The baby on arrival and after

What attributes does a baby possess when it enters the world? We have already identified in Chapter 3 that most babies born 'at term' (i.e. at 9 months gestation) are 'primed for action', and although the frontal cortex is 'waiting for experience' a baby comes equipped with a fully functioning brain. Babies can vocalize by crying, are able to hear well and see sufficiently to detect large patterns. Their inability to see fine detail prevents overstimulation of the visual sense. Babies are also sensitive to touch, taste, heat, cold and pain. Combined with this are a number of reflexes, such as rooting, sucking and grasping and the basic neural pathways for movement are in place. This is demonstrated by the existence of the 'stepping reflex': when a baby is held upright with its feet on a hard surface, it will make a 'step' movement. A further sign of neurological health is that the baby has in place the 'startle' reflex, which occurs when the baby's head is allowed to drop back suddenly when in the supine position. The baby flings both its arms out with the palms open and then brings the arms back to the body. This reflex illustrates that fundamental, life-protecting systems are in place, waiting for the fine tuning that experience will provide.

We humans have an inbuilt (or genetic if you prefer) response system to fear/anxiety with very well documented physiological response systems (sweating, pallor, sensations in skin and gut), and a response system that incorporates the 'freeze, flight or fight' response. It is important to understand that this system can be mediated by, and is connected to, cognitive processes in the frontal cortex but is separate from it – i.e. we respond first and think later. For example, we may react fearfully to a noise when walking home alone at night and then realize a cat has knocked over a plant pot. However, if there was danger, we would already be physiologically ready to respond.

A further important fact is that the brain system which responds to fear is closely linked to the neural systems which seem to be the focus of activity for feelings of 'rage'. The logic of this is obvious when we consider that one of our possible responses to fear is 'fight'. Fear and rage may also interreact to modify a response – for example, we may feel very angry about something but fearful of what the consequences might be if we act angrily. At other times of course, this combination of fear and rage can lead to more aggressive outcomes. Dependent on our experiences, we can also feel fearful of our own anger.

Although the display of fear does not appear to be obvious in babies until around 6 months, as I said above we are born with the 'startle' reflex. This is likely to be the precursor of the fear feeling as, if the baby is startled there will an accompanying sensation. Such a sense is vital as being afraid is such a strong survival instinct. However, babies are reliant on carers to keep them safe and are also not capable of independent movement, so a classic fear response is not necessary in the early weeks in evolutionary terms. However, carers can be fear-inducing, especially if mentally ill or under the influence of drugs or alcohol. Babies may react with startle/distress and/or anger in these situations and this may result in a 'freeze' response in some babies and continued rage/fear in others. Flight is not an option for babies! However, in more ordinary circumstances, the distressed cries of a very hungry baby do have an element of anger in them and it is certainly possible that this rage/distress has elements of panic/fear in it. These responses highlight that there is a strong emphasis on survival in very young babies.

Obviously survival is also helped by communication. As we saw in Chapter 2, very young babies can differentiate between sounds of all languages but lose this ability by the age of 12 months. In other words, we as babies come ready to deal with whatever language we are going to meet and later the brain filters out what we don't use or need. As babies, we also seem to have an innate sense of cause and effect, although obviously we don't 'think' about it that way. A baby as young as 42 minutes was able to imitate poking out his tongue, which if you try it as you are reading this will demonstrate graphically that you need to be proactive – it doesn't just happen!

As mentioned above, when born, a baby is able to see quite well as the eye is nearly mature. However, in newborns the ability of the musculature of the eye to adapt to objects at different distances is restricted. In our eyes, we have visual receptors known as rods and cones which are situated in the retina (the bit at the back of the eyeball). The rods are more numerous and are sensitive to black and white. Cones are less numerous but are sensitive to colour. Interestingly, the cones fall into three types, each type being more sensitive to one of the primary colours of light – red, blue and green. The area in the retina where the cones are most numerous is called the fovea, and it is to this area that over the first three months of life cones migrate. This 'migration' is only *fully* complete when we reach about 11 years, but it is in those early months that the fastest migration occurs.

As usual in development this is all very logical. The opportunity to see colour in depth is not necessary *in utero* but needs to be developed as soon as we are born – an example of 'experience expectant' development. By about 3 months, a baby's colour vision is similar but not so fine tuned as that of adults. Scans of the brain have shown us that this visual part of the newborn brain is the most highly active, which explains why infants are so visually alert early on, especially towards human faces.

What is important for carers is that babies are fascinated by objects close to them and their visual field encompasses the distance between the carer's face and where babies are usually held – at breast level – very nicely. The significance of acute hearing at birth and how this skill supports a baby's learning and contact is that the baby listens to the sound of say, its mother's voice and seeks visually for the source of the sound. This helps the baby to use both eyes together and the varying pitch and tone of the voice means that the infant keeps looking and tracking, demonstrating how the senses combine to provide information to the baby and encourage the next stage of development.

The newborn also has in place a rudimentary 'regulatory' system. As a foetus, the baby demonstrates regular patterns of spontaneous movement from around 12–16 weeks post-conception and researchers feel that this demonstrates the beginnings of organization of experience as opposed to genetic 'blueprint' activity in the central nervous system, which starts before birth and not at birth. In other words, before we are even born we begin to respond and instigate activity which is independent of, but dependent on, the sound workings of the DNA programme which builds us from cell to baby. We can only instigate activity if there exists a neural memory of that activity that 'pulls together' all the different workings of brain, nerves and muscles. Hitting a rattle for the first time means that there is a coordination, a basic pattern formed, between arm and eye.

Self-regulation

A fundamental task for all of us is to learn how to manage our own emotions and actions. This is often termed 'self-regulation'. The 'work' of the newborn is to begin to do for itself those tasks for life which were performed either by the mother while the baby was in the womb or in partnership with her. These tasks can be physiological, such as maintaining a normal body temperature, a combination of both physiological and behavioural, such as adapting to day and night, and psychological – for example, the soothing of inner feeling states, which eventually leads to the managing of emotions, including being able to actively control our behaviour and focus our attention. The achievement of self-regulation across all these domains involves:

- developing a relationship and communicating with the carer(s);
- learning and memory.

The intense care that very new infants require provides the corner-stones that allow the basic internal physiological and emotional rhythms to develop. Comforting, feeding, soothing, touch, taste and smell all combine to form a web of experiences which are organized into memories by the brain, providing the first steps in the organization of emotions and behaviour – the quality of which will depend on the quality and sensitivity of the care (as discussed in Chapter 3) and be demonstrated through communication. It may be useful to point out that in some western countries babies are expected to adapt quickly to the lifestyles of the parents without necessarily a full acknowledgement, realization and/or acceptance that adaptation/regulation takes *time*.

Newborn babies are often calm and alert for the first few hours after birth and then for the next three days or so can be much more unsettled. This is not surprising. Their brains are coping with a myriad of new experiences and are also having to adapt to the caregiving routines, whatever they are, of the parents (or hospital). What new parents may not realize is that very new humans have a wide range of 'states' including active and quiet sleep. Patterns of crying, attention and rest begin to emerge, although obviously they are still rather unstable. Parents must be aware of what mood or 'state' the baby is in when talking, feeding, changing and playing, and adjust their own interactions accordingly. Of course, many parents and carers do this almost instinctively, but not necessarily so. This means that it is important for those working with babies to bring this need for awareness to the parents' attention and/or be aware of it themselves and help to promote positive and mutually satisfying interactions. For example, it is not usually possible to distract a crying infant with toys. They usually need soothing behaviour rather than additional stimulation. After all, what would it feel like if you were crying and someone asked you to dance?

Babies are not indiscriminate beings. Even newborns show definite individual characteristics. These may relate to the baby's innate temperament (see Chapter 3), or what Levine *et al.* (1999) terms 'behavioural style'. Although this 'style' is variable, especially in the early weeks, it gives a general picture of the baby's usual responses to stimuli along with its individual levels of alertness and its sleep and feeding patterns. Some newborns already demonstrate 'fussiness' or startle easily, while others appear to be 'bomb-proof'. As Levine *et al.* describe, these individual differences can bring understanding and comfort, or confusion and conflict. The individual styles of the parents together with the behavioural style of the baby are mutually influential. Parents who are anxious and rigid in their style or who are rapid in thought and behaviour may not tolerate the distress of a cranky, fussy baby and respond in ways that increase the baby's anxiety. Parents who are too laid back may also not calm the baby but, through lack of interaction, may up the ante in the baby's world.

In Chapter 3, aspects of brain development in the womb were outlined. After birth, the process of connections between neurons really takes off. At birth, a newborn's brain is only about one-quarter of the size of an adult's. It grows to about 80–90 per cent of its adult size by age 3. Compare this to body size which at age 3 is only about 18 per cent of the size achieved in adulthood. This rate of growth alone should indicate the importance of the early years and the sensitivity of the child to adversity. The brain receives the myriad of information the baby is experiencing and then millions of connections take place, the ones that occur most frequently strengthening as they go. I must add that contrary to popular 'folk wisdom', as we get older we can still make connections between neurons – thank goodness!

As babies we need a wide range of experiences to help us consolidate the connections we need, because we are born with all the neurons that our brain will ever have. In the uterus, we actually produce many more but these are already being pruned before we are born. However, each neuron produces many dendrites (the receivers of information from the axons of other neurons – each neuron has dendrites and an axon so that it can receive and transmit). It has been well established through the use of positron-emission tomography (PET) scans (which image activity in the brain) by people such as Harry Chugani and Michael Phelps at the UCLA School of Medicine, that the brains of babies and young children actually overdevelop in the production of connections in the early years.

There are two important things here for professionals and parents to consider. First, the axons (the senders of the signals) from each neuron gradually develop a coating called a 'myelin sheath' which acts like the covering we see on electric wires, allowing the electrical transmissions from the neuron down the axon to be clear and speedy. At birth, while some axons have myelin sheaths (those in the primary motor and sensory areas) most do not, and the 'covering' process begins at birth and takes years. The process is most rapid in the first two years of life but then continues until we are about 30. The implication of this process of 'myelination' is that infants process information slowly – about 16 times less efficiently than adults. This is the reason why parents and teachers are advised to talk to children in clear, short, unambiguous sentences so they do not get 'overloaded' with information and can fully understand what we adults are 'on about'. It is equally important that very young children are given time to respond.

Second, as I have already said, most of the connections between neurons take place after birth and the huge burst of connections or 'synapse' formation is so enormous that it has been termed 'the exuberant period'. However this exuberance varies between different regions of the brain, beginning in areas such as vision and movement, and later occurring in the temporal and frontal lobes of the cortex which are more involved in sophisticated emotional and cognitive processes. When neural connections link together in a way that forms a pattern, a shift in development occurs. For example, a baby will move all its limbs in an effort to, say, touch a bright object. Through constant repetition, the connections 'form up' and the baby gradually refines its movements so that a wide swipe with one arm achieves the desired effect. Our brains need experience to practise what we need to know within the wider framework of how our innate development (such as myelination) is progressing.

In the first three months of life, the rapid myelination of the axons and the increase in the branching of the dendrites gradually allows the patterns of daily life to emerge, linked with the innate biological rhythms and needs the baby possessed at birth. This increasing regulation means that the baby spends more time in quiet sleep and remains alert and active for longer, and forms the basis for emotional as well as physical security. If we consider the cameo at the beginning of this chapter, we can see how each experience links together physiological and psychological networks within the brain. In the cameo, Baby A has learned that the carer is able to respond, most of the time, in a loving, caring way. Baby B, on the other hand, has little or no emotional warmth linked to the need for food. For Baby B, the experience is like eating alone at a bare table in a stark room. If these babies' experience in this situation is reflected by their experience in others, we can imagine the very different internal feelings each child will have. Care routines, such as nappy changing, bathing, feeding, playing and soothing provide an opportunity for a sensory 'bath' which can include being held, moved around from horizontal to vertical (thereby helping visual acuity), moving of arms and legs while being dressed and undressed, being turned from front to back, being spoken to and face-to-face, eye-to-eye contact. All these experiences teach the baby about themselves and the environment, about bodily sensations, space and movement. All this is particularly important because before language, actions and signalling through facial expression are the only way that babies have to let us know their needs. Over the first 12 weeks, parents will notice that the baby's physical movements become more integrated and babies can begin to look at their own hands and touch one hand with the other. The role that the carer has in helping these basic pathways to be formed may not have been formally researched but actions such as putting the hands of the baby together will help the coordination of involuntary/voluntary actions and muscular activity.

Babies, faces and communication

Two important clues to the emotional state of those around the baby are their voices and facial expressions. The latter provides one of the most powerful means of communication between infant and carer. Newborn babies come fully neurologically equipped to express what are termed the seven 'universal facial expressions'. These are happiness, sadness, surprise, interest, disgust, fear and anger, although they are much more readily and clearly identifiable by the ages of 3 to 4 months.

Studies have shown that what babies like best from a visual point of view is human faces, in particular that of the primary caregiver, which is most often still the mother. Take a moment to think about how most adults behave when with a baby. Intuitively we seem to understand that faces are fascinating and when talking to babies we not only tend to raise our voices to a higher pitch but also widen our eyes, exaggerate our mouth movements, raise our eyebrows and generally enlarge our expressions such as smiling or frowning.

Babies often respond to these exaggerated facial movements with huge delight and corresponding expressions. Recent research suggests that what we do without thinking when reacting with babies may be necessary for us as babies to learn about emotions. A study by Calder *et al.* (2000) demonstrated that adults identified increasing levels of exaggeration in the facial expressions seen as being more emotionally intense, even though the exaggerated expressions were rated as less 'face like'. In other words, we appear to organize expression (emotion) separately from facial features. We sort out what the expressions we see might mean before we know what a face is – which links with the developmental milestone that babies reach at around 18 months when they realize that the person they see in a mirror is them, to their great delight!

In addition, Ekman (1992, 1994) identified that expressions such as happiness (smiling), anger and fear have very distinct patterns of facial muscle positions, which indicates that when we first carry out these actions we begin to know what it feels like both physically and emotionally, and again, through familiarity, we begin to 'store' the experiences and can then 'recognize' a familiar expression or feeling. This also helps to explain why, if we try to smile when feeling rather miserable, it can actually alter our mood. The expression we adopt 'reminds' our brain about what it usually means and so the appropriate firing of neurons starts to take place.

Calder's study (Calder *et al.* 2000) also demonstrated that people were highly sensitive to changes in the intensity of expression. This work with adults again lends support to the importance of the work of people such as Janet Dean (see Chapter 3) who (along with many others) carry out detailed examinations of the interactions between carers and their babies, using freeze-frame videotape which identifies both the speed and responsiveness of babies to their carer's expressions and the speed at which emotions can 'play' across the face. The exaggerated emotional expressions we use with babies may help to 'imprint' both the expression and the feeling in the baby's mind. This is probably why changes in facial expression, no matter how fleeting, are felt by both infant and adult as being an indicator of the true 'emotional mood'. It is perhaps this combined experience of frequent face-to-face contact combined with the emotional expression on the face, together with the infant's ability to copy expressions and the accompanying physiological sensations, which help the infant get to know both the carer and how it feels to be with that carer. An interesting insight into how this process might work is demonstrated in a study by Forde and Humphreys (2000) of memory loss in people who have suffered brain damage. The study demonstrated that performance on simple tasks is better when someone is shown a task and then asked to imitate it. Studies on primates quoted by Forde and Humphreys have identified what appear to be 'mirror' neurons in the brain that are activated 'specifically within the context of an action being performed that mimics another action that is concurrently being seen' (p. 214).

This may help us understand how we learn about our own faces and feelings by watching and/or imitating the expressions of the faces we see in these early weeks. A further study by Ulf Dimberg in Sweden, quoted by Daniel Goleman (1996) found that when people view a 'smiling or angry face, their own faces show evidence of that same mood through slight changes in the facial muscles'. Interestingly, these changes are not visible to the naked eye. Freeze-frame analysis of videotaped interactions between mothers and babies also illustrate fleeting changes in facial expression, to which babies respond, which are also not visible in 'real time' playing of the tapes.

Studies also indicate that when two people interact, 'mood transfer' can take place – always from the more forcefully expressive to the more passive. This helps to explain how a positive smiling face can lift the spirits while a face full of rage may also transmit some of the fear that is associated with it. For an infant beginning to learn about emotions, such an association must be terrifying and this process may also suggest why a depressed, worn-out parent may feel angry helplessness in the face of a screaming infant or raging toddler as the baby's 'state' impacts on the mother.

By 10–12 weeks, babies can recognize their parents but are still quite a long way from being able to realize that when they cannot see them the parents still exist. This is the concept known as 'object permanence' and recognizing the familiar helps form the foundation towards this sophisticated understanding. A study by Atchley and Atchley (1998) identified the potential role of the right hemisphere in processing global information about objects which would seem to logically tie in with right hemispheric dominance in the early years and the infant's need to 'get the picture' before filling in detail. The level of visual acuity would also support this.

Through the constant flow of multi-sensory information, we can imagine in the cameo how Baby A and Baby B are learning about their world through the response of their carers. Once again, it is the consistency of response which allows for more specific patterning of the organization of experience within the brain to emerge. It can be seen how the different caring experiences of Baby A and Baby B can lead to very different internal states and thereby influence the type of strategy each baby adopts to deal with its positive or negative experiences.

Links between care and emotional regulation

In order to demonstrate how different aspects of the daily life of the infant help to establish the beginnings of emotional regulation, it is helpful to consider some of the basic routines which are essentially the 'life experiences' of a new baby – for example, crying, sleeping and feeding. In western cultures these life experiences may be regarded as 'problems' and therefore the information given will not be about the self-regulatory process specifically.

Crying

Crying is the baby's means of communication and can be related to the calling signals of other species to attract attention to themselves and obtain the care they need. Anecdotally, parents (usually mothers) state that they can tell by the quality of their baby's cry whether the child is hungry, lonely or in distress (e.g. cold and wet). As females are generally able to hear higher sounds than males, it is not surprising that women may be more biologically attuned to hearing both a cry and its different tonal quality. The immediate reaction for most adults (and children) is to soothe the child and cease the crying. Nature has been very clever (as usual) in that the cry of a new baby has an urgency, pitch and tone that generally provokes a rapid response. Sadly the very qualities that make it such an effective signal can also cause negative responses in some adults who find the cries intolerable to a destructive degree, and it is certainly true that an exhausted, stressed carer has to find reserves of patience and tolerance towards the baby which may prove very difficult. This is why practical support for parents, information about crying and increased understanding by the parents that the baby is not being deliberately difficult or demanding can help defuse potentially explosive situations.

Babies do cry – a great deal, particularly in the first three months and especially if suffering from colic (see p. 84). What makes it so difficult for parents is that babies can often continue to cry even after being picked up, fed and changed. Babies of course, cannot explain what is wrong and so the helplessness induced by a crying baby can feel very frightening. However, parents can be informed and reassured that for an infant to cry is normal and that infants across cultures do it and follow a similar pattern (including clusters of crying in the late afternoon and evening hours, just when parents are at their most tired!).

One of the least helpful bits of advice that can be given in these very early weeks is not to respond to the baby's cries as it might get 'spoilt' and/or become even more demanding. Grandparents, friends and sadly some professionals sometimes even say that the baby 'has got to learn'. However, contrary to what might be expected, the reverse seems to be the case. The underpinning principle behind the idea of not responding to the baby every time it cries is the notion arising from 'behaviourist' style concepts that 'rewarding' a behaviour reinforces it. In fact, we humans are more perverse and complex than this. If babies are responded to quickly in these early weeks, the crying may not actually become less but the babies can be soothed much more quickly and therefore spend less time actually crying. On the other hand, it is as Schonkoff and Phillips (2000) point out, babies brought up in understaffed institutions, cease crying by about 3 months. These babies have *learned* not to cry because no one ever responds, so on one level the behavioural principle is correct – but at what potential cost to the inner world of the infant? What is more striking is that behaviourists also say that the best way of ensuring a behaviour continues is to reward it sometimes and not others, and studies do show that parents whose response is somewhat intermittent seem to have babies who are more fussy and whiny. Babies' behavioural strategies in response to the care they receive have interesting echoes when considering the rationale for the categorization of attachment qualities (see Chapter 6).

Studies across cultures demonstrate a frequency peak of crying at around 6–8 weeks, gradually settling down again by about 12–16 weeks. Babies still cry after that time, but not so frequently. What differs across cultures is not the fact of babies crying but the types of response to, and rates of, soothing. A study quoted by Schonkoff and Phillips (2000) describes the different caregiving practices between the !Kung tribe and North American babies. The !Kung babies cried *as often* as the North American babies, but cried *less*. The main difference seemed to be in that !Kung mothers carry their babies with them all the time and thereby respond quickly to any cries. However, studies illustrate that even for American and British parents, those who are able to respond 'consistently and readily' to an infant's cries are rewarded by a reduction in crying over time.

When considering why babies under 3 months cry so frequently, it may be useful to consider what is going on in terms of the infant's overall development. We have already spoken about the enormous changes which take place in the brain together with the impact of brand-new experiences and it does not seem illogical that babies are in a state of mental 'confusion' and therefore may be generally more prone to feelings of diffuse distress without any specific cause. For example, imagine how you would feel if trying to concentrate while at the same time music is playing, a television is on, someone else is listening to a radio and yet another is playing a computer game with the accompanying bleeps and whoops. For very new babies all experience is novel, with only consistency and repetition over time allowing 'shape' to emerge from the confusion – which again helps to explain why, by 12–16 weeks, most babies have begun to settle, are less fretful and more relaxed.

Again, parents and carers must take into account the child's innate temperament and adaptability.

Some babies wake immediately into a state of 'quiet alertness', others may cry on waking. It is possible to compare how we wake from sleep as adults. Some people are grumpy, hard to waken and wish to be left alone, others are lively and alert from the moment they open their eyes. Babies are no different.

Colic

One of the most distressing events for parents of very new babies is that their baby appears inconsolable and this is often related to a condition referred to as 'colic'. Suffering babies are in real distress, often red in the face, with knees drawn up and are extremely difficult to settle. The pattern of crying follows that of other babies, with a peak at around 6–8 weeks, gradually diminishing by about 12 weeks (which can seem like 12 years to the exhausted parents). Because colic produces 'cramp-like' pains, treatment generally consists of gentle, abdominal massage and warm (not hot) towels placed on the abdomen or on the lower back.

A general guideline as to whether a baby is suffering from colic is if they: fuss or cry for more than three hours per day, for three days per week for three weeks. This is Wessel's famous 'rule of three' (Wessel *et al.* 1954). However, while this is a very useful aid to separating 'excessive' from 'normal' crying, babies vary widely and parents can record that a baby with colic is crying for most of the time and sleeps proportionately less!

The true causes of colic are still unknown. Intuitively, the problem seems to be linked to the digestive system, but many studies have shown that only about 5 per cent of babies with colic have an identifiable pathological cause. Given that in western cultures the incidence of colic can be as high as 10–20 per cent, this leaves an awful lot of babies (and their parents) in distress without a potential reason.

A clue to this apparent digestive distress lies in two areas. First, by the 3–4 month mark, the vast majority of colicky babies settle down and a happier baby with an easier temperament emerges. This hints at some kind of developmental process. Second, a study of adults with irritable bowel syndrome (IBS) found that rectal tone alters when people with IBS are exposed to emotionally-laden words expressing anger, anxiety and sadness (Blomhoff *et al.* 2000). While the researchers accept that there are difficulties in the study, they nevertheless feel that it clearly shows a 'close interaction among mind, brain and gut' and that 'gut motility may be a dynamic indicator of level of stress or emotional state'. While babies are going through this early developmental phase, which I contend may be quite stressful, some may be even more sensitive and so become colicky.

Sleeping

New parents learn to their cost that a very young baby can wake up anything between five and seven times during the night. Inevitably the amount of time a baby sleeps (and when) can become an all-consuming focus for exhausted parents. What may come as a surprise to some new parents is that we are not born with the ability to sleep during the night. We do, however, have a biological, internal 'clock'. This clock, which includes the sleep/wake cycle and other 'circadian' (24-hour) rhythms, is synchronized with the earth's rotation by means of factors in the earth's environment such as changes in light and temperature. However, biological sleep/wake cycles, plus the usual routines adopted by carers to settle and soothe their child such as rocking, stroking and feeding combine together to synchronize both the infant's own internal clock and their adaptation to the circadian cycle. Sleep irregularities are therefore quite normal up until around 6 months, but at the same time a night/day 24-hour rhythm can begin to be noticed anything from 2–6 weeks and a gradual lengthening in the time infants sleep during the night can begin at around 4 weeks.

Infants also are sensitive to family patterns of sleeping/waking, and over time adopt a pattern which reflects the household's attitudes to sleep. For example, a regular night-time routine helps establish a sleeping pattern while parents who are much more flexible about bedtimes may find their infants are difficult to settle. However, some researchers have asserted that up to 10 per cent of all babies still don't sleep through the night at around age 1.

The importance of establishing a sleep pattern is reflected in studies such as those by Pollock (1992), who in a very large national study reported that children with sleeping difficulties during the first six months of life were three times more likely to have sleep problems at 5 years and twice as likely at 10 years. Some other interesting facts emerge about sleep and sleep problems: boys appear to have a predominance in night waking and countries that have strict bedtime routines (such as Switzerland) report fewer sleep problems. Conversely, in cultures where there are high-density households, patterns of sleeping, eating, etc. are seen as of little importance, according to Harkness *et al.* (1999). Such children often find adjusting to routines once they enter day care or school more problematic.

Knowledge about the 'average' baby's sleep and crying patterns can help parents (and professionals) to respond to the baby in a more realistic way. Images of angelic, smiling babies in magazines, on television and in films, who sleep between feeds and all night do not reflect either reality or experience! Babies need help when they are born in sorting themselves out and parents must come to their rescue. It is a difficult situation for professionals as respect and sensitivity has to be shown to different lifestyles. In order to meet the needs of babies, professionals need to help parents understand that providing their babies with some consistency of experience is a potentially positive, long term, beneficial move. It is also very important to emphasize to parents that babies need to *learn* the routine, and so the regularity and rhythm of the day are essential to help the baby sort out the initial jumble of sensations, thereby establishing 'order' – a step towards the integration of experiences and self-regulation.

The more I read research on babies, brains, emotions and learning, the more it seems that the cornerstones for 'sorting out' experiences are stability, consistency and repetition.

Feeding

The cameo at the beginning of this chapter linked with the other information so far will emphasize the importance of feeding in the life of a baby both in terms of self-regulation and in terms of links between physical and emotional experience. The feeding of a baby is paramount in the lives of the parents and carers especially in the early weeks. How much and when are key issues for carers but in the emphasis on these practical considerations professionals also need to keep in mind the baby's emotional well-being.

One fact that professionals may want to remind parents (and themselves) about is that normal expected rate of weight gain in the first six months of life is greater than at any time during the lifespan and overall most infants will expect to double their birth weight in the first four months. Alongside this, as we know, the central nervous system is also developing at a galloping rate. This all amounts to a great deal of activity which requires a great deal of energy, and the 'hungry' baby is often just that, because it to needs the calories required to ensure optimum growth. The high levels of sugar and fats in breast milk are nature's way of ensuring that babies receive enough energy to fuel brain and physical growth. Myelination, for example, is a potential reason for babies' need for high fat levels in their diet until they reach about 2 years, as myelin is a very fatty substance.

Feeding demonstrates how a 'natural' need of the infant provides a frequent opportunity for carer/infant interaction, including 'talking', eye contact, holding and touching. It also inevitably involves the sensory inputs of taste and smell. In other words, the giving of food by either breast or bottle allows the mother or other carer and the baby an opportunity to learn about each other. Incidentally, myelination begins in the motor and sensory areas first, such as those pathways that receive information from the eyes, ears, nose, skin and mouth, so those experiences are transmitted more quickly, even very early in the baby's life. This again highlights the importance of the whole feeding experience.

The infant also learns about their environment through growing familiarity with repetitive experiences that are, in the normal state of things, extremely rich in sensory input. They are learning in other ways too – for example, the sucking reflex gradually becomes more under their control, so they are able to suck for comfort as well as food. Starting and stopping sucking becomes a more definite and purposeful activity, and the baby begins to acquire the first vestiges of independence through 'control' of feeding timing, pace and quantity.

The fats and sugars in breast milk stimulate taste buds that in turn are linked to opioid (natural painkiller) pathways which diminish the sensation of discomfort in hunger. Touch around the mouth also seems to set up a chain of chemical reactions that influence the brain pathways controlling distress. Thus it can be seen how feeding is accompanied by a range of physiological and psychological effects which combine to soothe and comfort the infant – far wider and more diverse than simply the mechanical act of 'being fed'. Add to this eye contact, holding and voice and the amalgam of these bodily responses provides a rich and powerful source of experience, linked inexorably with the caregiver(s). It is no wonder that eating and food are often laden with emotional and social overtones. The giving of food has an essential role in friendship in many cultures, can also be an emotional 'battleground', and is used by both children and adults as a way of self-soothing.

Links between feeding and sleeping

One of the most contentious issues for parents is night feeding and sleeping. It may be helpful (or not!) for mothers of breastfed babies and their partners to realize that according to Wolke (2000):

- breastfed babies start sleeping through the night later than bottle-fed babies;
- breastfed babies sleep less than bottle-fed babies over a 24-hour period.

The genuine distress through tiredness that this can cause is, according to Professor Wolke, one of the main reasons for women choosing to stop breastfeeding. The position is complicated by the fact that those babies who have a so-called 'easy temperament', wake up less in the night and generally feed less frequently may, in fact, not grow so well as they are not getting the nutrition they need. Many breastfed babies do need to feed during the night in order to double their weight. Perhaps it is not fully recognized by parents and professionals that essential growth requires calories.

Once again, mothers have to tread the fine line of allowing the baby to feed as it requires and at the same time not be seduced by the attractions of the 'good baby' who may be too 'laid back' for their own well-being! Of course it is also possible to overfeed, but this is more common with bottle-fed babies and is more a reflection of parental behaviour than the needs of the child. Advice from health professionals and the visible cues of a growing baby (clear eyes, alert and responsive) will help reassure parents that the child is receiving sufficient nourishment.

A final point regarding the link between sleeping and feeding is that some babies who had been breastfed in the first five months appear to have long-term sleeping problems (e.g. at 20 months of age). However, this seems as much to do with the mother's style regarding night-time feeds as with breastfeeding *per se*. Wolke (2000) uses the phrase 'feeding into submission' as one example and this seems to be a key factor, as other studies show no increase in sleep problems when the breastfed babies got older. The strategies used to 'get a baby to sleep' can sometimes engender further sleep problems. The reason is that the baby has difficulty in self-regulating and literally can't get to sleep without the parents adopting such strategies as rocking the infant to sleep in their arms, taking them for rides in the car and so on. If the difficulties get to this stage, compassionate and supportive help regarding behavioural strategies seems to be the most successful form of intervention.

Summary

How we learn is tied in with the brain's capacity to integrate experiences together with the associated feelings which accompany these experiences. The responses of carers to the basic systems of sleeping, feeding and crying outlined above will become part of what the baby learns – part of its sensing and forming of patterns.

Even in the early weeks of a baby's life, carers will detect subtle changes in how they behave which demonstrate how this integration of experience works. For example, by about 3–4 weeks babies can control very simple actions, such as looking towards a moving object or looking away from it: they have control over their own 'looking time'. By about 7–8 weeks infants, if sitting facing the carer, will respond to the voice by looking into the carer's eyes, cooing or smiling – or all three. At 2 months the baby's vision has improved considerably, resulting in a more complex response which combines physical and emotional behaviours. The most complex abstract thought, sensitivity, empathy and care has to begin somewhere and the first three months of life are the start of this road. The achievement of potential, the ability to learn, adapt and interact all start here, through simple, everyday care routines which, for the baby, are loaded with sensory experiences and also provide time for the baby to begin to settle to life outside the womb.

5 FROM SMILING TO WAVING (ALMOST!) (3-7 MONTHS)

The central theme of this chapter is the growing 'organization' of the baby and a sense of it reaching out into its world, both physically and mentally. Between 3 and 7 months, a baby's basic physical systems are settling down, vision becomes more acute and the baby's repertoire of signals increases: most babies are now fully smiling and obviously enjoying interactions. As the months go by, the baby achieves some amazing new skills: it can coordinate its lips and tongue in order to swallow thicker foods; it learns how to reach, grasp and bang objects together.

As well as transition from one capacity to the next, development can also be described as the growing ability to become steadily more independent and able to function socially and emotionally within one's own society and culture. Babies in this period are becoming more active 'agents' in their own environment – for example, their increasing physical skills allow them to reach for an object rather than simply have it handed to them. Their opportunities for 'knowing' are growing, including getting to know their carers and the objects around them. The world is expanding for our new baby.

According to Schonkoff and Phillips (2000) some cultures celebrate a child's 'first' birthday, three months after birth. This not only implies an acceptance that development/life begins at conception but also coincides with a 'biobehavioural shift' in development. Between three and four months after birth there are marked changes in almost every aspect of a baby's functioning.

This shift is striking and shows up in several ways. The amount of crying decreases (parents heave sighs of relief all round) and sleeping patterns also change. As we saw in Chapter 4, babies have very variable sleep patterns including the patterns of 'dream sleep' (REM sleep) and non-dream sleep, but by about 3 months or so the much more rigid patterns of dream/non-dream 'adult' sleep begin to emerge. Electroen-cephalogram (EEG) studies of babies at around this time demonstrate an actual shift in brainwave patterns.

By this stage, physical development has become much more coordin-ated, vision is much improved, the baby is more obviously looking, smiling and interacting and their repertoire of sounds is expanding. The baby's brain develops by being active and studies have shown that by 3 months the baby's brain can distinguish several hundred different spoken words.

The importance of talking to a baby, not just during the first three months but throughout its development, is demonstrated by Hart and Risley (1995) who found that the amount of speech children hear from their parents has a strong correlation with the child's own vocabulary growth. Hoff-Ginsberg (1991) also demonstrated that children whose mothers talked more during day-to-day activities had larger vocabular-ies. The brain organizes itself around those words that have been heard repeatedly within daily family life and begins to make connections be-tween these frequently-heard words so that it comes to recognize those sounds that are part of daily language. Repetition of words/sounds forms a network of connections in the auditory cortex so that over time com-prehension emerges. A similar thing happens when listening to a foreign language. If you are able to listen long enough, over time certain sounds will become familiar and that familiarity, linked with context, will lead to a gradual understanding of what the words mean.

By the 3 month 'landmark', the baby is emerging as an individual, with their own unique personality and temperament/behavioural style. It does not seem illogical to suggest that the first three months, with its emphasis on fundamental care, sleeping and feeding, provide the infant with the necessary emotional and physiological 'space' to begin to adapt, both to the particular rhythms of human life and to the specific type of care they are experiencing. Now that the baby's physiological systems are virtually adjusted to the new life outside the womb, they can get on with the important business of learning about themselves and the world.

Izard *et al.* (1984) tell us that the 'first exposure of a stimulus gener-ates an orienting pattern with its particular response topography and autonomic and visceral correlates' – in other words, we activate neural pathways and also react with feelings, actions and bodily changes. At around 11–12 weeks, carers will notice a greater coordination of actions emerging. For example, an infant can look at the carer's face, listen to their voice and smile (Fischer and Rose 1994). The infant, over time, has learned to put all these 'greeting' responses into one seamless action. Another example is that the infant can now make efforts to reach for a toy and open their hand at the same time. Later still, at around 15–17 weeks, babies can begin to make movements that show a greater degree of hand/eye coordination – for example, they can now reach for a moving ball and adjust their movements to take into account where the ball is on its continuum. This also illustrates a growing sophistication of visual development allied with muscular development and intention. The baby is attracted by the moving ball and wants to reach it. What adds to the attraction, of course, is that colour vision is also now improving. The magic is, of course, that the brain interprets particular colours as constants due to the working of different cells which compare the different colour signals from other surrounding objects. Being able to see an object as a constant colour helps the baby to further identify similar objects.

The classic works of Piaget, and more recently research studies such as those by Baillargeon *et al.* (1995) and Gopnik *et al.* (1999) demonstrate that infants as young as 3–4 months have already attained much useful knowledge. For example, that inanimate objects need to be propelled in some way into moving (such as shaking a rattle to make a sound); that stationary objects are moved when something comes into contact with them; and that objects cannot be suspended in mid-air. The presence of an innate sense of gravity has been demonstrated in studies of astronauts who have great difficulty catching a ball when in zero gravity (McIntyre *et al.* 2001). They persistently act 'as if' the ball will descend at some point, and so do babies!

When investigating babies' abilities, researchers use habituation. Once something becomes familiar, it no longer excites attention but if something novel happens then babies are again interested. Babies like looking at interesting things and have used this liking for novelty or strangeness to work out whether infants notice something unusual in the midst of something familiar, or if they are attracted by something that seems 'impossible' (remember how learning is influenced by 'novelty'). Carefully thought through and carried out experiments with things colliding, appearing on apparently invisible platforms, going down slopes and reappearing somewhere else have all demonstrated that infants look longer at the unexpected. This shows that infants are not 'fazed' by unlikely events and so possess some innate understanding coupled with what they are learning by experience. At 6–8 months, for example, babies are able to notice if the number of different items displayed to them on photographic slides changes. The numbers are kept small (two or three items on a slide) and once their 'looking time' has dropped with slides of say three different items, babies then perk up and show interest when they are shown a different number of items. The items themselves were not the same (the sides showed different household objects), the only commonality was the number. This research demonstrated that we, as babies, have an innate sense of number in an abstract form (Butterworth

1999). Infants around this age are also able to notice when things are added or substracted to a range of items, again by perking up and showing interest. They may not know what the items are but they have grasped that there is a difference.

The beginnings of 'Object permanence'

Babies have to learn about people and 'not people', things that move of their own volition (like people, animals, insects and so on), inanimate objects which require an outside force to move them about and pesky things in between like trees and flowers which are living things but stand still! How do we as babies begin to sort out what is what?

By about 6 months, adults will notice that babies have become excellent explorers of things. They will turn things around, taste, smell and obviously look. When looking, the patterns of light make an image which is sent to the visual centres of the brain. The information linked together and occurring simultaneously is what provides the brain with the overall information which allows learning about the environment and what is in it to take place.

During these early months the brain has to 'wire up' or make a 'map', 'representation' or 'schema' of the whole body, which includes a well-formed sense of where every bit of the body is in relation to every other bit. When asked to touch our toes, we don't have to think about it, even if we can't reach! We can also touch a part of our body with our eyes closed. However, if by some tragedy we lose a limb, there is every likelihood that the brain will still pass a message saying that the missing limb is 'itching' or 'feels' pain. In such cases, the neuronal connections fire spasmodically until they eventually reorganize to the new state of affairs. When we play 'heads and shoulders, knees and toes' we help toddlers learn about the body. By playing finger games with babies, we help to create the pathways of physical 'mapping' as well as cognitive and emotional experience – the latter providing the context which gives meaning to the experience.

By about 4–8 months, babies can find a partly hidden object and will 'track' something that is moving vertically. However, they still do not look for something if it has been hidden, even if they see it happening. Gopnik *et al.* (1999) describe the excitement a 6-month-old baby will display when shown something stimulating such as a jangly, shiny bunch of keys. However, if you put a cloth over the keys, in full view of the baby, they are deeply put out and will only get excited again when you pull the keys out from under the cloth. One (unsatisfactory) explanation for the baby not seeking the hidden keys is a lack of physical coordination in reaching for the cloth and pulling it off. However, if a transparent cover is used, allowing the baby to *see* the keys, they will retrieve them quite successfully. As with all aspects of learning, the qualitative leap of understanding that something unseen still exists requires a great deal of learning rehearsal: our brains need to assimilate a whole range of experiences before we can grasp even a rudimentary sense of an object's continuing existence. It is not until around 8–9 months (see Chapter 6) that babies will reliably look for the keys where they have been hidden. Another point of interest here which again demonstrates the temporal quality of development is that Gopnik *et al.* also suggest that the concept of 'disappearance/existence' is still not fully functional even in a 15-month-old baby who will look for objects where they last were rather than where they might be. Gopnik *et al.* clearly demonstrate that the permanence of objects moved from one place to another is something that has to be painstakingly learned.

Studies of memory in infants using heart-rate responses as an indicator of interest have shown that memory systems gradually improve over time, illustrating how innate development helps to support learning. A study by Frick and Richards (2001) showed differences in recognition memory for something briefly seen in infants of 14, 20 and 26 weeks of age. The study also made intriguing comments as to individual differences in development in babies within the groups, which seemed to link to the babys' physiological responses. Heart-rate variability, for example, is linked with attention/looking patterns and as heart-rate is also responsive to emotional states this again illustrates how emotions and learning may have mutually influencing effects on all aspects of development. As I have repeatedly said, babies need adults who are prepared to note their activities and interests and help them find out more. 'Babies lead and adults follow' is a pretty good rule to have! The concept of object permanence for people and things is discussed further in the next chapter.

Language

As noted previously, babies have an acute sense of hearing and a wonderful ability to differentiate tones in speech. They can also differentiate between what is speech and what is not (e.g. birds singing, cats meowing). From 2 months, they have begun to show a preference for their 'home' language, by about 4 months they 'like' words and by 6 months they show evidence of differentiating between sounds that are familiar to their language and those that are not.

Research also shows that babies like sounds and lip movements to match. We all know how distracting a dubbed film can be and babies are apparently not keen either! Discordance is difficult for babies on every level. As said previously, the brain makes patterns from repeated experiences and takes in all the information surrounding an experience in order to set a context for feelings, responses and actions.

Research carried out with a 13-month-old child nicely illustrates the importance context has for helping children to understand what is happening to them. A little girl was put in her high chair and given an apple. She was then asked to eat it. Obligingly she bit into the apple. She was then handed an apple when playing in a playpen and was asked to throw it. Again, the obliging child did as she was asked. However, when placed in her high chair and asked to throw the apple she bit it, and when asked to eat the apple when in her playpen she threw it. This sensible child had learned what usually happens in her high chair and what she usually did in her playpen. When we are very young, we need 'markers' to help us make sense of the world. The infant or very young child's growing comprehension of language is based on the usual contexts in which they hear particular sounds and it would take some additional experiences before this little girl could understand fully the terms 'throw' and 'eat' and that they could be applied in different contexts. It is the social, emotional and physical context of a word which helps the child 'catch' the meaning and from there associate the meaning with the sounds of the word.

As babies and children learn about language from listening to language, parents, carers, etc. should talk to their babies as much as possible. It is a heartwarming sight to see a parent out with their baby in the supermarket, giving a running commentary in a natural, unforced way, using an instinctive high-pitched tone with lots of 'swoops' in pitch, asking their baby whether they should buy the pasta or the rice, showing the baby the packages and so on. The parent does not expect a response, but frequently gets one in the form of smiles, gurgles, coos or babbling. What is sometimes called a 'proto-conversation' is taking place, with its proper pauses, turn-taking and interest – all leading to the baby learning about sounds, context and meaning.

'Motherese', or high-pitched and exaggerated speech helps babies to learn about sounds in a very special way. If you listen to someone talking like this to a baby, you will notice that the sounds of the words are enhanced. For example, 'Hello, how are you today?' might sound something like '**Hellll**loooh . . . **howww** are **you** today?' with bold type indicating potential emphasis or changes in pitch and tone. It is much easier for a baby to discriminate between sounds when listening to this type of speech. The greater emphasis on rhythm and pitch will also be accompanied by greater mouth movements and facial expressions (wide eyes, big smiles, raised eyebrows and so on). Sounds fun – and of course it is. Through this type of interaction, babies learn about their language and continue to practise making their own sounds in response to this wonderful 'noise'. 'Reading' and singing to a baby in this age range is all wonderful grist to the baby's language learning mill. Of course, it does not have to be only adults who do this. Siblings, older children and so on are all part of the learning process and as almost everyone who talks to babies uses the instinctive high pitch mentioned above, babies get to listen to what they like – adults talking in an interesting way, just to them.

Another way in which direct, baby-targeted speech can help development is through supporting the association of sound and vision. We know that even very young babies are perturbed if lip movements and sounds don't match. Vision and sound work together to help us make sense of what we experience. Sometimes visual cues provide the 'stronger' clues, but sometimes auditory stimuli 'win out' instead, especially when timing of events occurs. The example given was as follows: researchers flashed a circle on a computer screen and played a single beep at the same time. Viewers correctly stated they had seen one flash. However, when two beeps were sounded when viewers saw the single flash, they stated they had seen two flashes. Dr Shinsuke Shimojo, who carries out much of this research, is also doing studies on infants that demonstrate babies younger than 5 months still appear to have some difficulty integrating visual and auditory cues. For example, depth perception is not fully developed at 3 months and focusing is still inaccurate. If we think of the way the brain is developing, this is not surprising. Information reaches different parts of the brain for processing at different speeds (e.g. emotional information transmits faster than cognitive information). The synthesis of all this information into a coherent form requires time and the provision of day-to-day experiences to support the gradual integration of physical and psychological experience.

Babies who may be spending considerable time in day care need to have staff who recognize their need for language, routine, individual care and consistency of experience. Language repeating the baby's sounds, providing a variety of sounds including soft sounds to help them discern differences in sound (which ultimately helps reading skills as well as spoken language), and ensuring the setting is not too noisy all help provide a pleasurable language and learning environment. Carers, whether in the home or in a day care setting also need to remember that sometimes it is nice for the baby simply to practise babbling and cooing on their own. The interest in what sounds might be produced will be wonderful, with the baby realizing that they can squeal, blow raspberries or just repeat a sound and have fun in this way. A noisy environment with adults shouting, televisions blaring, radios playing and computer games zapping will reduce the opportunity for babies to familiarize themselves with sounds and decipher what it is that they are hearing through all their senses.

Weaning

One of the hallmarks of these months is that of 'weaning', when babies begin to move away from total breast- or bottle feeding and demand (in no uncertain terms in some babies!) to have something more solid. What is surprising is that babies have to *learn* how to swallow something thicker than a liquid. They do this by:

- using their tongue differently and 'synchronizing' their swallowing in relation to their food intake (this can initially cause gagging and spitting up as taking in food and swallowing it get confused);
- repetition of the learned procedures so that the brain adjusts to the new task – those patterns again.

While it is often tempting for parents/carers to put weaning foods in a bottle, as it can appear to pacify very hungry babies, it is not only inadvisable nutritionally, because babies don't get the required 'eating' practice. Taking solids off a spoon is much more appropriate.

The change from liquid to food is an intricate process, regulated by the brain and bodily physiology in tandem with the particular baby's own specific needs. It provides a new sensory experience of different tastes and textures. The introduction of baby rice is an exciting event, although those of us who have tasted it might wonder why! Many babies will reject a new taste first time, but the reintroduction of it on another occasion will help the baby make this exciting transition. Babies will have learned to spit out food by this stage. This does not necessarily mean rejection of a taste, but is also part of an exploring activity, a kind of 'look what I can do!' As the baby gets older, it will become more and more interactive at feeding time, reaching and grasping and, if bottle fed, will try to hold the bottle. The baby will also be much more vocal, expressing pleasure at the prospect of food and crossness at having to wait.

The success of early feeding depends critically on environmental conditions that are favourable towards building upon the first reflexes and oral skills (e.g. rooting and sucking), linked with age-appropriate shifts in psychobiological control and self-regulation. Carers will have to 'pace' the feeds for the baby, but the baby also can 'demand' by crying and then utilize different behaviours to 'tell' the carer its needs. A baby may indicate they have had enough by stopping sucking, head turning, active lip closing or, at a later stage, pushing away. Similarly, they will continue to suck vigorously or cry to indicate they want more.

By about 3–4 months, babies are also sufficiently confident about feeding to be able to express interest in what others might be eating, and have usually learned their feeding routine. As with everything else what happens to infants, the style and behaviour of the carer towards any aspect of interaction influences the baby's understanding and subjective experience. To give a rather sad illustration of how the style of the carer's actions can affect the infant's later attitudes to food and eating, I will cite an example from one of Janet Dean's (see p. 66) videos. It was striking to observe a 15-month-old child who had learned that feeding time was extremely distressing. The child had a hostile mother who pushed food mechanically into its mouth, with frequent exhortations to 'look at me' while the child desperately tried to reduce her distress by looking away. In the end, the child would turn her gaze frequently to the ceiling. The child's body language was interesting too, with the arms held out, flexed at the elbows, palms outward towards the mother, parallel to the head and neck. This child's whole reaction was both emotional and physical, showing distress, vigilance and behavioural adaptations to the painful experience. She also showed her compliance through the mechanical opening and closing of her mouth as the spoon went in and out. One can imagine how this child was 'introduced' to more solid food and possibly how she was fed in the initial weeks. Although this is an extreme (but sadly not uncommon) example, it demonstrates clearly how the style, attitude and approach of the carer towards feeding a child affects not only the actual physiological intake of food but carries with it a much wider impact on emotional and behavioural responses in the child. Remember that there are opiate pathways in the area around the mouth which relieve distress. The confused messages that the child in the video was receiving only added to their confusion and difficulties. One can imagine that food will not be a pleasurable part of life for that little girl.

Weaning does not *have* to occur at 3–4 months, 6 months or 9 months. In some countries, it is delayed as breast milk remains the most nutritious (and safe) food available. Apart from iron intake and some vitamins, generally breast milk remains sufficiently nutritious until the baby is about a year old (Stein 1999), and differences in cultural feeding practices need to be taken into account.

However, because of the increased use of day care, the transfer from breast to bottle often occurs sooner. Day care raises an important and difficult issue for those working in nurseries or as childminders. What might be the implications for the way in which mealtimes and snack times are managed in care and learning settings? What are the feeding/snack or mealtime routines and what is the style and behaviour of the staff? Unfortunately there exists in some settings a lack of realization that feeding/mealtimes are such an important part of an infant's life and 'group feeding' of two or more babies by one member of staff is not unknown. Look again at Cameo 1 in Chapter 1 (see p. 2). Having read this far, what do you conclude?

It can only be wondered at what 'messages' the babies in the cameo are receiving about themselves, their food and their world when fed by a harassed member of staff who is trying to cope with more than one baby and who may not necessarily or practically be able to time the offering of the food to the needs and style of each baby. What makes matters even worse is that the member of staff is talking not to the babies but to other members of staff in the room, so the emotional 'space' between the carer and each baby is qualitatively empty. A further point that professionals should consider is what a child's feeding/eating experiences have been prior to their admission to day care. This is particularly important when dealing with babies who are 'difficult' at mealtimes.

The importance of interaction during mealtimes and the use of language is illustrated by Gopnik *et al.* (1999) who identified research which showed that infants display a distinct preference for tapes where adults speak in 'motherese'. Babies were not so keen on tapes of adults talking normally, as if to other adults. So our babies who are being fed by someone who is not interested in them or talking to them are losing out on an daily opportunity for fun and enjoyment.

Communication

Although we have talked about language, we know very well that language is not the only form of communication. Alongside language we have non-verbal 'speech' which includes facial expression, body language and gesture. For babies, the sounds they hear are particularly set in a context of non-verbal language, whereas once we become proficient in language we are less consciously aware of what the non-verbal language of the other is saying – although we still 'read between the lines'. For babies, sounds, pitch and tone are an integral part of communication, and so interaction between parent/carer and baby needs to take into account the parent/carers attitudes, beliefs, values and style as well as their capacity to interact with the baby.

Communication involves not only the interaction between two people (whether between two adults, an adult and a baby or even two babies) but what each brings to the interaction. The response we receive from our communication, whether verbal or non-verbal, elicits a response which in its turn provokes a further response – i.e. the *transactional model* of communication. As we saw in Cameo 1 in Chapter 1, the particular responses to the babies cues set up a very different 'chain reaction' of responses and therefore, ultimately, behaviour (see Figure 5.1). As you will notice, both baby and adult interpret the meaning of cues (non-vocal/vocal and/or behavioural) and responses and interpretation involves assumptions.

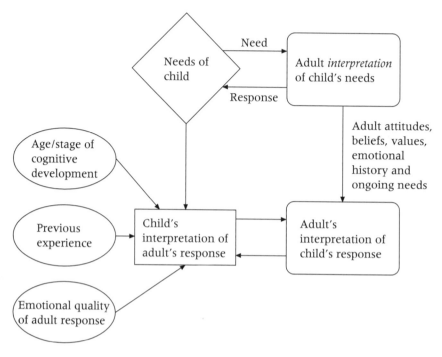

Figure 5.1 Illustration of the transactional process between baby and adult, demonstrating just one episode in an ongoing, dynamic process of day-to-day interaction

The child's interpretation is heavily influenced by their stage of cognitive development, which may or may not be linked with age, their previous experiences with that adult and the emotional quality of the response (e.g. adult responds with a smiling or angry face). Adults for their part will also interpret according to the three 'staples' – attitudes, beliefs and values – which, in turn, will be influenced by their own memories of parenting, emotional experiences with family, friends and partners, expectations of the types of response they usually receive (friendly, hostile, etc.), expectations of the child, beliefs surrounding childrearing and their ability to separate out their needs from those of the child. In addition, the adult will be influenced by their current social and emotional circumstances.

What is most important is the baby is not cognizant of what circumstances may be prevailing in the adult's life and can only respond to adult communication *as it appears and feels to them*. If a parent talks about having to leave the child to cry for a long time because they were feeling fraught due to personal circumstance, the child only knows what it feels like to be crying alone. As adults we can be sympathetic towards each other but the baby has no choice but to feel what is happening to them.

Summary

Communication between adult and baby during months 3–7, when the baby is becoming more proactive and increasing synthesis between sensation, internal physiology and ongoing experience organizes the infant's view of the world, is paramount. Adults in reality do not have to do anything very special. A 'rich' environment for a baby means loving adults who are sympathetic and responsive to the baby's needs, who take time to talk, sing and play, who carry out daily care tasks with sensitivity, who handle the baby with confidence and not roughly or as if the baby is about to break, and who share the baby's distresses and joys. This, of course, also applies to babies in day care, whether in a group care setting with a childminder or in their own home with a nanny. Whoever is the primary carer for the baby needs to focus their attention *on* the baby. Babies need to feel safe and secure and the way to achieve this is for adults to provide this care through holistic communication.

It is through our vocal/verbal and non-verbal interactions that we begin to consolidate, modify or change a baby's first impressions of the world. As mediators of the child's environment we can give the baby opportunities and resources to explore their environment: bath toys, board books to chew, things to pull and shake, objects to feel and grasp, experience of textures, new tastes, warm bedding, soft toys, mirrors, music, sounds, being lifted high in the air, swooped and rocked. We give the baby their world and we also provide them with experiences which are the precursors to future relationships, future learning and the ability to adapt to their own particular lives. Experience may be the sculptor of the baby's mind but it is we adults who provide the chisel.

6 PEEK-A-BOO AND WHERE ARE YOU? (8–12 MONTHS)

This chapter covers expected development and transitions between approximately 8 months to 1 year. Within this time several key changes occur which are the precursors to more sophisticated behaviours later on. It is useful to note that at 8 months we have twice as many neuronal connections between the cells in our brains than at the age of 12 years. Around this time too, EEG recordings show a heightened degree of both coherence and strength in brain activity and there can also be a spurt in head circumference.

Changing perceptions

First, we need to remind ourselves that development occurs across domains simultaneously but at differing rates and intensities, influenced by unfolding, temporal, innate processes within the brain, and by environmental stimuli. We learn a new skill or acquire new meaning because particular domains of development have linked together with gradually increasing complexity – with some connections having an 'Aha!' quality. A child's ability to handle a small brick is dependent on physical development, sensory integration, the opportunity to reach and grasp together with the provision of objects to grasp and reach and the motivation or curiosity to do so. Emotions also play a large part – the stronger the emotion, the more likely a child will remember an experience. Babies and young children will also be more receptive to new experiences if the general emotional tone of their previous experiences has usually been positive. Negative emotions also influence a child. If these are very strong, then this can override their capacity to learn. A distressed child will not want to, or will be reluctant to, play with small bricks either in the short term (such as a stranger wanting them to 'perform' for a development check) or in the longer term if they have been neglected or abused.

Key developmental areas at this time are the emergence of *object permanence* and *separation anxiety*. These developmental milestones are interlinked and also mark another stage in the formation of the relationship between a baby and their carer. The nature and quality of this relationship will have been affected by the quality of the interactions between adult and baby, and in tandem with this will be the growing formation of the 'internal working model' or template discussed in Chapter 2. The ongoing questions are whether the baby is learning that they have a secure base from which to further explore their world or whether they are learning strategies to cope with the more negative sensations that are their daily experience. The quality and type of relationship or 'attachment' of the baby towards its carer(s) has also been developing through their daily interactions and in this chapter we think about attachments and *attachment theory*. A third key area is that of *joint attention* which is linked with the concept of *social referencing*.

Development, like the Roman god Janus, looks both ways: into the past and into the future. Each experience adds to the endless summation of experiences that, from moment to moment, intertwine the past with the present and herald future behaviour across all areas of development.

Understanding learning in these early months is of necessity hampered by the fact that infants cannot tell the adults around them what they are experiencing. Adults should work on the assumption that the infant world is very different from the world of the toddler and the preschool child, just as many of the attitudes and beliefs of adolescents can be very different from those in middle life. All researchers can do is make assumptions from their findings which in turn depend on their particular hypothesis plus their own individual belief system as to how human development occurs and what influences are primary. For example, if you believe as I do that emotions are primary influences on learning and that children who are distressed are unable to learn, then the findings of some of the studies discussed below will provide food for thought as to what might be going on in the mind of the baby and their resulting behaviour.

During this time, babies move through a very well documented transition of skills and emotions. A child of 8 months has gained a much richer repertoire for investigating all those interesting objects now within exciting reach, especially when they have gained a degree of mobility either through crawling or bottom shuffling. For example, a baby can use its more sophisticated visual skills to work out how best to reach for a toy, as it is now able to work out where the object is in relation not only to other interesting objects but also to the baby – far away or close by. If we think back, at 3–4 months, babies can track an object smoothly because their eyes are working together. Over the next few months this skill becomes more refined.

Pinker (1998) describes the work of psychologist Richard Held who maintains that the neurons in the receiving part of the visual cortex 'sum up' the input from each eye, but gradually the neurons in this part of the brain develop a 'favourite' eye and the information can be more smoothly integrated – the brain 'knows' what direction the stimuli are coming from. This has implications for babies and children who have a different visual capacity in each eye. The stronger eye's neurons 'elbow out' the information from the 'weaker' eye – the so-called 'lazy eye'. Strabismus or 'squint' is caused if one eye is far-sighted and the baby struggles to focus on near objects, and this struggle pulls one of the eyes inwards. If uncorrected this means that vision is impaired and there is a sensitive period here as surgery to help line the eyeballs up is not effective after the ages of 1 or 2. It is no coincidence that it is around 8 months of age that health visitors in their routine developmental checks are looking out for any signs that a baby's eyes might not be working together.

Once a baby has reached a desired object, it can be brought close to the face for minute inspection, turned over, mouthed, fingered and felt. One of the traditional health visitor checks at this age in the UK is to hand a small brick to the baby who obligingly takes it. The health visitor then gives the baby another brick. Many babies of this age will transfer the first brick into the other hand in order to reach for the second brick. This indicates an awareness of both sides of the body, the ability to focus, the use of two hands and much more independent action – i.e. the baby can reach quickly and purposefully with a smooth movement. Health visitors also note the way in which a baby reacts to this 'testing' by someone who is most probably an unfamiliar figure as well as the baby's general level of interest and enthusiasm, bearing in mind of course the context, such as time of day, whether the baby is hungry and so on.

Shared perceptions

From the age of 6 months, infants use gaze in an increasingly complex and social manner and it is at around 9 months that most babies actively take part in 'joint attention' – the ability to shift attention between an object and a person. This means that both baby and carer can focus and pay attention on the same object such as a toy, but the magic difference is that the baby is aware of their own and their carer's interest in the same thing. Let us just think about that for a moment. The baby now knows that 'I am looking' and 'you are looking', and so 'we' can look together. So begins the first understanding of a shared meaning and experience. This mutual sharing is probably built on the type of 'turn taking' that baby and carer have previously engaged in during their 'conversations' over the past months and is logically a precursor for understanding other mental states.

Researchers working with children with autism often discover in the history of the child that this shared looking is minimal or absent at this stage and one of the key theories regarding children with autism is that they have great difficulty working out what other people might be thinking or feeling and alongside this is a reduced ability to 'read' expressions, which also links with what has been termed *social referencing*. This term is used to describe how, when faced with an unknown experience, a baby looks to the carer to assess reaction and a positive or negative reaction on the part of the adult will influence the way the baby responds to the new experience.

A study by Kingstone *et al.* (2000) underlines how brain development influences the 'coming together' of various developmental strands. The researchers illustrate how shared looking involves developing cortical processes, including those areas in the brain that process upright images of human faces and interact with those areas that process information from the eyes. A shift in gaze involves identification of where another person is looking and the ability to purposefully shift the gaze as a consequence. This 'paying attention' to a shift in someone else's gaze is very powerful. Try looking upwards, for example, and notice how may people will openly (or furtively) glance upwards too. Parents often follow the gaze of their infant, pointing out a bird or a plane, and this practice may also help the baby, when the brain is sufficiently developed, to look alternately between the object of interest and the adult with whom they wish to share the moment. Incidentally, pointing at an object also occurs within a similar time frame in the latter half of the first year and this method of inviting shared attention further enhances the opportunities for the baby to realize that both it and its carer are seeing the same thing and sharing the same world view. A study by Johnson *et al.* (1998) considers what mechanism is at work which prompts infants (and adults) to follow the gaze of another and 'intention' certainly seems to be a strong contender – i.e. an understanding that someone might be thinking 'this is interesting'.

An important part of both sharing and learning is that we 'pay attention'. For example, a baby looking at an interesting object. Paying attention or noticing involves a whole body assimilation of information and response. Dawson (1991) describes the physiological changes which occur simultaneously when babies 'orient' or pay attention to a stimulus. The body becomes momentarily stilled, pupils dilate, brain waves desynchronize, there is a response in the skin, breathing and heart rate slow and there is a decrease in peripheral (outer) blood flow. If we bear in mind that learning is accompanied by an emotional context and that both emotions and attention are more actively processed in the right hemisphere of the brain, then we can see how all experience, especially in these early months, works towards the integral relationship between emotional, cognitive and physical experience – and that future learning will be influenced in turn by the qualitative interplay of ongoing whole body/mind experience.

One of the most famous pieces of research which linked together social referencing, innate development (i.e. the ability to crawl) and behaviour is the 'visual cliff' experiment with 1-year-olds (Sorce *et al.* 1983). By this age, social referencing is well established and the research showed how the facial expression of emotions such as joy/interest, sadness and anger/ fear in mothers influenced how their babies behaved when presented with a potentially confusing or scary situation. In the research, infants were presented with a visual situation that gave the appearance of a 'drop' or 'cliff' on one side. The mothers were asked to give different facial cues to their babies as the infants moved towards the 'cliff', in order to assess the impact that their expression had on the children's attempts to 'cross'. The findings showed that the infants behaved in accordance with their mothers' responses. For example, in one phase of the study an anger face resulted in no babies crossing the 'cliff'. A fear face produced a similar response although some babies did cross. Joyful or interested faces gave most of the babies confidence to cross while a sad face produced more confused responses as the babies tried to work out what was going on. That the babies had a sense of 'danger' was elicited by the very laid back responses of those who were presented with a very much shallower 'drop'. Anger and fear were both found to be powerful inhibitors of the babies' behaviour. Similar experiments using mothers' varied reactions to toys demonstrated that infants of 12 months reliably respond to novel toys in a manner consistent with the responses of their mothers, even if the toy might seem attractive and appealing in itself.

An important aspect to consider in mother/baby interaction and parental responses is that parents frequently exaggerate their emotional response to a person, situation or object when with an infant – often totally unconsciously. If the baby crawls away and then comes back, it is often greeted with an effusive response that heightens the pleasure at reunion and also the positive feelings associated with the carer. This has a twofold outcome. First, the baby becomes confident in the continued loving presence of the parent, even when they move away, and second, being with the carer is associated with a positive, pleasant experience. However, whether the emotions are positive or negative, the often greater expressiveness of emotion means that the baby is much more likely to 'attend' and so the meaning of the emotion becomes more established as the baby 'mirrors' the expression in its own way.

Attention and learning

Infants become more able to share interest and attention during this phase of development. Much research has been devoted to how 'attention' and developing language might influence learning ability. Sigman *et al.* (1997), for example, compared information available on visual fixation (what the baby was noticing) and home rearing conditions in 93 infants and the results of the same babies' cognitive test measures at 18 years. They found that the greatest predictive association for positive results was the extent to which children were spoken to between 8 and 24 months of age allied with the amount of time children spent looking at objects. This study and others dealing with infant development and links with later cognitive ability also highlight the interlinking of different aspects of development. It would seem that infants who spend shorter times 'looking' are processing information more efficiently while 'long lookers' are taking in the information more slowly. As we know, infants generally spend longer looking at novel or unexpected happenings but it is the amount of time they spend 'digesting' this new information that is a factor in later outcomes. As always, the impact of the carer must not be forgotten or underestimated in this process: the findings in the Sigman *et al.* study also included the impact of adults talking to the babies.

Rose *et al.* (1999) studied 'attention' to a learning task in 5-, 7- and 9-month-old babies. They found that positive emotion (or affect) appeared to be associated with 'long-look durations and slower learning'. Another longtitudinal study of infants between 3 and 11 months also looked at the relationship between emotion and attention. It found that infants who were distressed for shorter periods of time, were also 'short lookers', the implication being that these babies were able to regulate their distress and concentrate. This ties in with research indicating that children who are in emotional distress (acute or chronic) don't learn well. On the other hand, Rose *et al.*'s study raises the intriguing possibility that if we are enjoying ourselves a great deal or are emotionally 'occupied', we don't learn as well then either! Perhaps babies are most receptive to learning when in a quiet, alert state without too many distractions. We learn best when we are alert, generally calm and in an atmosphere which is not overly distracting. This has implications for parents and caregivers who need to allow babies to explore without too much interruption and intervention.

Of course, individual temperament is also important. Some babies are more able to cope with noise and constant stimulation than others. Another angle to consider is that the part of the brain linked with 'attention' is also the same region associated with the hands. Thus, babies' love of handling objects and their fascination with their hands contibutes to their ability to 'attend' over time to experiences beyond those that directly influence or interest them. It is noteworthy how playful activities facilitate, support and enhance learning in preschool children and that these activities are often multisensory, automatically involving the hands (e.g. building bricks, water play, sand play, finger paints, planting, modelling, measuring, cooking and so on). Conversely, as Dr Linda Nathanson-Lippit in Atlanta pointed out in a communication to an internet paediatric development debate, it is not surprising that many children diagnosed with attention deficit disorder (ADD) have problems with sensory integration.

This raises some interesting questions about the trend to provide quite formal (as opposed to playful) learning experiences for very young children. The right hemisphere of the brain is more dominant in the early years and is active when children pay attention to where someone else is looking (Schore 2001). The right hemisphere is also more concerned with the 'overall' meaning of experience, which means that learning what other people think and learning about the environment through movement, touch, etc. are linked. Consequently, giving children tasks more orientated to the *left* brain before they are developmentally ready may adversely affect their ability to attend as well as impacting on other aspects of development.

Before we move on to thinking about the change in language – babies are now usually 'babbling' in a speech-related way – I would like to identify some changes in sleeping and feeding which occur during this period and which link with the other aspects of development which are coming 'on line' for the baby.

Sleeping

Most babies are sleeping most of the night by this stage, but it is not uncommon for babies to develop some different behaviours when falling asleep such as head banging, rocking and restless leg movements. Head banging is particularly common and in the absence of other difficulties is not usually a sign of pathology. However, the development of the ability to finally understand that what is not seen still exists also means that babies who may have settled into a nap and/or bedtime routine now become fretful again. The baby during this time needs help in learning, in this new context, that being settled for a nap is a safe and secure business.

To understand this it is useful to ask ourselves: how do we know, when we wake in the morning, that we are in the same place as when we went to sleep? Most of us have had the unnerving experience of waking up, perhaps in a hotel, and not being sure of where we are. This shift in development – being able to understand *permanence* – takes a great deal of 'rehearsal'. Reassurance, soothing actions and the use of comforters such as a favourite toy, a piece of blanket or a dummy can be helpful here. These 'transitional objects', as they are sometimes called, are things that help babies in the transition between external comforting and 'internalizing' the comforting feeling. The baby is learning to self-soothe and self-regulate their distressed feelings, with help from understanding and sympathetic carers. In this way the baby is able to build up an emotional 'security bank account'.

Feeding

As we have seen, the baby's skills in handling small objects, its hand-eye coordination and its fine motor movement are now becoming increasingly noteworthy. From now on, the baby gradually begins to assert independence, for example by trying to hold a spoon and attempting (but usually failing) to feed themselves. Finger foods are an attractive option here and the ability to get the tasty object into one's mouth is satisfying and rewarding. Parents need to be encouraged that exploration, including exploration of tastes and textures in food, is a natural part of development and babies of this age will not usually be 'tidy eaters'. Once again, the temperament and attitude of parents and/or carers will affect this area of development. A baby who happily spreads their hands into a plate of beans is not being 'naughty' or 'dirty'. The beans may taste good, but they also *feel* good and smell good too! However, if the parent is someone who cannot abide mess or who finds a bean-covered baby off putting, then they need support and guidance to help them in not taking out their dismay and frustration on the baby. Angry wiping of a baby's face may not seem like abuse but the subjective experience of the baby, associated with the angry or disapproving face, tone and pitch of voice aligned with the experience of mealtimes bodes ill for both parent and baby.

Many babies, especially after the age of 10 months will find dropping food off the table and watching it fall to the floor an interesting game which links very well with the concept of object permanence which has now reached the stage of the baby realising that out of sight still exists.

Language

We have already considered the importance of language with babies from the moment they are born. Babies learn about the rhythms, pitch and sounds of their language from hearing their home language around them every day and being spoken to them. By about 6 weeks, 'term' babies (i.e. those born at the usual gestational time) have already picked up the rudiments of turn-taking, due to their interactions with their carers. By about 9 months, babies are beginning to recognize the particular emphasis or stress patterns on syllables that a particular language uses. For example, in English the first syllables in a word are usually stressed while in many other languages it is the latter syllables. The rhythms of language in different countries which share a common language are also different. For example, Australian English and American English differ in this way, and so Australian and American babies will learn different cadences and stresses. Babies are now babbling and interestingly produce similar sounds across cultures. 'Babababa' or even 'Dadadada', much to the disgust of some mothers who think that all their care has been set aside by this baby who is busy calling for their father!

Some physiology

There are definite 'language centres' in the brain, evidenced by a myriad of techniques and research including the study of people who have lost speech or the capacity to vocalize thoughts in a particular way. Although these language centres have a specific purpose, the actual way the brain processes the information is very complex. Specific areas that have been identified are *Broca's area* (for speaking) and *Wernicke's area* (associated with hearing words).[1] Both these areas are in the left hemisphere of the brain. Interestingly, when the brains of people who are deaf are imaged, signing produces activity in the left hemisphere of the brain also (Neville *et al.* 1998). These areas are, of course, not the only active regions. When someone is 'silently generating words' or seeing words, then other brain areas are active. As Panksepp (1998: 333) points out, communication 'can be elaborated by other brain areas, especially when we are young'.

The complex processes associated with language are highlighted when we look at development 'backwards', in people who have had damage to areas related to speech – for example because of a stroke. If there is damage to Broca's area, the ability to speak coherently can be greatly impaired but the understanding of language remains intact. Interestingly, the motivation to use language appears to lie in an area of the brain called the anterior cingulate cortex, which is also very involved in social motivation, emphasizing again that we are born with the innate potential to communicate on a wide range of levels with our fellow human beings. Damage to this area results in people still being able to speak but not particularly wanting to communicate. There is also a difference between the ability to use words and understand the meaning of them, so a person can speak fluently but not necessarily understand what they are talking about. It is rather like a child who appears to be reading fluently but on closer questioning has memorized the word shapes and sounds but has no idea of the sense of the story. What is fortunate is that if damage occurs to the left hemisphere early in life, then the right hemisphere takes over to a great extent and normal speech can be obtained. The right hemisphere is involved with what Panksepp calls the 'emotional melody' of language, so that someone who has lost left hemispheric speech may still be able to sing express-ively! There are also corresponding areas to Broca's and Wernicke's in the right hemisphere. The corresponding area to the former influences our ability to express emotional meaning while the corresponding area to the latter allows us to interpret the emotional tone of speech. This all ties in rather beautifully with recent brain research which indicates that different types of experience create different brain rhythms and that emotionally 'charged' experiences can 'tune in' to frequency ranges that have special biological meaning.

There are also possible gender differences with regard to speech. It has been suggested that males are more dependent on the left hemisphere for organization of their speech, while females appear to use both hemi-spheres, although some studies of brain activity during language process-ing show an emphasis on left brain activity in both sexes (see e.g. Shaywitz *et al.* 1995; Frost *et al.* 1999). Carers need to take note of these possible physiological gender differences and should not have expectations of similar language acquisition in the early years for girls and boys. They should take care to sing to, talk to and read to babies to ensure the best possible environment for language and meaning connections for both males and females.

Language is one of our richest modes of communication, but words are not 'sterile'. Each word has a meaning and as babies we learn about not only labelling of 'things', colours and shapes but also the emotional meaning that words carry together with the emotional tone with which all our utterances are subtly or powerfully imbued. If we are bored, people can often tell even if our words are 'breezy'. Think of the phrase, 'I'm fine' and consider the emotional minefield that this common utter-ance can imply! Just as babies can 'read' facial expressions with stagger-ing rapidity, they can understand the nuances of the emotional tone and the meaning of utterances long before they have caught on to the 'language'. This is supported by the fact that people are more likely to remember emotionally meaningful words if they hear them in their left ear (which is 'governed' by the right side of the brain). If heard in the right ear, they are more likely to be forgotten. Other research (Frost *et al.* 1999) also supports this 'left ear'/'right brain' advantage for such stimuli as musical chords and melodies. An interesting piece of research could be to see which ear adults 'in love' might instinctively choose when whispering sweet nothings! Yet another fascinating aspect is that females across cultures and independent of whether left- or right-handed, show a distinct preference for cradling infants in their left arm, which means that the left ear of the baby is uppermost when they are being fed or cuddled, the right ear being nestled next to the body of the carer. Such a distinct cradling preference is not demonstrated in men.

As babies are developing their language skills, they are also learning about the world around them, learning about their world's reality is through increasing mobility, the ability to practise and/or rehearse and the ability to play in different ways.

Mobility

Around this age and onwards most babies are usually beginning to be mobile. Crawling babies are able to be more proactive and some babies discover that they can crawl along while holding an object in one hand. Crawling, of course, means potential access to a much wider range of fascinating household objects and this is when the 'no' word can come into the carer's vocabulary! Of course, it is going to be many more months before the baby really gets the idea that what they are doing is not what their carers want them to do and it is often far less stressful for adults and babies to adjust the surroundings so that the baby is not 'set up' for negative responses. A useful way of doing this is for the carer to crawl about on the floor and view the room from the baby's point of view.

This can be a taxing time for the carer as the baby's new-found skills mean that it is not only beginning to give expression to its own curiosity but also its need to be close to the carer. The baby will become distressed if it cannot see its carer. This is the time when 'separation anxiety' begins. Infants can sometimes become 'velcro babies' – attached to their parent's leg! However, for some parents, the lesser degree of helplessness and the ability of the child to play with a toy on their own can lead to a sense of not being 'needed' or as vital to the baby's survival. If the parent(s) have an unrecognized, unconscious need to be needed which has been met by the absolute dependency of the baby, then the gradually emerging independence of the baby may be met with efforts to 'control' that baby. Such control can be rationalized quite logically and realistically as keeping the baby safe, and professionals may find a subtly controlling parent difficult to spot. However, persistent anxiety that the child will hurt themselves, swallow something and so on may have its roots in trying to keep the baby 'helpless'.

To emphasize how different types of development interlink, there is some very fascinating work by Fox *et al.* (1994) which links the experience of hands and knees crawling with cognitive competence – i.e. the ability to retrieve a hidden object when moved to a different location, as in Piaget's classic 'A not B' task.[2] Fox *et al.* noted that babies who were more successful at finding a hidden object were also those babies who had a few weeks' experience of hands and knees crawling. Their study included EEG monitoring of brain activity and indicated that there is a surge in connections between frontal/occipital and parietal occipital regions in the cortex linked to the onset of locomotion. The brain patterns of babies who had not yet started crawling were different from those who were 'early crawlers' and they were different again from experienced 'movers' who showed evidence of pruning of the neural pathways. The brain appears to over-produce connections until the pattern required to carry out the action or understand the meaning is obtained. Unwanted connections are them pruned.

The parietal lobe of the cortex is involved with spatial skills, attention and sensory pathways to the hand, so greater stimulus for spatial awareness may in turn influence the baby's ability to locate an object in 'space'. Fox *et al.*'s intriguing study illustrate the depth to which different areas of development are intimately connected and how not only the ability but also the opportunity to develop skills (e.g. space and encouragement to crawl) supports the unfolding of innate processes.

Learning and remembering, practising and play

One of the strategies we use to remember something is rehearsal/repetition/practice. For example, we learn a poem by saying it over and over again, we learn to drive by practising and this same process of repeating a particular movement or intention is one of the strategies that enables us to learn about everyday life. We also use 'summarization', another memory strategy for checking understanding: If we can summarize something it means that we have grasped its essence. By grouping together similarities, our brains extract a concept or meaning and again, like Janus, they work in two directions. The complex interlocking of neural patterns means that the brain can put together items of information and then, as we become more familiar with basic ideas, we can actively break down this information into specifics. Once we recognize the features that mean 'bird' we can then discover the different types of bird using these self same features to differentiate between them. However, if we miss out some of the basic ideas, subsequent knowledge and/or experience may never quite fill in the gaps – only bridge them. This notion is useful when thinking about the difficulties a child may have in learning: what are the 'gaps' in their previous experience? This is as true for considering emotional learning such as attachment formation (see below) or for those who never quite understand how to work out percentages, volume or distance other than by a mechanical formula which may give the correct answer but leaves understanding behind.

Most babies are sitting very steadily by now, although some may still require a cushion or other support at the back to stop leaning backwards. This ability to sit brings with it a whole new wonderful experience – the opportunity to explore a 'treasure basket'. This method of supporting infant learning was devised by Elinor Goldschmied and was initially aimed at infants who sit steadily but are not yet crawling. However, the principle can be adapted and used for children up to preschool age. The concept, detailed information and other valuable advice and guidance for children under 3 years in day care is given in *People Under Three* (Goldschmied and Jackson 1994). A brief summary of this delightful way of supporting infants in the exploration of their world is well worth a mention here.

The treasure basket idea was in response to the identified 'boredom' of babies around this age, and was designed to help parents realize that everyday objects are a wonderful source of stimulation, interest and exploration. All the objects in the treasure basket (of which extensive lists are given in the book) are objects easily obtainable at little cost, such as large pebbles, fir cones, large corks, a shaving brush with those lovely rounded ends and soft bristles, objects in rubber, fur, metal, and so on. There is no plastic! Perhaps the most salient point here is that when early years workers are shown a video of infants and older children playing with treasure baskets they are often astounded at the degree of concentration and attention displayed. Infants have been known to play with the items for up to an hour, taking out objects, testing them, returning them, retrieving them, exploring, tasting, passing from one hand to another and sometimes sharing their pleasure with a responsive adult. What is so wonderful about the treasure basket is that this method of introducing exploratory objects matches perfectly the developmental stage of the infant in the second half of the first year. As we saw above, this is when mouthing takes second place to exploring with the hands and sensory input from the hands links with attention.

The role of the adult here is that of attentive watcher, providing the baby or babies with the security and comfort of an adult presence with whom they can share an object, if they choose, but whose interested, unobtrusive and non-interventionist presence gives the baby the freedom to explore at his or her own pace. Adults are discouraged from helping the infants to explore as the adult would wish – as Goldschmied puts it, not to 'offer' objects to the baby or help them to hold the 'right' end', and so on. It is often very difficult for professionals and parents to simply let a baby be and allow them the emotional and cognitive 'space' to find out for themselves.

Goldschmied also points out that in group situations, babies involved in such play are very aware of each other, with shared smiles and glances. However, it is not proximity alone that prompts this – it is the previous secure experiences of the babies with adults that have led them to be confident enough to explore and interact. Goldschmied's work with abandoned infants in post-war Italy demonstrated that the infants did not interact with each other at all even though 'they had spent all their waking hours lying or sitting together in a playpen'. These children could not socially interact because they had never experienced a consistent, caring, sensitive adult who was responsive to them. The innate potential for contact with other human beings had not been developed because of the lack of the first stage in the process – a main carer who provides the baby with the sensitive, focused interaction so necessary for survival.

One final point here is that treasure basket play is essentially an exploring type of play, different from rough and tumble, tickling and crawling about games. Babies need both, and as they get older and more physically competent, opportunities to rush about, slide, swing, jump, wrestle and climb are also part of their *necessary* repertoire of learning about the world. Unfortunately, the value of physical activity and the use of the outdoors to widen, enhance and promote children's learning is sadly underestimated, with outside play often being seen as an opportunity to 'let off steam' monitored by, at times, uninvolved adults, rather than the rich and varied experience it could be.

We now move onto one of the most important transitions at around 8 months is the beginnings of understanding object permanence introduced in the previous chapter. This has interesting links with a baby's emotional development, and it is to this that we now turn.

Object concepts, permanence and separation anxiety

Object concepts and object permanence

As a baby learns about their physical and emotional world, they need to learn about the permanence of objects, both seen and unseen. A prominent researcher into infant cognition and their understanding of objects is Rene Baillargeon (1987a, 1987b, 1994), who identified three important concepts that babies need to learn:

- something that is hidden still exists;
- the hidden object retains all the properties it had before (i.e. a yellow ball is still a yellow ball even if we cannot see it);
- the hidden object will still behave in a predictable way and is still 'subject to regular physical laws' (Baillargeon).

This all seems very obvious to us adults. Our lives are based around such assumptions. Things that are dropped, fall, things we cannot see, still exist. When we leave a room we do not anticipate that the furniture will move around or that it will have changed shape or structure (although we might wish it if we are fed up with our current chairs!). Magicians' shows 'work' because something unexpected happens. Rather like babies, we pay attention to the unusual and the unexpected because so much of our lives is based on fundamental assumptions which include physical laws such as motion, gravity and time, all founded on our everyday experiences with falling objects, night and day, locomotion and other creatures. We expect people in general to have two eyes, a nose and a mouth and two ears, and faces to be the right way up (we have great difficulty recognizing faces if they are upside down). We expect arms to be on the upper body and legs on the lower body. We have learned about heat and cold; that feeling heat is not quite the same thing as learning about temperatures; we know that if we hit something with something else, the first object will probably move or break, or both. In essence, we can only live our lives if we make these assumptions, otherwise every day would be a day of discovery and uncertainty. We develop a sense of 'reality' built upon a logical process of synthesis of experience.

However, we do not start out knowing these things, nor is our sense of individual 'reality' universal, especially when concerning people and ourselves which I will discuss further in the section on attachments (see p. 125). Regarding our understanding of the reality of 'objects', while there is much debate as to when babies begin to acquire the idea that things hidden still exist and can be found, there is a general agreement that it is not until about 8 months that most babies will reliably look for an object, such as a toy which has been hidden under a cloth (see p. 130). This milestone is far from the end of the story, as the concept of objects existing when not visible is far from fully developed in all its aspects. The next step from being able to retrieve an object from its known hiding place is to realize that the object might be hidden in a different location.

The three ideas listed above are crucial to our survival and our ability to interact with our environment. The understanding that objects can remain the same in different locations is as difficult as realizing that it still exists if we cannot see it, and the struggle to fully appreciate this 'wonder' underpins much of early play. If we look at children from around 1 year to 18 months using the treasure basket mentioned above, we see them exploring in very similar ways. The children are fascinated by objects being put inside other objects and by tipping them out again. A child will often reach inside the container and feel around to find the objects, retrieve them and then 'post' them again. Any parent or carer will know the popularity of the toy with different shaped holes in the lid and the efforts that children will make to push the objects through the holes and then retrieve them. Children will repeat an experience over and over again. What they are doing is making strong connections between those parts of the brain which will organize the results of the hiding and retrieving game.

Consider how popular is the game of peek-a-boo. Babies love this game and will play it for ages, but you may have noticed that some babies will become distressed if you don't 'appear' quickly, so adults need to adjust their timing accordingly. Some babies may find the suddenness and/or the 'boo' rather upsetting and such babies will need the adult to adjust their behaviour to help – perhaps by only partially hiding initially, or by playing different games. Others babies will be quivering with excitement, anticipating your appearance and the accompanying 'boo' greeting with squeals of delight. This is where carer sensitivity to the baby's individual temperament and consequent 'behavioural style' comes into play so that the baby can receive stimulation which is developmentally appropriate but also in tune with their own specific needs. Novelty and surprise can also be stressful and therefore the way new experiences are handled – even if inherently positive and enjoyable – can influence the ongoing reactions of the baby.

At this age, babies have a fascination with dropping things. They will than watch and wait for an adult to retrieve the object so that they can drop it again. Instinctively many parents and carers know that the child's playing is part of their learning, and will patiently keep picking up the teddy or the piece of toast or whatever. Other parents may see this behaviour as 'naughty' or frustrating, not appreciating the degree of practice needed to provide the security of permanence. Parents can be greatly helped by the professionals with whom they come into contact if the reasons for this repetitive and exploratory behaviour are explained. Parents can cope much better if they realize that the baby who tips up the plate of spaghetti hoops is actually on a voyage of discovery and not doing it to annoy their carers and make a mess.

As they get older, children remain fascinated by appearance and disappearance, and love those push-up, cone-shaped toys, where pushing up on the stick makes a teddy or other animal appear. Think too of the 'jack in the box', where again children will push down the lid and wait for the appearance of the toy over and over. I mentioned magic shows above, and some of the flavour of this 'magic' occurrence for babies is still with us when we are amazed as the rabbit emerges from the hat or the egg from behind the ear. From all these games, including (later) 'hide and seek', babies and children learn the permanent existence of objects in the widest sense and with greater complexity of understanding.

Separation anxiety

Although the timing varies between babies, it is at around 7–8 months that many parents begin to notice that their baby suddenly seems afraid of unfamiliar people. This comes as a surprise because previously the baby was friendly with everyone. The reason for this change in behaviour, known as 'separation' or 'stranger' anxiety, ties in with the realization of object permanence. The baby's experiences over time have helped them to distinguish between those they know and 'others'. The baby has developed a 'template' of familiar faces that has arisen through an association of repeated experiences. Development in the frontal cortex of the brain, the area associated with the ability to regulate emotion, think and plan, probably underlies the emergence of these behaviours. The baby can hold the image of familiar caregivers in their mind and compare it to the image of 'other' – either a new person or a friend or relative who visits infrequently. Maturation of memory and repeated experiences help the baby to distinguish between people they know well and those they do not. This awareness of familiar and unfamiliar, comes alongside the dawning realization that it is not only 'things' that still exist when not seen, but also people. The security linked with familiarity (and even negative experiences can feel 'familiar') means that the baby still likes the parent to be close by, and if they leave the room they will try to follow (if physically capable) or will cry or fuss. The baby has learned to organize themselves so that they keep close to a few familiar people. In particular, if distressed and/or fearful, they will turn to the person who they have learned will prove responsive to them and whom they know well.

Attachment and attachment theory

One of the most influential and debated theories about the process of emotional development is that of attachment, with its implications for cognition, social interaction and emotional well-being across the lifespan. It must be emphasized that attachment formation can continue throughout life just as cognitive development (both social and intellectual) also continues throughout life. Attachment theory is the subject of a vast range of literature and therefore can only be briefly discussed here. However, I hope that this brief overview of the background to attachment theory and the later work on classifications of attachment will serve as both a refresher for those who are familiar with the theory and a stimulus to read more about it for those who are not.

The term 'attachment' was used by John Bowlby ([1969] 1991) to identify this particular form of relationship between the child and its mother. Although the theory originally dealt only with the mother/baby relationship, it can and does encompass a child's or adult's relationships with others which retain the particular qualities of 'attachment'. A discussion about the concept itself will follow in the next sections. What must not be underestimated is its importance. Schore (2001) states that Bowlby recognized, more than 20 years ago, that attachment theory can frame specific hypotheses which could link early family experiences to 'different forms of psychiatric disorders, including the neurophysiological changes that accompany these disturbances of mental health'. He adds: 'It is thus no coincidence that attachment theory, the dominant theoretical model of development in contemporary psychology, psychoanalysis, and psychiatry, *is the most powerful current source of hypotheses about infant mental health*' (Schore 2001, emphasis added).

In addition, Schore (2000) emphasizes the neurological underpinnings of the formations of attachment and points out that the right brain is centrally involved not only in processing social and emotional information, but also in the associated functions of bodily survival and management of stress levels. In addition, he emphasizes that the capacity to prefer the familiar and to tolerate new situations with minimal or managed stress is fundamental to an individual's ability to move onwards in their development.

The integration of neurobiology and attachment theory has helped support an understanding of the process of how an infant learns to function emotionally and behaviourally, and in addition how it feels to *be* that individual.

A brief historical background of attachment theory

Attachment theory was developed by the English psychiatrist John Bowlby in his book *Attachment and Loss* ([1969] 1991, [1973] 1991, [1980] 1991). It has been further developed in the UK and USA to the present day. Karen (1998) describes the theory as one of 'love and its cultural place in human life'.

John Bowlby was born in 1907 and became interested in developmental psychology while studying medicine at Cambridge University. It was while working in a small residential unit for maladjusted children that his attention was drawn to two children in particular. One followed him around like a shadow and the other was an isolated and remote individual. He became interested in family influences at this point and his early writings give indications of how his thinking regarding attachments was already developing. One of his key works was a paper called 'Forty-four Juvenile Thieves'. His work with this group of boys demonstrated for him that 'had it not been for certain factors inimical to the healthy development of the capacity for object love, certain children would not have become offenders' (Bowlby 1944: 53).

Bowlby then began to focus his work on mother-child separation. His theory was the result of not only his own particular experience, work, research and psychoanalytical training but also of considering information from other sources such as ethology (especially the work of Robert Hinde, Konrad Lorenz and Harry and Margaret Harlow) and cognitive psychology (in particular the work of Piaget). He also considered the work of social workers, in particular that of James Robertson, who joined Bowlby in his 'sanatorium study' which was designed to follow up children between the ages of 1 and 3 who had been hospitalized. Robertson made the famous (and at the time notorious) film *A Two Year Old Goes to Hospital*. This remains a classic and is still used as a powerful training tool in understanding the impact of the separation of children from their carers. In its time, it forced a review of hospital practice with children. James Robertson's wife Joyce joined him and Bowlby in this work and contributed greatly to a further series of films.

Bowlby maintained that infants are born with instinctive attachment-seeking behaviours which in turn combine to attract caregiving behaviours, and that the strength of the primary affectional bond persists throughout life. Later attachment workers emphasized that children can make powerful attachments to others, including influential teachers, and that as we get older other strong relationships take centre stage while the relationship with parents may become less important. However, many therapists would contend that an adverse primary relationship can 'get in the way' of understanding relationships with current partners, and the work of Mary Main (Main and Kaplan 1991) in the Adult Attachment Interview, which examines the relationship between adults and their children, also emphasizes the importance of adults' primary relationships.

Bowlby was the object of a great deal of misinformed criticism when certain groups took his theory to indicate that women were 'prisoners' of their children. As Ornstein (1997) points out from his own experiences regarding the 'hijacking' of right-brain theories as being against rationality, if an idea is bound up too much in the social and cultural influences of the time, then the true meaning and implications of that idea may be lost. In fact, Bowlby had nothing against, for example, a 'good' nanny although he emphasized the importance such a person would have on the life of a young child. He also advocated sensible advice regarding getting a child used to small separations and stressed the importance of a well-known (to the child) full-time loving 'caretaker' (e.g. father or grandparent) if the mother had to be absent. However, Bowlby firmly believed that a loving mother was crucial to the child.

Perhaps the most fascinating aspect of the development of attachment theory is that it was a dynamic process, with Bowlby refining and thinking about his work all his life, listening carefully to the interpretations and additions of others and collaborating with highly skilled people like Mary Ainsworth and Colin Murray-Parkes, who was responsible for highly influential work on bereavement and the grieving process. The brilliant but troubled psychiatrist R.D. Laing was also part of Bowlby's cohort in the 1960s.

Bowlby's thinking was originally stimulated by two main issues. First, the finding that many maladjusted adolescents had suffered a lack of 'mothering' in one form or another. Second, the very real distress displayed by very young children on separation from their mothers. The final component of the 'secure base' came later with the work of Canadian psychologist Mary Ainsworth (e.g. 1985) who was rather charmingly described as the mother and grandmother of attachment theory, being the mentor of many attachment researchers.

A comprehensive and masterly overview of the role of attachment in the organization of behaviour is given by Schneider-Rosen (1990: 185) as follows:

> The establishment of an attachment relationship is considered to be a critical socioemotional task that must be accomplished during the infancy period, that provides the basis for competence and effective functioning and that prepares the infant for the successful resolution of subsequent developmental tasks in the socioemotional and cognitive domains . . . Once an attachment relationship has developed during the first year of life, it is characterised by a pattern of behavioural organisation that is mediated by affect . . . and that operates in transaction with other organised behavioural systems that regulate the infant's interactions with her [*sic*] environment.

A final point before we move onto Mary Ainsworth's work on the classifications of attachments is a further reminder that Bowlby recognized that attachments were a *dynamic process* and considered that how an individual developed was due not only to how caregivers treated them in infancy but also throughout childhood and adolescence.

Attachment classifications

Much of current thinking on attachment theory has been highly influenced by the work of Mary Ainsworth who, before she met Bowlby, had already studied under William Blatz in Toronto. In his studies regarding abnormal psychology, Blatz had developed his 'security theory', which considered how a young child was able to acquire the confidence to leave its mother and explore its particular environment without (too much) fear.

Ainsworth moved to London with her husband and applied for a job with Bowlby, analysing the data that the Robertsons were bringing in. She worked with Bowlby for three and a half years and during this period also learned from the Robertsons about the power of observation. Her husband meanwhile obtained a job in Uganda and Mary went with him there. With no formal role, she began to think about her past experiences and re-established her thinking about mother-child relationships and the development of security. She started observing mothers and babies in their own homes and over time she visited 28 babies and their mothers twice a week for nine months. She gradually began to notice a difference in both how the mothers reacted to their babies and how the babies acted and reacted. She identified different phases of the development of attachment including a consideration of the secure base.

Some years later and now in Baltimore, USA, Ainsworth set up a project which involved naturalistic observations in the home (which incidentally showed up the difference between what can really happen and self-reporting by adults). She then decided to test her hypothesis (that if a child has a secure base they are more able to deal with unfamiliar environments) by comparing the activities of the Ugandan infants with American infants. What she finally devised was the now classic 'strange situation' technique.[3] She found great similarities between the behaviours of children from both countries, demonstrating clear links with the parental behaviours previously observed. She also found two main categories of attachment – 'secure' and 'insecure' – the latter being subdivided into insecure-avoidant and insecure-ambivalent. These categories not only indicate the quality of the mother-child relationship at the time but also the child's internal working model. The behaviours illustrate how the child feels about, and can cope with, stressful situations and the reliability (or otherwise) of their main carer.

The main classifications of attachment fall into the following categories:

- avoidant (A);
- secure (B);
- ambivalent (anxious) or resistant (C);
- disorganized-disorientated (D).

An in-depth discussion on patterns of infant attachments can be found in Ainsworth (1985), but the following gives a broad outline of the different categories as set out by Slade (1999). Slade points out that these categories identify *patterns* of behaviour in response to important persons when the child is under stress – and that these patterns indicate how the child has formed both a view of their experiences and a systematic way of responding.

The 'avoidant' category (A) is characterized by the 'dampening down' of feelings (and even thought when older) related to attachment experiences. The 'polar' opposite is that of ambivalent/anxious/resistant attachment (C) whereby feelings appear to be heightened with the child (and adult) showing behaviours which are meant to encourage care and concern by others. The secure category (B) is illustrated by behaviours which seem to be reasonably managed – i.e. both positive and negative emotions are expressed in a way that appears coherent and appropriate to the experience. For example, a child falls over and may cry but is easily comforted and soothed. An avoidant child may hide, not cry, not seek adult comfort and so on. An ambivalent child might scream and cry or appear angry as well as distressed. The first three categories also have extensive subdivisions indicating a wide range of behaviours which nevertheless point to a particular style of response to stressful situations.

The final classification (D) was a later addition – the outcome of considerable analysis and study of many 'strange situations' and the interactions of mother and child. This category deals with the incongruous behaviours demonstrated by some children at reunion. For example, a video I saw during an attachment classification training week showed a child who stroked the wall when the mother entered the room. This was only one of several bizarre and unsettling behaviours the child demonstrated on reunion with the mother, while still demonstrating distress when left alone. A study by Heller and Zeanah (1999) shows how mothers who were still struggling with feelings of grief and helplessness had their children assessed as having disorganized attachments, which further supports the notion that it is the quality of the mother's emotional availability and expression which influences the way in which the baby experiences the mother. The classifications themselves refer to the types of behaviour that children at the age of 1 year demonstrate on separation and most particularly reunion with both mother and a 'stranger' in this laboratory situation, thereby giving a clue to the child's view of the world.

It is important to emphasize that the links between the behaviours seen in the strange situation and parental styles were based on thousands of hours of observed interactive behaviours in the home by Ainsworth and her teams. Since then considerable work has been done across cultures and continents which has replicated these broad categories, although of course the findings are not without critics. Nevertheless, I feel there is sufficient information available as well as what can be witnessed in the everyday behaviour of infants, children and our own behaviours with partners, friends and family at times of stress to indicate that our feelings of emotional 'safety' are closely linked with some of our close relationships. Many of our behaviours at such times echo those thought of as being indicative of attachment rather than other 'relational bonds' and these attachment behaviours are set out by Weiss (1991: 68) as follows:

- *Proximity seeking* – the child will attempt to remain within the protective range of their parents. This range is reduced in strange and threatening situations.
- *Secure base effect* – the presence of an attachment figure fosters security in the child. This results in inattention to attachment considerations and in confident exploration and play.
- *Separation protest* – threat to the continued accessibility of the attachment figure gives rise to protest and active attempts to ward off the separation.

Weiss also gives additional 'properties' of childhood attachment which include the important point that the infant/child will form an attachment to the primary carer despite the quality of the adult's care of that child – what Weiss terms 'insensitivity to experience with the attachment figure', which is discussed further below.

Stroufe (1981: 3–4) summarizes the power of very early interactions as follows:

- Individuals are biologically disposed to form intimate (attachment) relationships and development takes place in the context of these relationships.
- The earliest relationships are of special significance because they provide the context for the emergence of the self and because they represent prototypes for later relationships.
- Early prototypes are carried forward through the attitudes and expectations the child forms concerning the availability and likely responses of others and the outcome of their own efforts to cope with stress.
- A prototype behavioural organization will be manifest in different though coherent forms in different circumstances and at different points in development.

According to this approach and considerable longtitudinal studies (e.g. Shaw and Vondra 1995; Lyons-Ruth 1996; Shaw *et al.* 1997), the quality of these primary attachments has a great influence on future development. However, the formation of attachments is not a static process and both the quality of attachment and the attachment relationship(s) can and do change. As infants and very young children we can also form secure attachments with other primary caregivers such as fathers and grandparents, nannies and sometimes older siblings. As we grow older we can form attachment relationships with close friends and partners. It is very likely, however, that the prototype of these first relationships reverberates, no matter how faintly, throughout the life cycle, finding its expression in the qualitative style of our relationships. One of the most fascinating aspects of the growth in early brain development research is that the findings are beginning to illustrate why and how early or primary attachments remain so important. As we know, the right brain is dominant in the first three years of life and a wide range of research implicates this hemisphere in unconscious processing of information and early learning, especially about the *emotional* value of experiences.

It is therefore important for those working with babies and young children not only to be aware of the concept of 'attachment' and the background to it, but also to think about how the attachment is actually formed, what influences its quality (i.e. the classifications) and how the attachment influences the child's behaviour through the strategies the child adopts on a daily basis to deal with life.

The attachment process

I would like to tell you first of all about Amy, Gordon, Charlie and Lucy. Amy was abandoned by her mother shortly after her birth and was 'brought up' by a succession of people, finally finding a long-term home. When she became an adult, she formed a rather volatile relationship – she found intimacy difficult and could only tolerate brief episodes of touching and contact. She did however become pregnant and a baby, Gordon, was born. He was a very sickly baby and Amy found it almost impossible to be with him and could not tolerate his need for affection, closeness and care. He was quickly removed from her and taken into foster care. Contact was maintained with his mother and eventually combined care was established. They are together now, although Amy still finds Gordon's needs almost too much at times and he often finds his needs for affection and emotional security met by being with other adults.

Charlie is an adult who was severely abused over many years by his carer and now, while terrified of violence, nevertheless can still 'throw' great rages when upset.

Lucy is now 2 years old and was neglected and beaten by her carer from birth. She finds it very difficult to relate to others and clings to a 'security' blanket which she carries everywhere with her.

It may surprise you that these are not human beings but monkeys. Gordon and Amy are orang-utans while Lucy and Charlie are chimpanzees who now live in various family groups in a primate sanctuary. The keepers are very happy to talk about the animals' case histories and there are videos available for purchase at the sanctuary which give very clear illustrations of the primates' day-to-day behaviour. Their needs for security and love have very strong echoes in our own basic needs. The behaviours they show when they are the victims of physical cruelty, neglect or lack of mothering are not too far way from how human children and adults respond to their own emotional distress. From the stories about the primates we can discern how the work of Harlow[4] and Konrad (on 'imprinting') inspired Bowlby's thinking that the attachment process was an innate biological one demonstrated by the infant's heroic efforts to elicit care from surrounding adults.

The crying and later smiling of the very young baby, in most circumstances and across cultures, arouses the caretaking responses of the carers. Women seem particularly attuned to the infant cry, which in evolutionary terms is just as well, and some breastfeeding mothers find that the 'let down' reflex which ensures that the milk supply is ready and waiting is activated not only by the baby 'rooting' at the nipple but simply by hearing the cry. Just as human babies are born with the requisite brain structures in place ready to socialize, learn languages and so on, so women are physiologically 'primed' to both nurture the foetus and provide the first nourishment for the new baby. The extent to which both baby and mother fulfil their innate potential depends very much on circumstance. The mother, for example, has all the 'equipment', both physical and physiological, to breastfeed but may choose not to. The baby is ready with its signals to keep the mother close and to care for it, but the mother may find the baby's cries unbearable for a variety of reasons and so will not respond. The emotional world of the mother will have a powerful influence on her own capacity, both physical and emotional, to nurture her baby.

Attachment is much more than the baby learning to 'love' – especially as we all have very different interpretations of what 'love' means. We have already seen in previous chapters what 'loving' a baby really means for parents in practice! Babies, however, as we know very well, come into the world helpless and dependent. They are totally reliant on the adults around them to provide everything they need and to help them take the first literal and metaphorical steps to understanding who they are and what their world is all about. I would imagine that in most families there does emerge a primary caregiver and in many circumstances this will be the mother. This supports the idea that infants/children form a kind of 'hierarchy' of attachments which only becomes obvious under stress. Infants and young children can display very similar attachment-type behaviours to both parents depending on the quality of their relationship. However, if children are distressed and both parents are present they usually display a clear preference for one particular parent – even if the attachment relationship with both has been classified as secure. I agree with Karen (1998) that something 'fundamental seems to get established' in the relationship between infant and

mother in the first year or so of life, illustrated perhaps by the profoundly moving tales of desperately wounded soldiers on the battlefield
calling for their mothers at the time of their greatest need for safety and
comfort.

I believe this may be due to the propensity of females in general to be
more vocal, more facially and emotionally expressive and more socially
adept at reading faces. Although this does *not* mean that women are
somehow 'better carers' than men it may be that 'nature', via biological
and evolutionary necessity, has endowed females with the potential for
these skills because these are the ones needed for the psychological
health of a new human being. As we know, the right side of the brain is
at its most active in the early years of life and the emotional quality of
our experiences appears to be strongly linked with right-brain function.
Perhaps unsurprisingly, it is also the right brain which appears to be
most involved in the process of recognizing faces (Kim *et al.* 1999) and
so there is a direct early link between recognizing faces and the emotional experience which accompanies such recognition. A baby's first
experiences are dependent upon their limited communication signals
being understood and it is therefore in the baby's best interests that their
carer is both skilled at 'reading' facial expressions and body language
and also expressive in their own responses.

Time and again, in research paper after research paper, the issue of
adult sensitivity to the infant and child surfaces as the one factor that
seems to profoundly influence their responses: emotionally, physiologically and behaviourally. Parents and other carers need to respond to their
child in a loving context and with the ability to self-reflect – i.e. to be
able to separate out their own feelings from those of the baby and to
think about the baby as an individual. Schore (2001) points out that the
sensitive or 'psychobiologically attuned' mother is able to 'tune in' to
her baby. She will allow the baby to disengage from her at appropriate
times and will notice the baby's cues for more interaction.

Of course, this does not mean that the child never experiences emotional discomfort or that the carer is always 'in tune'. On the contrary, it
appears that the ability of the caregiver to *reattune* following a mismatch
between the baby's cues and the mother's responses enables the baby to
learn that negative feelings can be tolerated and are finite. As the baby
has no sense of time, this experience can help establish the beginnings
of an understanding that experiences have beginnings and endings. It is
also important to recognize that emotional experiences have two components: what we feel and the intensity of that feeling. For example, we
can feel pleasure at seeing a well-loved friend but have the same feeling
but with much greater intensity if we have not seen that friend for some
time. The physiological impact of interactions can be demonstrated by
the dual heart-rate speed up and slow down when infant and mother

smile at one another, which is influenced in turn by two systems in the body known as the sympathetic (the speed up process) and the parasympathetic (the slow down process).

Earlier, I mentioned that women generally have a tendency to cradle their infants on the left side (see p. 112). This means that the left eye (governed by the right side of the brain) is also accessing the facial cues of the infant and the mother's right brain hemisphere is attuned to the emotional impact of the baby's face as much as the baby is attuned to the mother's face. The right hemisphere is also tuned in to the sensory input from touch, and close bodily contact provides yet another medium for the formation of a melody of emotions which is mutually positive and enjoyable and which heightens the intensity of the individual emotions involved. To identify with the feeling, just think of when we gaze at loved partners or friends with affection and care or when we are on the receiving end of a 'loving look'. If a baby does not receive this tender holding and experience the loving scanning of its face by the parent then an unfortunate and sad 'gap in experience' will be the result. Babies who are 'not seen' in this way may already be turning off their ability to interact with others – unless there are other adults who are able to provide the missing experience at least to some extent.

The formation of attachments by the baby to its primary carers is a slow, evolving process, built up from pre-birth and accompanied by the innate potential of both mother and baby to forge this relationship – the baby with its signals, propensity for faces, identification of smell and voice, and the mother with her potential for particularly sensitive interpretation of face, voice and expressive signals. Each partner begins to learn about the other and the baby gradually learns about others in their particular social world. Through the close, shifting, evolving, dynamic interaction between baby and carer, a process which when in actual contact is a microsecond by microsecond attuning to one another, a picture builds up which is emotional in both context and impact. If we believe that conscious thought implies language, then pre-verbal experiences are experienced cognitively in the sense that memory and learning are involved, but not thought about except through mental images/representations. How then are needs and wants expressed if not through the motivation engendered by a feeling state? Feelings motivate the child and the emotional content of the responses provides the foreground in the early years of what the child experiences. The relationship with carer(s) is founded on the emotional interplay between them, expressed through voice, gesture, facial expression and touch, and accompanied by smell and taste.

The sensitive atunement of parent to baby is not only an understanding of the baby's signals, it is an overall acceptance of who the baby is – the individual temperament, pace and rhythm of this particular child.

The parent is able to accommodate and adjust their own temperament, pace and rhythm to that of the child, allowing the child room to be itself while learning about the mother and in turn learning about itself. Attachment therefore is more than a relationship – it is a fundamental requirement for the emotional/mental well-being of the human baby. This may explain why a lack of broadly secure relationships can lead to the chronic activation of attachment behaviours – i.e. seeking and separation protest – which include attempts to guard against the pain of loss. Such strategies inevitably involve avoidance of, or anxiety about, relationships with others.

The need for a close relationship which provides a secure base, no matter how this may be expressed, is demonstrated by an interesting study of attachment security in older children with autism using an adaptation of the strange situation. The study showed that it is possible to 'separate out' the behaviours associated with autism and those directly linked to attachment classifications, including that of 'disorganized' – an important point for those working with children who demonstrate a myriad of unusual and/or stereotyped behaviours to help them cope with their world (Capps *et al.* 1994). This reinforces the fact that no matter what the social or cognitive abilities of a child, professionals must never forget that the child has an emotional world which will influence its behaviour.

I believe that the effects of insecure attachments of whatever type rarely lead to overt pathology, unless severe and compounded by a global lack of nurture. Rather, they lead to the vague and unnamed chronic unhappinesses and frustrations encountered by some individuals who seem to repeat patterns of failed or unrewarding relationships throughout their lives.

Summary

During these final months in the first year of life there is an increase in the complexity of a baby's internal and external world. Over the past months, the baby has been learning about the people around them via their faces, emotional expressiveness and behaviour. Inwardly the baby's brain has been sifting, sorting and filing the diverse stimuli, gradually organizing them into patterns of expected consequences, linking feelings with behaviour, culminating in the emergent comprehension of 'I' and 'you' through early 'conversations' and in the ability to share interest in a common stimulus such as a toy.

'I' and 'you' is also 'we'. Up to this point, the baby can only understand others via their external behaviours – now comes the first glimmerings of understanding that others have an internal world too. The baby has also learned to look to familiar carers to give clues to the acceptability or otherwise of new experiences and new people. Babies around this age, and indeed until around 2 years, are often more wary of strangers and it is suggested that this is both an evolutionary safeguard (increased mobility means contact with people you don't know who may be 'dangerous') and that it 'sets a limit' on the number of attachment figures. The infant shows a very clear desire to return to the safety of a familiar adult when unexpected or novel situations arise. This shift in behaviour appears to occur across cultures, no matter whether the norm has been to have single or multiple caregivers (Marvin and Britner 1999).

Understanding this 'normal' behavioural change helps carers to understand the child's possible upset at being introduced to, or left with, unfamiliar adults (the intensity of which will depend on the individual child), and the need for further observation if a child within this age range is noted to be indiscriminately friendly to unfamiliar people. What must be understood is that novel experiences inspire both wariness *and* attraction. It is the degree to which the infant can begin to overcome a 'natural' wariness after a few moments which helps them organize behaviour. Clues to how to react come from social referencing where the infant looks to the adult for guidance and reassurance.

The increasing mobility of the baby also means many more opportunities to actively interact with the environment, both physical and social. Formerly, the baby had to totally rely on carers to introduce playthings – to bring the world to the baby, so to speak. Now the baby can begin to move outwards towards the world, to choose a toy of interest, to reach, to move towards and away from surroundings. The baby's horizons have suddenly widened but it is the quality of security of attachment which allows the baby to explore with confidence, diffidence or recklessness.

Notes

1 For detailed information regarding the exact neuroanatomy of these areas, there is a wide range of literature including texts on language development etc. as well as anatomical texts.

2 In the A not B task, the baby is shown an attractive toy which is then hidden under a cloth, 'A'. Babies around 8–9 months can typically retrieve the toy. During the sequence there is another cloth, 'B', next to cloth A. The action is repeated several times with the baby successfully reaching for the toy under cloth A. The toy is then hidden under cloth B with the baby looking on. Between the ages of 9–12 months many babies will look first at cloth A to find the toy – i.e. where the toy was usually hidden. Some babies may investigate cloth B but will then go back to cloth A (Oates 1994). Some researchers (Diamond 1985; Harris 1989) have found that if the baby was allowed to look for the toy immediately, there was greater likelihood of successful looking and retrieval.

3 The procedure consists of several coded episodes involving child, mother and a stranger (researcher). The episodes are devised to exaggerate the child's attachment-seeking behaviours. Note that 'strange' in this context means 'unfamiliar'.
4 Harlow's famous experiment discounted that the primary need of infant primates was feeding. Infant monkeys were presented with feeding contraptions – one merely wire, the other covered in soft cloth. Both provided milk but the monkeys demonstrated a clear preference for the soft device, strongly indicating that food alone was not enough for these little animals, and nor is it for humans.

7 UNHAPPY BABIES

This chapter concerns loss – loss of care, loss of nurturing, loss of emotional responsiveness. The reasons for such loss are fundamentally to do with the emotional world of the adult: the outcome for the baby will depend on the consistency of the experience, the form the lack of care and nurture takes (such as active abuse, passive neglect or emotional withdrawal) or a combination of all or some of these. Outcomes will also be influenced by the innate temperament of the baby, how the baby responds to circumstances and the influence this has on modifying or reinforcing the attitudes of the carers. Key topics here are maternal depression and abuse/neglect of babies.

Unhappiness in babies

The concept of 'unhappy babies' seems to be a direct contradiction to the traditional and thankfully much more common view of them – i.e. generally contented, alert and expressing 'happiness' through smiling, chuckling and so on. However, babies are capable of a range of powerful emotions, although a true fear response does not usually emerge until around 6–8 months – a time which coincides with growing mobility, stranger anxiety and separation distress.

Unhappiness itself is something most humans try to avoid at all costs, although life has a way of ensuring that most of us have to learn to both cope with and survive it. As we saw in the section on attachment in Chapter 6, as babies we need to acquire enough resilience to emotionally survive separations from our carers so that we are able to meet the 'arrows of misfortune' with the fundamental belief that we can overcome loss in a way that is ultimately positive. Of course, we learn all the time as we go through life, but the first experiences of care and nurture bring with them the building blocks of our emotional health.

Loss of any kind can bring distress, and can take the form not only of separations/bereavement from family, friends and pets – loss of face, lost opportunities, loss of respect/social standing or self-esteem are all rooted in our basic feelings of self-worth and can all cause distress. How we deal with it depends on the strategies we learn. All these losses bring unhappiness and feelings of sadness which can feel physical in their intensity, almost as if we are breaking up inside: we often refer to great distress as 'heartbreak'. When we are teenagers, a failed relationship, being left out by peers, 'stood up' or simply not feeling part of the group can feel devastating. If we have lost a parent, close friend, partner or a much-loved pet we know the utter devastation and desolation such a loss brings with it. A child's reaction to separation and loss is every bit as powerful as an adult's, and possibly more so. The core feeling for the child or adult that underlies separation and loss is that of being abandoned – whether emotionally, physically or both. Traditional folk and fairy tales are replete with stories of children being lost and found and suggest that the fear of being abandoned is universal and timeless, part of the fundamental human condition where we intuitively know what we most fear.

Verrier (1993: 105), in her book about adoption, says: 'The primary or core issues for adoptees are abandonment and loss. From those two issues, the issues of rejection, trust, intimacy, loyalty, guilt and shame, power and control and identity emanate'. I would add that these are core issues for all humans, although obviously for those for whom separation from the mother has taken place there is perhaps less doubt about the issues listed above, although as ever the degree to which any or all of them will occur will depend on individual circumstances and felt experience. Notwithstanding this acknowledgement, a baby's innate striving for contact has much to do with ensuring nurture and care and guarding against what is both physically and psychologically dangerous to the baby – abandonment. When babies do not receive consistent loving care in the sense described in this book, they have to fall back on their own devices. The problem is that babies have very few 'devices'. Adults have a range of strategies to draw on, learned from past experience. They can also rationalize what might be happening or find ways of coping through belief or value systems. For the infant and very young child such strategies are not available. Cognitively and emotionally they are still in the very early stages of understanding themselves, let alone others, and so are reliant on adults to help them deal with and understand experiences through external comforting and soothing. The necessary inner resources are not yet available, or are at a very primitive stage.

In the discussion on attachment in Chapter 6 we saw how the quality of attachment to formation carers led to the different ways in which we frame the world – safe and loving, or dangerous, deadly and without any shape at all. Why are emotions and their influence so powerful? One reason may be that emotional pain is as real and as potentially all-consuming as any physical pain. There is no reason why this should not be so. Animal studies illustrate that the areas which process separation distress are very close to the areas involved in the perception of pain, and it would seem that sadness and pain processes are interlinked. Infants who, for whatever reason, suffer emotional neglect, lack of everyday care and/or abuse have a powerful, feeling response to those events. However, the impact of neglect and/or trauma on an infant is often very difficult for adults to bear and we sometimes play down the potential significance and impact for the child, for our own sakes. This is also true in loss situations of varying types, such as:

• when parents separate;
• if a parent is ill and/or dies;
• removal to foster care;
• day care settings when there is a frequent staff turnover;
• multiple carer changes through a variety of circumstances (e.g. if foster placements break down, ad hoc care by relatives and friends).

In cases where there is death, divorce or other trauma, the adult's own ability to bear the pain and their own responses will influence how far they can support the child and also how far they are willing to understand the situation from the child's point of view. In earlier chapters, the power of unspoken communication was discussed and although parents may say that they 'never row in front of the children', children (and babies) are very sensitive to both 'atmosphere' and non-verbal body language, including facial expression. They may not understand what is going on, but they are certainly aware of discord, unhappiness and suppressed rage. Angry adults are often so involved in their own needs that they are unaware of, or dismiss, the trauma of children who witness violence, whether verbal, physical or both. A salutary quote from Coplan *et al.* (1998: 473) serves to remind us of the reality that we may prefer to avoid: 'current developmental neurobiological research reveals that growth-inhibiting, adverse early rearing experiences have longstanding and complex effects on a range of neurochemicals relevant to emotion regulation'.

The fundamental point is that as adults we need to be ready to acknowledge that babies and very young children have feelings and memories and that just because much of their experience is pre-verbal, this does not lessen their impact. What babies and young children are asking of us is not an avoidance of suffering on their part, but an active aware-ness that they *can* suffer and that their carers will provide alternative means of comfort and nurture. If we deny the emotional impact on babies and children of what we do to them in order to protect ourselves, then we cannot even begin to try to remedy the situation.

Depressed mothers – sad babies?

The first issue we are going to look at is that of maternal depression. There has been a considerable amount of research surrounding this topic and the very real challenges it poses to mothers, their partners, family, friends and involved professionals together with the parallel concerns of care for the baby.

Before we begin to consider depression in mothers and its potential effect on their babies, we need to clarify the difference between depres-sion which might have existed prior to the birth of the baby, postnatal depression and 'baby blues', which is a common occurrence for many women following the birth of their baby and which is relatively short-lived.

Identifying the symptoms

Eisenbruch (2000) describes a large body of evidence which suggests that 'maternity blues', which run the whole gamut from so-called 'baby blues' to postnatal depression, appear to be somewhat 'biologically or-chestrated' rather than a symptom of, for example, western culture. The way such feelings are experienced by both the new mother and her family and the meaning given to her emotions and behaviour are, of course, affected by the cultural context in which she resides. One of the most difficult things for midwives, health visitors and social workers to do is to differentiate between what might be 'normal' feelings of low mood, tiredness and lack of motivation or interest, which are essentially short-lived, and those feelings which are the precursors to postnatal depression. Some controlled studies have shown that around 12–16 per cent of women suffer a post-birth depressive episode and the figures are reportedly higher for younger, adolescent mothers. What is useful for professionals to remember is that the research on depressive episodes following birth is not in total agreement as to when the post-birth or postnatal period actually begins. A definition of postnatal or postpartum depression (PPD) describes it as a major depressive episode occurring within four weeks of childbirth, but other studies report that symptoms may manifest themselves in the 6–12 weeks following delivery. Some researchers have even extended the period to 6–12 months! So those working with babies and their mothers need to be alert to the fact that depressive symptoms can occur within a wide time scale, with the concomitant potential effects on the quality of interaction between mother and child.

The importance of recognizing postnatal depression is highlighted by two studies quoted in the December 2001 newsletter of the Association for Infant Mental Health. The first study by Seeley *et al.* (1996) found that 40 per cent of postnatal depression present in the research group went undiagnosed by general practitioners (GPs). The second, a recent study in Reading found 'only nine and a half percent of depressed mothers were seen as such'. The implication is that a depressed mood is seen as 'normal' in the early weeks postpartum rather than a situation requiring additional surveillance/assessment. Another very important issue that Rosenblum *et al.* (1997) point out is that depressed mothers are often reluctant to seek help in caregiving as this seems to compound their general feelings of failure.

Biological risk factors are: the mother has had a depressive illness in the past; the mother has suffered a depression in a previous pregnancy (or pregnancies) either during the pregnancy or after the birth; and/or there is a close family history of postnatal depression. Other potential psychosocial risk factors that may contribute to a heightened risk of depression during pregnancy and postnatally include poor social support, adverse life events such as a bereavement and marital instability, and ambivalence towards the pregnancy.

In very rare cases, a woman may develop psychosis postnatally. This is very serious but symptoms do occur very quickly, usually within the first 48–72 hours and up to a few weeks after delivery. Symptoms include an excitable or very 'high' mood, disorganized behaviour, mood swings and hallucinations or delusions. In extreme cases, the risks of suicide and/or infanticide are high, and such women require rapid and skilled treatment which usually involves hospitalization. Thankfully, this dramatic and fearful state of affairs is rare but fathers, family and professionals who come into contact with mothers in the first weeks after birth need to be aware of the possibility.

Many women will experience 'tearful' days or some mood swings, feelings of tiredness, etc. but these remain part of an overall picture which is essentially positive, with the mother able to enjoy and care for her baby for most of the time. Professionals must also remember that some mothers may suffer depression before the birth and there is some evidence that depression during pregnancy is more common than PPD. This has important implications for the potential effect on foetal development that may be influenced by changes in the mother's chemical/

hormonal make-up brought about by depression. There is some research on rats, for example, which indicates that environmental stress during the latter part of the pregnancy promotes internal neurochemical changes in the mother rat which affect the gender/sexual tendency of the rat pup (Panksepp 1998).

Potential implications for babies

It is important to remember that a woman can suffer from 'depression' separately from any connection with the actual birth. Worldwide, women are said to suffer from depression more than men. To counteract this, suicide rates in men are far higher, again across cultures, than in women – although women often make more attempts than men. There is a debate about whether the indicators of depression are too 'female orientated' and whether male depression has different cognitive, emotional and behavioural manifestations. For example, despite women being nearly always found to be more emotionally expressive than men, research on emotional reactions using different criteria (e.g. physiological changes measured through heart rate, skin reaction, etc.) shows little gender difference, with men sometimes showing more reaction, especially in fear situations, than women. However, whether the depression is related to the birth or not what is important for babies is the interaction with their primary carer – usually the mother, especially in the first few months. We have to remember when thinking about depression and its potential effects on babies that the condition is not static – the mother can sometimes feel reasonable and at other times may feel much worse. Nor is depression only an influence on mood – physiological changes take place too, such as changes in sleeping and eating patterns – a mother may hardly eat at all, or may 'comfort eat'. Sleep patterns are also frequently disturbed, often compounding the effect of the baby's own needs and subsequent interruptions into parental sleep. It is not surprising therefore that Tiffany Field, a very well known researcher on infants and young children, found that infants of depressed mothers have disturbed sleep/wake behaviours (Field 1998). An Australian study also found a correlation between the reporting of sleep 'problems' and maternal depression scores (Hiscock and Wake 2001).

A great deal of research has been carried out on the relationship between babies and mothers who suffer from depression, and the potential effects on the baby if – and this is crucial – unmitigated by other relationships or circumstances. A research paper by Schuetze and Zeskind (2001) demonstrated that both severely and moderately depressed women responded differently to the taped cries of newborn babies compared with non-depressed women. The women in the depressed group seemed to be less responsive to the cries especially the high-pitched ones. Unfortunately, high-pitched cries in babies usually indicate a greater degree of distress as a result of hunger or pain. Severely depressed women seemed particularly unable to hear the distress in the cries of the babies and consequently were far less likely to provide caregiving responses such as picking up the baby and soothing it. Non-depressed women, in contrast, rated the cries as getting more urgent and/or indicating sickness or great distress.

This raises an interesting point: if and when depressed women do pick up their babies, what kind of mood do they convey by their touch? Hertenstein and Campos (2001) demonstrated that touch which had a negative impact (tightened hold around the baby's abdomen accompanied by a sharply inhaled breath) caused the babies in their research group to be less confident in exploring and touching objects and also resulted in a more general negative effect.

Depression may also have an impact on the life of a baby due to the reality of the baby's developing systems. We have seen the developmental changes that take place in the first year: the growth of attachments, the formation of relationships and the influence of experience on both physical growth and mental well-being. The ordinary, everyday, up and down moods of an ordinary adult are different in both severity and persistence from those of someone who is depressed, and it is the essential quality of the ongoing interactions between the depressed mother and her baby that influences the potential effect. As we saw above, some depressed mothers may not 'hear' the cries of their babies until the babies are 'desperate'. However, as with everything else, depressed mothers are not an amorphous mass but are individuals who display variations in how they deal both with their own depression and with their babies. Some depressed mothers become emotionally 'unavailable' to their babies, simply feeling too swamped by their own feelings of hopelessness and misery to respond to the cues the baby signals to them. Others respond differently and react over-intrusively or angrily, speaking and acting towards their babies in a hostile manner. Still other depressed mothers will still manage to set aside their own feelings and respond in a caring way to their babies.

What seems to make a difference is the particular background and current circumstances of the mother concerned. If she has a supportive partner and/or family who understand, are sympathetic and share in the care of the baby then the mother is much more likely to be able to have some emotional 'room' to respond to the baby because her own needs are being met with compassion. Research studies support this contention. For example, studies quoted by Schonkoff and Phillips (2000) revealed the powerful influence of fathers – involved and supportive fathers were able to 'buffer' the children from the effects of their mother's sadness.

Obviously the opposite is also true. Zelkowitz and Milet (1997) compared attitudes towards the parental role and their baby's behaviour between two groups of fathers, one group of which had partners suffering from PPD. Fathers who had high stress levels and low support showed less psychological well-being and therefore were even less able to support their depressed partners. Work-related stress was the most strongly associated factor for 'adjustment problems and negative attitudes among fathers' (Zelkowitz and Milet 1997). It behoves professionals to consider what fathers might be experiencing and how this impacts on the dynamics of the family. The birth of a baby affects all the adults involved as well as any siblings, not just the mother. Her role within the family and her control or dependency on other adults in the 'usual' run of family life will influence how her depression impacts on the rest of the family as well as the baby.

Fathers have a powerful role to play in the family and as we know babies can make attachments to other significant caregivers. Hence the father may provide an 'alternative' perspective for the baby by being active, positive and providing the child with playful experiences. However, if maternal depression is compounded by discord either with partners or with other family members, financial problems, drug/alcohol problems or poor parenting history it is easy for the needs of a helpless baby to be lost: the child's demands for care, sensitivity and nurture are simply too 'tall an order'.

Another factor which has been shown to influence maternal (and therefore infant) well-being is the mother's own knowledge and understanding about child development. Realistic and appropriate expectations of an infant's behaviour may help the mother rationalize and deal with her baby's demands. An interesting study on maternal depressive symptoms following premature birth demonstrated that knowledge about infant development positively influenced the way the mothers responded to their babies and that prematurity *per se* was not specifically identified as a stressor (Veddovi *et al.* 2001). Again, maternal coping styles and emotional support networks were influential in both the reporting of depressive symptoms and the efficacy of interventions.

Some brain information

As we know, the right hemisphere of the brain appears to be dominant in the first three years of life and is particularly involved with the processing of emotions. From around 18 months, the left hemisphere begins its growth spurt and is the dominant hemisphere in most adults, possibly because of the power of verbal communication. In research studies, when non-depressed adults are shown movie clips carefully chosen to evoke negative emotions, the right hemisphere is most active. However, a shift from left to right dominance is displayed as a 'norm' in depressed adults, indicating neurologically that 'mood' is pervasive over their more logical functions. Measurements of toddlers' ECGs showed that children of depressed mothers demonstrated a similar pattern of right-sided dominance (at age 3) even when they were 'at rest' or doing an activity with someone other than their mother. Interestingly, this seemed to be linked more with children whose mothers were depressed in the second and third years of the child's life rather than the first year. However, the children whose mothers had been depressed in the first year of life showed higher levels of cortisol than the others, cortisol being a substance in the body which is naturally produced in response to stress. This indicates that the timing of the maternal depression in the child's life may itself mediate the biological or chemical bodily response to the experience. It also indicates that the more helpless the baby, with limited capacity to monitor face-to-face interactions, the more likely is an increase in actual physiological stress response. This would indicate that the different behavioural manifestations that certain depressed mothers may display to the baby can induce a different kind of physiological stress response in that baby. For example, a baby may respond fearfully to overly intrusive behaviours such as poking, an angry face or rough handling while a baby who is faced with a sad, unresponsive type of carer, may try to stimulate the carer by engaging in much activity or by actual 'withdrawal' – i.e. a 'depressed' baby.

Studies illustrate that babies as young as 2 and 3 months will try to attract an unresponsive mother. The famous 'still face' experiments carried out by several researchers including Tronick and Cohn (1989) illustrated the varying responses babies displayed when their mothers showed an unresponsive face but that distress was inherent in all of them no matter how briefly. A small but important longtitudinal study by Edhborg *et al.* (2000) examined mother-child interactions and attachment classifications in mothers who were classified as depressed using the Edinburgh Postnatal Depression scale, which is used countrywide in the UK and also abroad. The mothers and babies were filmed when the babies were 2 months of age and then again at 15–18 months. As is often the case, there was no simple 'cause and effect' finding and variations were apparent in mother and baby behaviours and in the type of interactions. However, there was a general finding that some babies whose mothers had high scores on the Edinburgh scale were less joyful and curious and more easily distracted than their counterparts. The variations between the group may be indicative of differences in maternal support and also of the parent's original 'way of being', which might supersede the cumulative effects of day-to-day low mood. It would appear that some babies reflect in their own behaviour the behaviours they have experienced in their mothers. In other words, they give to adults a reflection of their own experience. A study by Field *et al.* (1995) demonstrated that depressed mothers and their babies who were aged 3–6 months showed similar patterns of right frontal EEG activation. Jones *et al.* (2001) also demonstrated greater right frontal EEG asymmetry in older infants of depressed mothers. These findings reflect other studies such as that by Feldman *et al.* (1999).

It may be that the individual temperament/behavioural style of the baby influences which babies adopt this strategy. As we know, communication between mother and baby is not a simple one-way process but a two-way one, with the child influencing the mother's behaviour. This transactional process can have an accumulative effect. For example, a baby who has a behavioural style which is already 'quiet' may have this trait confounded by a mother who is withdrawn and unresponsive and who, in her turn, may find a less demanding baby less challenging to her own mood. However, an angry, depressed/hostile mother may find the temperamentally quiet baby aggravating and perceive this behaviour as reinforcing her own sense of failure and worthlessness, becoming even more hostile as a result. An active baby, on the other hand, may become part of an increasingly angry and distressed cycle of mutual behaviour. Conversely the active baby may respond to a withdrawn mother either by withdrawing in its turn or by becoming 'hyper' in order to elicit some response, with their agitation being associated with anxious and fretful behaviours.

In addition to both the individual behavioural manifestation of depression in the mother, her basic temperament and the baby's own behavioural style, a further part of the equation is to consider what effect depression may have in altering, reinforcing or changing how the mother actually feels about the baby. As we know, a mother's perception will also influence the 'how' of the interactions between mother and child. In a study by Hart *et al.* (1999) mothers of newborns were asked to rate their infant's behaviours using a modified version of an infant behaviour assessment scale. The ratings were for such items as the 'cuddliness of the baby'.[1] The findings were that mothers who self-rated as depressed were much more likely to rate their newborn baby's general behaviours more negatively than objective observers and by 1 month old the babies concerned showed a downward trend in their behaviour in that the observers rated them less positively at this stage. To quote:

> By 1 month, infants of depressed mothers received lower ratings of state organisation . . . suggesting lower levels of alertness, poorer abilities to respond to social stimulation such as the sight of an adult face and the sound of an adult voice and weaker coping and

self-soothing skills. These findings support reports noting inferior progress among infants of depressed mothers within only 1 month of development.

(Hart et al. 1999: 207)

What is interesting in this study is that the very positive perceptions of their babies by non-depressed mothers were matched at 1 month by the observers, which indicated that a mother's perception of her baby (such as fussy, cuddly, irritable) influenced the way the mother interacted with that child and her expectations of that child. The depressed mothers more negative views of their babies seemed to suggest some kind of 'self-fulfilling prophecy'. Research on schools and teaching has indicated a similar process. When teachers have high or low expectations of their pupils, subsequent pupil performance reflects these expectations. It is therefore not unreasonable to attach great importance to parents' perceptions of their children – a view already stated in earlier chapters which is well supported by research from a variety of sources (e.g. Abrams *et al.* 1995; Lundy *et al.* 1996).

What is important for professionals is to note how a parent talks about their baby, what language is used, what emotions are evident, what impression the teacher, social worker or childminder have about how the parent views the child. Careful notice must also be taken of body language. A tired and anxious mother may still turn towards her baby with a smile while talking of lack of sleep or demanding feeding. She may still cuddle the baby close even while in tears or soothe and stroke the baby's face while telling a health visitor about the stresses she is enduring. For the baby, it is of no consequence whether the perceptions the mother has of them are based in reality – what is important is what the perceptions *are*, because it is those beliefs that will provide the context for the powerful daily interactions between parent and child. Also important is how far the mother can separate out her own needs from that of the child.

What the professional must do it twofold. First they must assess how far the mother is 'aware' of the infant as a person in its own right and second they must find out about the beliefs the mother has about the child. If these beliefs are negative or 'blaming' then the professional may be able to provide the mother with an alternative view without undermining her self-esteem, which may already be at rock bottom. For example, a health visitor or nursery staff member could say, 'Yes, he does cry but look how he turns towards you with that special smile, just for you', or 'Yes, she does take a long time to feed but thank goodness she has a mum who is willing to give her time'. In other words, the professional finds something positive and special to offer the mother to help her see her baby in a better light. These findings also reinforce the fact that proud parents of 'normal' infants should not have their beliefs dented! Happy is the baby whose parent(s) delight in its presence.

In contrast, Beebe and Lachmann (1994) quote studies that illustrate how babies who have intrusive carers develop an interactive style which is characterized by distress and protest. As we know, babies learn through familiarity and adaptation to regular experiences. If the regular quality of interaction is forceful and generally hostile, the baby will learn to react to this expected event. There is no evidence to suggest that the baby somehow understands that the style of the parent may not be that experienced by most babies. The baby only knows what it knows – that this carer, who is the baby's main carer, usually acts in this particular way. It is beyond the baby's capacities to know that there are other ways of being, unless these are demonstrated consistently by someone else.

A study by Diego *et al.* (2001) emphasized the importance of matching interventions to the mother's style, noting that withdrawn or intrusive mothers responded differently to different approaches. For example, withdrawn mothers did better when coached on trying to attract their infant's attention while intrusive mothers needed coaching on how to 'see' their baby's cues for regulating interactions.

To summarize, the effect on babies of maternal depression, whether as a pre-existing condition or exacerbated by the pregnancy/birth is difficult to assess in that so much depends on the individual mother, her support mechanisms, her own ability to see her mood and feelings as separate from the baby, and of course the baby's own temperament. However, enough research exists which indicates that prolonged depression can influence the type and quality of interaction between mother and baby with a 'knock on' effect on the child's ability to relate to others and to learn. Once again this is not to 'blame' the mother but to face reality. A woman cannot help becoming depressed. Therefore, a positive approach is to identify the signs and symptoms of depression and explore with the parent(s) and their families ways in which both mother and baby can be supported. The mother may need to be helped in a sensitive way to maximize the pleasure of her interactions with her baby and alternative sensitive care needs to be provided as far as practically possible for those times when the mother may feel the needs of the baby are too much. In practical terms, resources may be limited but there is much that can be achieved by acknowledging the problem in the first place, recognizing its importance for parent and baby and involving, via the lead worker (such as a health visitor), such agencies as may exist in the area, not forgetting the GP. In addition, an adult mental health team may be able to provide additional skilled support to the mother and to her family.

Possible influences of gender on the impact of depression

A final point is there is some evidence to suggest that male babies are more affected by maternal depression, especially if it lasts beyond a year and that a male baby's cognitive ability (and therefore learning potential) may be reduced if no intervention takes place. Male babies are generally more vulnerable to adverse circumstances and these gender issues need to be borne in mind. This is not to suggest for a moment that female babies will be 'all right' without interventions, but simply that there may be an additional vulnerability in boys in the early years. Girls seem to become more vulnerable in adolescence and this may be a focus for research as to whether brain changes in adolescence render a greater sensitivity to life pressures in females. It is always wise to remember that 'blanket' solutions for any aspect of development, whether it be social, emotional, educational, language-based, etc. may not be developmentally or physiologically appropriate and that gender issues perhaps need to be more realistically assessed without the handcuffs of political correctness, feminism or other ideologies.

Infant depression and failure to thrive

Guedeney (1997) asks the question, 'Why is infant depression so hard to recognize?' He feels that there is something about infant depression that hampers the ability or willingness of adults to acknowledge its existence. The usual view is that infants do not get depressed, although on an intuitive level we recognize the sad and/or troubled baby with its lack of positive emotional expression, withdrawn behaviours, lack of curiosity and irritability. Other signs that a baby may display are wariness or a somewhat fixed gaze on adults, a lack of eye contact with the carer, a lack of vocalization, an engagement in self-stimulatory activities and resistance to cuddling. Quite correctly, you may say that a wide range of circumstances and conditions could produce the above symptoms. While this is true, professionals involved with babies and their families must nevertheless be courageous enough to notice such behaviours, their context, frequency and general circumstances and brave enough to think the unthinkable: that this is an unhappy baby.

Of course, we cannot know how an individual baby feels, nor can most of us remember what it felt like to be a baby, sad or otherwise. However, we do know that as infants we feel, we remember, we have physiological responses to our experiences and we develop strategies. The depressed or 'withdrawn' infant does exist and pictures of babies in overcrowded, grossly understaffed and poorly equipped orphanages is testament to the reactions of babies to such circumstances: we see withdrawn, mute infants who rock or stare unsmiling at their world. Unfortunately it is all too easy to see depression in adult terms, whereas the capacity for hopelessness is probably there from the beginning.

Guedeney (1997) focuses on the emotional aspects of 'failure to thrive'. This term is something of a 'catch all' to describe a variety of symptoms, usually associated with very slow weight gain or actual loss, and concurrent general developmental delay. It has been found that many of the cases of failure to thrive do not have an 'organic' (i.e. disease or physical) dysfunction but are due more to difficulties in feeding and general care. However, even in those cases where there is an organic component, there is also a non-organic element – few cases are purely organic. Even in countries where malnourishment is prevalent because of acute food shortages, babies and very young children suffering from severe malnutrition still display psychological effects as well as physical ones. It is important to remember that mothers in these situations are also individuals with their own personalities and ways of coping, as are their babies.

In the general scheme of things, if a professional notices that a baby appears to be gaining weight very slowly or is actually losing weight, appears listless or anxious and is fretful then it may be that failure to thrive is apparent. However, it is important that the professional looks at the whole picture, as the baby may simply be a slow feeder, or the mother may find the baby's style difficult. This is not to 'blame' the baby, but is a recognition that for each baby who is suffering in this way there will be a particular individual and family context. Sometimes an anxious parent may try all sorts of ways to make a baby eat but the outcome is increasing tension at mealtimes and an ensuing vicious circle of a baby who is not relaxed enough to eat and a carer who is potentially running out of options.

The baby's perspective

The baby's own style is important, as infants who may be termed as having an 'easy temperament' can be at greater risk of being malnourished because of their temperamental bias towards not making a fuss. In addition, where, when and how the baby is fed are also issues that any professional needs to take on board when looking at a baby who is not 'thriving'.

The importance of the relationship between parent(s) and child cannot be overestimated and must be the subject of scrutiny when early years professionals are concerned about a baby. However, as Guedeney (1997) points out, the baby's own reactions and what effect these reactions might be having on the child's overall development must not be forgotten either. If you have a row with your partner or a close family member or a friend, you may be able to analyse the reasons for the argument – i.e. the style and quality of the relationship between you. What is yours alone though, is how *you* feel and it is these feelings that you have to deal with, as well as thinking about a new strategy for next time. Depending on the context, frequency and type of row, the results of the interaction will compound your feelings of rage, shame, bitterness, sorrow, humiliation, despair, determination – whatever. A baby also has its own inner world to experience as well as what is coming at them from the outside. A sad baby is the result of their experiences, both internal and external.

A note here about 'withdrawal'. While a 'withdrawn' baby is a candidate for further observation, professionals must also differentiate between the very normal technique of 'withdrawing' in order to regulate (slow down) an interaction and the chronic listlessness of a baby whose 'sparkle' seems to be extinguished. Babies must be able to withdraw and they do this by turning their heads, generally averting their gaze or actually moving away, if sufficiently mobile, in order to let others know that, for a few moments at least, they have had enough. We all need to withdraw at times! Withdrawal is both emotional and physical, and infants who have endured troubling experiences will often make every effort to withdraw from what they see as a potentially adverse situation.

Children exposed to abuse and neglect

American statistics for the year 2000 from the National Child Abuse and Neglect Data System (NCANDS 2000) show that the youngest children are the most vulnerable. Children younger than 1 accounted for 44 per cent of child fatalities and 85 per cent of fatalities were younger than 6 years of age. Some 3 million referrals concerning the welfare of approximately 5 million children were made to child protection agencies throughout the USA. The most common form of abuse is child neglect, and approximately 879,000 children were the victims of various types of 'maltreatment' (categories include general neglect, medical neglect, physical abuse, sexual abuse and psychological abuse). Almost two-thirds of child victims (63 per cent) suffered neglect, including medical neglect; 19 per cent were physically abused; 10 per cent were sexually abused and 8 per cent were psychologically maltreated. It is interesting to note that in spite of the prevalence of neglect much more attention is given to other forms of abuse, in particular sexual abuse. Studies such as those by Azar *et al.* (1998) and Zuravin (1999) point out that 'neglect' is often itself neglected, with inevitable adverse consequences for children.

UK statistics of the numbers of children and young people on child protection registers from 1996 to 2000 show a steady increase in the number of children on the register because of 'neglect' (11,200 in 1996 and 14,000 in 2000). Unfortunately, it is unclear what kind of neglect is assessed as there is a further category of emotional abuse which shows a fairly static picture. However, I would strongly maintain that neglect, even if assessed as purely 'physical', of necessity carries with it an emotional component. In addition, all other forms of abuse must also carry a strong emotional response within the child. The emotional consequences of the type and quality of care received by infants and young children will pervade whatever the primary source of abuse may be and thus present a broader, more complex picture as to what might be the consequences for neglect and abuse of children in the early years, when children are vulnerable and when emotional development is at the forefront. Incidentally, sexual abuse, in spite of its exceedingly high profile, showed a slight fall in numbers in the UK between 1996 and 2000, and yet it is sexual abuse which often dominates both the media and child protection literature. Child protection workers often comment that 'neglect' is the neglected aspect of child abuse and can often be known to social services personnel, health visitors, nursery nurses and so on for years before proactive decisions are made regarding the health and welfare of the child – by which time, of course, the developmental clock has moved on.

Neglect differs from other forms of abuse in that it implies that something is lacking – care, nurture or love, for example – while other forms of abuse imply action against the child. The UK government paper *Working Together to Safeguard Children* defines neglect as: 'the *persistent failure* to meet a child's basic physical and/or psychological needs, likely to result in the serious impairment of the child's health or development' (Department of Health 1999: 6, emphasis added). The key word here is 'persistent', implying that *omission* of care is a part of the child's daily life. It is easy to see how neglect can pervade the unfolding of a child's development, casting a shadow over their basic temperament and leaving a gap where the child's sense of self-worth may reside. The neglected child, who may express their sadness through withdrawal, aggression or anxiety, lives with absence – a hole in the tapestry of development. Neglect can obviously occur via either parent but lack of nurturing by the mother seems to carry a particular significance, at least in the perception of clients of my experience and in the anecdotal evidence from friends and colleagues in their own work.

What early years workers need to remember is that neglect is most common in both boys and girls in the younger age ranges, with the highest proportion in the *0–3 age range*. What is also distressing to discover from the US statistics for example is that the *rate of recurrence* of neglectful abuse is also highest in this age range. The rate of physical abuse for males was highest in the 4–7-year-old and 8–11-year-old age groups.

The highest physical abuse rate for females occurred in the 12–15-year-old age group. The only form of abuse/neglect which had significantly higher occurences in females was sexual abuse, but this does need to be considered with caution as sexual abuse of boys may be under-reported.

Implications and ramifications

When considering the potential long-term outcomes of abuse and neglect it is important to take into account the possible emphasis that has been placed on measuring outcomes via cognitive and language development rather than the emotional outcomes of abuse (i.e. the way in which abused and neglected children deal with their relationships). Research on attachments, for example, indicates that adopted children reared in orphanages can make attachments to their new parents/carers even when relatively 'old' (Chisholm *et al.* 1995; Ames 1997). However, the quality of these attachments varies considerably, with some children displaying 'shallow' affections and experiencing difficulties in making lasting friendships. What tends to be overlooked – perhaps because it is difficult to measure – are the feelings of 'not being good enough' which can blight the lives of many who remain endlessly seeking the approval which will make them feel 'all right'. This search can take personally destructive forms, while cognition and language skills may remain relatively intact or even of high quality.

It is safe to say that the consequences of abuse and neglect are influenced by factors such as the:

- duration of the abuse;
- type of abuse and its association with developmental stage and age;
- context of the abuse (i.e. is the abuse directed at a child who is already suffering, such as physical abuse to a child who is having multiple 'out of home' placements, neglect when the carer may also have a mental health, drink or drugs problem, emotional abuse in the context of constant family rows and/or violence);
- relationship with the abuser and the presence or absence of other caring, supportive and nurturing adults.

The last factor can provide a powerful 'buffering' effect to a child. When I was a practising counsellor, I always remember a client telling me about his appalling childhood with abuse occurring within the home, in a subsequent foster home and also in a further placement in a children's home, where denigrating bullying was rife. He movingly described the actions of one social worker who would take him out for 'a burger' and chat to him. This one man seemed to hold a beacon of hope for my client and he probably never fully realized the impact that his concern had on this troubled and despairing child.

How does the 'buffering' effect work? Chronic stress means that the body's stress response mechanism is continually on 'high alert', and this then becomes the 'norm' for that child. A safe adult who is consistent in their behaviour in a nurturing positive way allows the child to relax, in turn allowing the stress-modulating system within the body to 'turn off' the stress response. The more this happens, the more that the stress effects will be counteracted. Safety and routine can additionally help this stress-reducing mechanism to activate. This process occurs on a daily basis with all babies and their carers – it is part of the growing ability to self-regulate: as the baby becomes distressed, the parent soothes it and so there is a fairly equitable balance between stressed and non-stressed states, with the latter being not simply an absence of stress but an absence plus the additional positive feelings brought about by co-occurring stimulation (holding, rocking, voice, visual contact, etc.). Over time the baby learns to cope with the stress and the positive feelings become paramount. It can be seen that if the baby is not soothed/responded to or is met with hostility and anger on a regular basis, the stress response will be heightened and therefore becomes the baby's usual state, influencing ongoing development. This process, of course, echoes that of the underlying mechanisms by which attachments are formed (see Chapter 6) and therefore may in turn affect the quality of the attachment between baby and carer.

Abuse and neglect of infants and very young children: some specifics

When parents get together, they sometimes share their own horror stories about times when they hit their child very hard, or shook their baby, or threw their baby on the bed in a rage. There are often nods and sympathetic murmurings as to the anger/despair that can be instigated in an adult by a crying infant or 'defiant' child. A man once described to me how he had broken the door of the bedroom by punching it instead of his baby; a mother once described how she threw her baby on the bed and then called a friend to come and help her. The needs of babies and the behaviours of children seem to arouse powerful feelings in us, and we can (and do) lose control.

People are generally covertly sympathetic to parents who occasionally 'go too far', though lines are drawn at 'systematic beating'. Even here, though, we seem to be somewhat vague about what is 'realistic' (slapping or hitting?) and what is not. When babies are picked up and generally 'handled' during caregiving routines such as feeding and nappy changing, the sensory input to them is 'multimodal' – i.e. all their senses are receiving information. Touch is a powerful communicator, and recent high-profile cases of abuse towards infants have highlighted the possible consequences of shaking a baby in anger. This has led to the identification of 'shaken baby syndrome' which encompasses the possible neurological consequences of violent handling/shaking of an infant.

A well known researcher in the field of abuse is Dr Peter Dale of the National Society for the Prevention of Cruelty to Children (NSPCC) who has recently conducted a study on 'serious injuries to babies and infants with discrepant explanations' (Dale *et al.* 2002). While the research mainly deals with the inexact and very difficult science of determining intervention procedures, infant safety and risk assessment, it remains pertinent to our discussion because, although it only examines the case notes of 21 infants under 2 years of age it highlights a number of salient issues – namely responsibility, professional responses and perceptions.

In terms of responsibility, both that of carers and professionals, in only 4 out of the 21 cases was there a clear acknowledgement of responsibility by the carers. It has to be noted that these 21 cases included very serious physical injuries such as burns, fractures, head injuries, severe bruising, poisoning and suffocation. Dr Dale points out that in cases of fatalities in babies, these have often followed injury to them without sufficient explanation by their carers.

In terms of professional responses, there were four fatalities among the 21 case histories, including a baby who was killed in a family where the father had already been acquitted of the murder of his 8-week-old baby by a previous partner. What was striking was the sheer number of injuries some of these infants sustained and the very young age of those presenting with severe injuries, ranging from 3–10 weeks. Dr Dale noted that in several cases the severe injuries had been preceded by more minor ones which had been seen by professionals and noted but not regarded as 'potential indicators of mounting parental tension'. Explanations such as 'the baby lying on a dummy' were apparently accepted. Professionals seemed willing to accept no explanation at all for the injuries to the children. Bearing in mind the helplessness of very young infants, acceptance of a severe injury being self-inflicted in a 6-weeks-old baby who was apparently 'boisterous' seems difficult to understand. However, some of these explanations came from articulate middle-class parents and this highlights another difficulty for professionals: perceptions of who abuses children.

It is far easier to consider abuse if the families present as stressed, in dire circumstances, poorly educated and so on. Abuse seems almost a consequence of the stresses and strains of daily life coupled with the needs of a new baby. Perhaps professionals feel emotionally and professionally 'safer' in intervening in such cases. The need seems so apparent.

However, what triggers violence in apparently affluent, well-educated parents? The apparent impossibility of parents recorded as 'nice' perpetuating abuse on their babies seems to paralyse professionals, as does the likelihood of resourceful parents bringing in the weight of family, lawyers, media, etc. In Dale's study there were five such cases where there was an absence of the usual 'markers' for abuse such as family violence and parental mental health issues. Perceptions and beliefs also figured in those cases studied where family violence was part of the context of the abuse towards the baby. Dr Dale and his colleagues noted that some of the cases involved mutual violence between partners and the violence of the mother became focused on the baby. There appears to be a tacit assumption that in cases of domestic violence the children will be safe with the mother, whereas her own violence may be a factor in the dynamic of the family situation. This is a difficult and sensitive issue, but denying that women can be violent towards their partners and especially towards their children means that the ultimate safety of infants and older children may be compromised. The unfortunate pairing of 'violence towards women and children' perpetuates the myth that only men are violent and that women, by default, are never violent towards children. Unfortunately, unless professionals in the early years, who are often themselves female, are prepared to acknowledge the darker side of their own sex, we are not protecting children. A very sobering passage from NCANDS (2000) states:

> Most States define perpetrators of child abuse of neglect as parents and other caretakers, such as relatives, babysitters, and foster parents, who have maltreated a child. Sixty percent of perpetrators were females and 40 per cent were males. The median age of female perpetrators was 31 years; the median age of male perpetrators was 34 years. More than 80 per cent of victims (84 per cent) were abused by a parent or parents. Mothers acting alone were responsible for 47 per cent of neglect victims and 32 per cent of physical abuse victims. Nonrelatives, fathers acting alone, and other relatives were responsible for 29 per cent, 22 per cent and 19 per cent, respectively, of sexual abuse victims.

Professional practice

Perceptions and beliefs about mothers and babies, fathers, men and women, family life, identification with adults about the stresses of crying babies and 'defiant' children all contribute to how a professional interprets signs of distress in a baby. In the next chapter I consider some of the aspects which may 'blind' professionals to the stories that infants are telling through their behaviour, but suffice to say here that professionals must try as far as possible to realize that babies can be and are maltreated, that maltreatment can be insidious (e.g. through emotional as well as physical neglect), and that the parent(s) belief systems about the child and themselves may offer clues as to what stressors may be playing their part in undermining the care of the infant.

Professionals must also guard against their own belief systems which, when working with a family may lead them to collude with the needs and wishes of either parent, only allowing them to see one part of the picture rather than the true situation: professionals must always give themselves permission to 'think the unthinkable'. While all this may seem obvious, the continuing suffering of children at the hands of their parents and the fatalities that occur still highlight the importance and dangers of the beliefs and perceptions about parents and other professionals held by those working with the family. These beliefs, if they combine with the personal emotional needs and beliefs of the family worker, can be a potentially dangerous cocktail.

Potential long-term consequences

Galvin *et al.* (2001) describe how negative early experiences with their accompanying bodily responses can lead to a concept of post-traumatic stress:

> When orienting, an infant turns toward a novel stimulus and suppresses bodily movement. Physiologically, orienting is accompanied by pupil dilation, brain wave desynchronization, increased galvanic skin response, suppression of respiratory frequency, decreased peripheral blood flow, and an initial slowing of the heart rate . . . These physiologic responses habituate with repeated exposure. At the upper threshold, overly intense stimuli elicit the aversive response characterized by heart rate acceleration and failure to habituate on repeated exposure. To the extent these thresholds are biologically determined, individuals may have an arousal/aversion range that typifies their ability to tolerate novel events *throughout the lifespan*. Meaning is contingent on memory systems that undergird internal representational models. Malignant episodic memories are psychobiologically linked affective, cognitive and arousal functions in stable toxic configurations; they are central to the definition of PTSD [post-traumatic stress disorder].
>
> (Galvin *et al.* 2001, emphasis added)

This serves to emphasize the importance of the first year of life and the potential long-term effects of negative experiences during this time and into early childhood. While the powerful effects of subsequent nurturing and loving experiences can counteract the impact of early chronic neglect and/or trauma, it may well be that these remain emotional 'sticking plaster' over the early rents in an individual's psyche. Positive experiences can include a child being adopted or fostered by a caring family or the way the child is treated by social workers, teachers, early years workers, childminders and relatives. If the counteracting experience comes early enough, the 'rents' may be repaired far more easily.

In terms of research considered on the long-term effects of neglect and other forms of maladaptive care of children, my own view is that not enough attention is paid to the everyday struggles of people who, on the surface, may be 'successful' but who are engaged in a lifelong struggle to keep back the demon of self-doubt with its mantra of 'you are not good enough'. Different people may adopt different defences but the demon can tap someone on the shoulder at unexpected times and leave them floundering in distress and despair which no amount of rationalization (at the time) can alleviate. In order to remain emotionally 'safe' I imagine quite a number of people retreat into 'disengagement' with the world using a wide range of strategies.

A fascinating study by Schiffer (2000) on 'split brain patients' (i.e. people who have undergone surgery dividing the two hemispheres of the brain as a radical treatment for epilepsy) demonstrated that in one man, who had suffered sustained bullying in his childhood, the memories still remained and invoked an emotional response arising from the right brain. Similar questions about the bullying directed to the left hemisphere were met with responses that denied the influence of the bullying. In other words, he had 'forgotten' his past emotional experiences of being bullied, but of course they were not forgotten at all and probably influenced his day-to-day decision making, and his personal and professional relationships without his being consciously aware of why he responded in different ways to different situations and people. As we know, the brain's 'halves' work in tandem – it is only in such unusual and dramatic circumstances that we can catch sight of how each half focuses on the emotional and cognitive perspectives of life's experiences.

Summary

Our awareness of the lingering effects of our early experiences helps us to put the care of babies into context. Babies are born to individuals at a particular time in those individuals' lives when relationships, work, home and community life may all be going well or badly. The parent, in addition, will be at a particular point in their own developmental journey and be carrying with them their past and their particular strategies for dealing with life in the present. For some babies (thankfully still a minority) the parents are in a state of flux where emotions, behaviour and understanding are still in a relatively early stage of development and are unable or unwilling to see the baby as an individual with needs and a temperament of their own. This can lead to inappropriate care, ranging from a general insensitivity to neglect and/or deliberate harm. Babies can and do tell us through facial expression and body language as well as by their weight and height that all is not well with them. Parents too often 'tell' professionals about the difficulties they are having through constant complaints about the baby's behaviour and by the way they talk about the baby and act towards it. Professionals, whatever their particular role, must be able to listen to what babies and parents are telling them. It is hard, because ultimately we see the vulnerability of babies and do not want a world in which they are treated harshly, neglected, abandoned, ignored, hit, shaken, burnt, thrown or sexually abused. We may not want to admit to ourselves that the perpetrator may be the mother unless the signs are obvious (such as mental health problems, abuse of drugs or alcohol). The growing evidence of neuroscience, which supports the insights of cognitive and psychotherapeutic thinkers, must be a clarion call for all of us to appreciate that we *have to* open our eyes and see what is there not just what we want, believe or wish to be there.

Note

1 The 'cuddliness' ratings were: When you pick your baby up and hold him/her in a rocking position (1) She/he often swings his/her arms and kicks her/his legs and squirms a lot; (2) He/she is limp like a sack in your arms; (3) She/he relaxes and nestles his/her head in the crook of your arm; (4) She/he nestles in your arms while moving his/her face toward you and reaching her/his hands out to grab your clothing.

Part 2
REFLECTIONS ON
PROFESSIONAL PRACTICE
AND PERSONAL EMOTIONS

8 THE PERSONAL IN THE PROFESSIONAL

The second part of this book concerns the emotional life of professionals, providing an opportunity to think about what attributes contribute to positive professional working and what factors may influence negative or difficult outcomes or relationships. Official reviews on certain tragic child fatalities carried out over several years have highlighted problems with communication and interprofessional relationships, and of course these difficulties are not unique to these particular circumstances. Every day, all over the world there will be situations arising where communications, whether between agencies or within agencies, break down or are difficult. Communication between adults and between adults and children can also break down in circumstances that are not overtly difficult but which nevertheless are compromised by misunderstandings and prejudices.

Good professional practice is enhanced by continued monitoring, reflection and consideration of the child's behaviour together with a full appreciation of our own part in the actual dynamics of any given situation. However, the capacity of any professional to do this, whatever an individual's particular expertise, range of knowledge and experience, will depend on their own emotional response to the situation and their ability to reflect on this response, situation by situation. It is this response which provides a possible explanation as to why in some situations perfectly competent and experienced professionals find themselves feeling helpless, de-skilled and confused. Occasionally, however, in the professional literature, the importance of our own individual response to situations can be overlooked and it appears to be assumed that we as professionals always behave objectively and are unaffected by our personal values, beliefs and past experiences. This chapter and the next take a brief look at what inter- and intrapersonal dynamics may be at work.

What's love got to do with it?

To talk about 'love' in the context of thinking about our humanity in our professional lives may seem overly romantic, but I want to focus here on the fundamental need in all of us to be loved, approved of and accepted. Winnicott (1965) suggests that the earliest human anxiety is related to being 'insecurely held', which could imply that the role of the carer, including the worker in a preschool setting, is to provide a safe, secure environment which emotionally protects the child. Loving is also about nurture, and what professionals who work with infants and their families actually do is nurture them, providing a secure base away from the home or encouraging security within the child's own home. The teacher cannot teach children who are anxious or fearful, who are without trust and who already feel unloved. Social workers must have as their priority the emotional as well as the physical well-being of a child and health visitors work towards the goal of supporting a nurturing home environment.

In our early lives, not only do we need to be loved but we also need to feel safe. The role of parents and other carers is to reassure the child and make sense of their fears. It is interesting that in infancy, the emotion of fear occurs in the latter half of the first year, an adaptive occurrence which helps keep the child safe. Babies have many fears: of heights, of strangers, of being away from their familiar person, of being alone and not knowing where the familiar person is. Anyone who has watched a child's sudden dreadful panic when they realize they are on their own somewhere unfamiliar can readily identify the very real distress and fear displayed, no matter how fleeting. To a child, such a situation is akin to how an adult can feel if they are alone in a foreign country, unable to speak the language or read the signs. The fear and panic can be quite devastating, until our adult resources kick in. What we have to think about is our ability to function with babies and young children and how childhood informs adulthood and vice versa.

The reasons for considering the emotional aspects of working with babies and young children arise from my own experiences, which include training to be a teacher, working as a counsellor and a health visitor, training others who work with children and researching and reflecting on human development. I profoundly believe that one of the great issues involved in thinking about good practice is that of the *personal within the professional*. In the past, I did sometimes wonder if it was only me who allowed how I felt about a situation, person or child to overwhelm my sense of good practice, stated professional standards and, most importantly, my capacity to think. In reality, I know that I was, and still am, far from alone. Conversations with professionals who work directly or indirectly with children and families helped me to recognize with some relief, that these troubled episodes in my professional life were far from unique. Case histories of the extreme tragedies of child abuse fatalities (e.g. Reder *et al.* 1993) highlight human frailty in episodes of rivalry, lack of communication and personal neediness. I imagine that some of you may be thinking that these extreme cases represent equally extreme difficulties, but I would contend that it is not just in the worst cases of abuse and neglect that such personal difficulties occur, nor is it only a question of the particular situation being, of itself, too difficult to deal with. Professionals in all fields can, and do, deal with a wide range of difficult and demanding situations and/or individuals but it is the individual's way of coping that is of interest to me and which provides the backdrop for this discussion. I firmly believe that professionals must be prepared to consider what renders them 'helpless' and why their professional work can lead to even greater stress and emotional burn-out. While it may seem that some situations or individuals appear relatively unchallenging, professionals can still find that difficulties working with a particular child or family can bring about disruption within day care, a classroom or a team.

I may appear to be emphasizing the negative here, especially as working with babies and young children can often bring great pleasure and laughter. However, it is because of the great sensitivity and vulnerability of children that it is so important that we think about our own reactions towards them so that we can optimize our relationships with them. This means, of necessity, being able to face the parts of ourselves that may inadvertently influence the way we behave when we are with children and their parents. As professionals we have the unique opportunity to be able to reflect on our behaviours with a greater objectivity than a parent can. We can adopt the professional mantle and examine ourselves and our colleagues with honesty. In fact, we must, because otherwise we cannot fully support those infants, children and parents who may be further troubled because we are unaware of our own needs. Therapists are obliged to undertake therapy for themselves in order that their own issues do not get in the way of their work with their clients and also have to have supervision for the same reasons. While teachers, nursery nurses, health visitors, social workers and so on are not therapists or counsellors (and should not take on these roles without specific training), nevertheless their involvement with their particular client group means that they form a relationship with the children and parents which is often powerful. The person within the professional is the yardstick by which the care and/or interventions will be deemed to be successful or not. It is who the professional is as a person and how they carry out their work that will ultimately influence what they actually do and how their interventions will be perceived and even implemented by those at the receiving end. It is *such* a responsibility that I often wonder whether we fully appreciate it when we undertake our initial training.

This leads me to another point, which is that there is strong anecdotal evidence that people who enter early years work are sometimes unconsciously looking for a solution to their own emotional needs. I cannot speak for other professions but I know that in nursing I came across nurses whose motivations for their vocation were very mixed and many further education tutors across the country would vouch for the very varied reasons that young women apply to become nursery nurses. For many of them, the opportunity to play when they are on their practical placements appears to be as meaningful to them as for the children they are meant to be supporting. In addition, research in many 'helping' organizations has highlighted how a group of professionals can find themselves 'acting out' the dynamics of the family they are trying to support. It is therefore very helpful for us to reflect, both personally and professionally (e.g. through practice supervision) on our own individual reactions to children's and their families' behaviours and how these might link with our inherent motivation for the work. For example, do we see ourselves as 'caring helpers', and if so what is our reaction if our help is consistently rejected? If we have control issues, how do we deal with missed appointments, people ignoring or challenging our advice or refusing to cooperate? We all have our individual emotional tender places. Thinking about why we have them will help us consider whether we are content with the way we respond and so may support us in continuing to regard with compassion the child or adult in front of us who is behaving in a way we find individually difficult. We may then find that we respond with more confidence in terms of the way in which we manage their and our own emotions.

Looking in, acting out

One of the most difficult things to accept about ourselves, especially if working in one of the 'caring' professions, is that we are human and that we have human frailties. There is a tendency to think that when we are adults we have somehow 'got it all together', especially in our working life.

Raths (2001), for example, indicated that problems in teaching teachers to teach were often due to the fact that people held beliefs about teaching that were difficult to change and sometimes ran contrary to what teacher educators were trying to instil in trainees as 'good practice'. To take an example, a teacher who believed that children had to sit quietly, be obedient and compliant in order to learn well would find their belief system challenged when told that young children learnt through play and playful experiences which involved exploration, moving around and discussing with each other. Cracks might appear in this teacher's teaching style when they tried to apply what they had been told through their planning, room arrangement and so on and yet continued to behave according to their beliefs. This mental 'tug of war' potentially exists not only in teachers but in all of us who work directly with other human beings. In professions where the interaction is often on a very personal level, where the professional is the primary resource, this acknowledgement of personal belief systems becomes crucial.

As an example, I recently heard on the radio a woman saying that 'all men are sexist'. This sweeping generalization, something on a par with 'all women are man-haters' was nevertheless something that the speaker appeared to truly believe. One can only imagine the assumptions she holds, the meaning she would give to what any man might say to her, how she would respond to a friendly male greeting, compliment or criticism. Her interpretation of her interactions with men would be coloured by her assumption that any remark must be couched in innate 'sexism' and so any compliment would be 'demeaning' and any criticism simply due to the fact she was a woman and not because of anything that she might do or how she might behave. It would equally justify in her own eyes behaviour towards men that might be perceived by others as challenging, defensive, offensive, demeaning and critical – her own 'sexist' attitudes.

It can be seen how a 'belief' can act as judge and jury on other people's behaviour and how a belief can 'blind' us to the realities of our own motivations and behaviour. Some examples include a health visitor who feels that she is more sensitive to a child's and family's needs than, for example, a social worker. She may then collude with the family against the social worker, subtly undermining the other's practice, advice or suggestions. Her belief about herself could be that she is kind, sensitive and caring – all of which may be true. At the same time, she may also have a powerful need for approval, to be liked, of which she is less consciously aware. In the context of her work this partly-glimpsed part of her character may lead her to blur the boundaries between personal and professional.

The need for approval, if unrecognized and unguarded, can lead to unhelpful behaviour in professional life. The health visitor in the example may work hard to be the 'friend' of the families she encounters and such a stance may render her helpless when trouble arises. She could be unconsciously dismissing or ignoring destructive behaviours or situations that she might say she would normally challenge or question. In many situations, emotional 'alliances' may be formed with clients that could lead to breakdown in communications with other agencies – for example, a professional in one discipline seeing themselves as the only person who really 'understands' or cares about what is happening with the child and family.

Examining our 'selves' is painful because it is hard to admit that our motivations may not be totally altruistic or that our belief systems may be blinding us with the assumptions that often trail behind those beliefs. For example, some social workers have negative belief systems about the police and vice versa and it will only take one negative encounter to harden such beliefs. Unfortunately, this may mean blocking communication or dismissing comments or concerns. When we examine difficult situations in our work we can start to spot the danger signs – we keep 'forgetting' to post off a report or make that telephone call or send that email. Suddenly meetings are at very inconvenient times or it is simply too much trouble to get the police or social worker to come along on a visit. If you find a pattern emerging, take note, the pattern is telling you that all is not well – with you.

To take another perspective, what might be going on when a social worker who has a variety of strong personal reactions to a case of child neglect is nevertheless able to cope with these feelings and work positively and professionally with the family whilst finding themselves completely 'at sea' in a similar or even a less obviously challenging situation? What might be the intrapersonal dynamics going on for a teacher who is driven to distraction by a child with disruptive behaviours when a colleague is noted to have few problems and both teachers are similarly experienced and knowledgeable?

I do not believe that any of us can totally set aside our beliefs and value systems, and most importantly our emotional strengths and weaknesses, when we are working with children, their parents and other professionals. We may adopt a professional stance but our personal feelings will often creep to the surface, especially in times of stress, and influence how we behave, affecting the nuances of body language, expression and influencing the decisions we make – even though we may be able to rationalize them to ourselves and to others.

Beliefs about others are not the whole picture, of course. We also have strong beliefs about ourselves that are just as difficult to challenge or confront. Our self-belief is entwined with our self-esteem – how we think about ourselves, whether we feel fundamentally good enough, kind enough, loving enough, strong enough. How far our self-esteem is bolstered by the esteem of others or conversely to what extent we can dismiss or ignore the opinions of others depends on the fragility or strength or our self-esteem and what form our defences against psychological destruction might take. In turn, this will affect our own ability, as professionals, to self-reflect on what and how we do our work.

Personal beliefs and needs also affect work with clients, whether they be children or adults. To illustrate this, I will give a very personal example. Many years ago I was a 'clingy' friend, desperate for approval and constantly seeking positive 'feedback' from others. I was fortunate in that I had friends who were able to tolerate my neediness and I undertook many activities which bolstered my self-esteem – taking part in soup runs, going abroad to work 'with the poor' and training as a nurse. However, although there was genuine care and concern in the choice of all these activities, there was also a strong but unacknowledged and unrecognized internal 'push' in that these activities were *approved of by others* and therefore *I* was approved of. A psychological wake-up came after carrying out a bedbath on a patient. As I walked away I was gratified to hear the patient say, 'What a nice girl, so kind'. The next second I realized to my horror that this was what *I wanted* to hear, *needed* to hear, what I unconsciously *waited* to hear. With a sinking heart, I recognized that some of my motivation in always offering to do extra shifts or unpleasant tasks was because of my need. I never challenged, never confronted because I was afraid that if I disagreed what would follow would be absolute rejection. It was an all or nothing scenario: if I was not seen to be doing 'good' then I was 'bad' – nothing in between. I will not go into the origins of this belief but will say that my behaviours often included strategies to avoid the terror of being abandoned. I am happy to tell you that now I can be something of an 'old bat', although still nice occasionally!

It is very hard for any of us to realize and face the fact that we may have needs similar to those described above, needs that have long and convoluted roots reaching back into our early years. The reality is that we all want to feel fundamentally 'loveable', or if you prefer something less 'fluffy', then 'accepted and valued'. If for some reason we do not, then we may seek situations whereby we either try to find what we are constantly seeking or we may bury our need in an apparent disregard for the opinions of others.

Crawford (1986) talks of a nursery nurse who needs to keep everything under control and is enraged by the unruly behaviour of the children in her care. In his sensitive interpretation of the dynamics that might be going on with the nursery nurse, her internal world, the children and their internal world, Crawford suggests that the children can sense her fear of her own loving feelings, thus leaving them angry and impotent, and their rage helps to satisfy a need for their own power and fulfils her fears of chaos. This scenario provides a clue as to why, in some situations, professionals can become helpless. For some nursery nurses an unruly group of 3-year-olds would not be a 'threat' but a positive challenge to try to find ways of engaging them and they would not be afraid of showing care and concern to those children. On the other hand, for the nursery nurse in Crawford's example, the fear of 'disaster' through chaotic behaviour renders her unable to show care but only control. This of course can apply to anyone who may fear 'chaos'. Consider the following situation.

> A teacher and a trainee teacher were working together in a
> Reception class. The children had been involved in painting,
> collage-making and so on. The teacher had to leave the room
> for a few minutes and on return found one of the boys crying
> desperately. She started to go towards him but the trainee held
> her hand out and told the teacher to stop as the boy had to
> 'learn'. He had disobeyed her and she had taken his hand and
> forced him to tear up the painting he had been working on and
> put it in the waste bin. The boy had spent most of the morning
> on his painting and was clearly genuinely heartbroken.

What had caused this woman to mete out this punishment which was not only out of proportion to the actual misdemeanour (which turned out to be a hesitancy on the boy's part in responding to a request), but was also cruel in itself? The trainee had received all the appropriate guidance during her teaching course, the teacher herself aimed to be consistently kind and respectful towards the children and expected them to be the same, so the ethos in the setting was caring and supportive. What did the trainee fear? Like the nursery nurse in the previous example, was she afraid that any non-compliance would lead to utter chaos, or did she feel that only by exercising absolute power could she experience any power at all?

These examples clearly illustrate how the inner world of the practitioner influences the quality of their interactions whatever the initial causes of that world might be. The emotional response and ensuing behaviour may also bear little relation to how someone might actually talk about situations or even think about them during training or meetings. In addition, the response may or may not reflect the behaviour of those around them or their own 'academic' knowledge. The actual response can be much more to do with individual needs and fears than the reality of the actual, current situation.

Of course the picture is complex if we think about what might be the 'triggers' which activate the emotional tender places in the individuals concerned. In the second example, it may have been something about the boy which negatively resonated in the trainee – something as innocuous as facial expression, a gesture, how he sat or stood, and it may have been this which brought into the foreground an incipient cruelty of a type which often has its roots in feelings of powerlessness. Powerlessness may also have led to feelings of competition with the teacher – that she (the trainee) could 'cope' with the class. Whatever the reason, the outcome betrayed both her fears and her coping strategy.

Back to babies

In Chapter 7 I talked about the 'sympathy' which can be expressed when parents are overwhelmed by their babies and also the very varied and sometimes confusing approach we have to 'hitting' or 'smacking'. It is generally acknowledged that when we smack children, we do so because we feel out of control – and we are. We do not condone violence towards adults and yet somehow we seem to suggest that smacking children is somehow not violence; that it is necessary for their own good (otherwise chaos); and, what else can one do? We can also be obsessed by control. What we have to ask ourselves is why does the care of a baby arouse such incredible highs and lows of emotion? Why does a baby who cries and will not settle provoke such alarming feelings?

The answer may be to do with the unmet needs of some parents, and this is demonstrated by the fact that many parents *are* able to tolerate distressed babies with sympathy and understanding. They may indeed feel tired, perplexed and so on but they are able to see a child's distress as its *own*, not as an accusation of incompetence by the baby towards its parents. However, for other parents the distressed baby is somehow *their* fault, suggesting that they 'should do better', and this ties in with fundamental feelings of 'not being good enough'. They will then react towards the baby from their own feelings of helplessness using strategies they have used all their lives: anger, or withdrawal or further helplessness. How such behaviour is expressed will depend on the individual. Some parents will channel their rage through activity – finding out information, buying whale music or rhythms of heart beats or surf pounding, or drive around the streets at two in the morning. Others will express their anger overtly by shouting or shaking, or covertly by leaving the child to cry or handing care over to someone else as often as possible.

The problem for professionals in such situations is that they can often see that the solution to the problem is quite mundane: the baby is hungry, or the baby is responding to the rhythm of family life which is chaotic and, although suiting the parents, is overstimulating for the baby, providing no 'markers' to help them self-regulate. Professionals may also be keenly aware of the distress of the baby concerned and feel helpless or inadequate as a result. How should professionals deal with the knowledge that the parents may completely ignore their advice or find every reason under the sun as to why it won't work?

One of the things a professional can do is seek help and nurture from their colleagues. However, this can bring additional complexities to the intrapersonal response of the individual. If we are in full-time employment, we spend about 50 per cent of our waking time at work and may make long-lasting relationships with others in the team, whose opinions then become very important. Friendships and rivalries abound in many offices and staff rooms, and there will usually be an overriding ethos surmounting individual relationships. This will be either one of cooperation or confrontation, with team members siding against management or cliques forming among the team itself. Whatever the scenario, there will be a personal cost to the life of the working professional. We may want so much to be accepted as part of the team that we end up repressing contradictory or challenging views in order to ensure our acceptance. For many of us, day-to-day practice will be influenced by how our colleagues perceive the work we do – especially for those professionals whose own self-esteem is low. It then becomes more difficult to discuss the worker's own individual problems in dealing with a family, especially if their problems are connected with concerns which seem to run counter to the accepted wisdom of the group.

The powerful feelings that babies can invoke (e.g. care and nurturance or fear and anxiety) transmit themselves into the professional practice of those working with them. The picture grows in complexity as the carer who 'needs to be needed' shows care and nurturance to the babies in their care but becomes so involved that they regard themselves as the 'indispensable' worker who is 'best' at feeding or playing with the babies and who may harbour feelings of resentment when the babies smile at someone else. Babies sense the truth and their own responses may indicate the realities of the underlying emotions of the adults who care for them. Babies respond to faces and behaviours microsecond by microsecond and the carer who needs a baby to need them will be more likely to induce anxiety in the babies than comfort. Of course, the very sensitivity of babies to the emotions of their carers whether professional or otherwise can help those observing babies to work out what is happening in their individual worlds.

Adults, babies and the baby within the adult

You may remember that in Chapter 1 I listed a series of questions that professionals might ask themselves when working with babies (see p. 8). Here we are going to consider three of these questions:

- What do I usually *see* when I look at babies?
- What do I usually *feel* when I look at babies?
- What is my understanding of how babies learn about themselves and others? *How does this baby react* to me, parents and other adults?

So, what might you see? A helpless bundle? A demanding, noisy little creature? An object of wonder? Something cute and/or adorable? A real person, albeit small and helpless? Do you see an individual baby *as* an individual with its own particular temperament and needs, or have the babies in your care become a kind of amorphous mass, with perhaps only one or two that you find particularly 'cute'? Does any one baby remind you of someone you care about or someone you don't like? Does this 'identification' affect your dealings with the baby? We know that parents can project their feelings about other adults onto a baby who reminds them of that person, so it can also apply to you (or any of us!).

What do you feel? Your feelings towards any one baby or a group of babies will be linked with your own attitudes towards dependency and vulnerability, either positive or negative. You may feel overwhelming tenderness and a sense of protectiveness. If this is the case, what form does it take? Will your feelings of protectiveness mean that you find it difficult for others to also work with the baby and the family? How 'protective' is your protectiveness? Does it imply protection against physical or emotional harm, or both? What may be your own issues about power and control? What does being powerless actually feel like to you as an individual? Does it frighten you or make you want to control something else? Do you like to feel in control of every aspect of your life and how then do you cope with parents who are chaotic in their care for their baby? What does this actually do to you, inside? What are you aware of when you talk about such families? What are your sentiments?

All these questions are hard, but they do need asking! Otherwise, it is easy to find ourselves dismissing of some parents and not others, finding some parents more acceptable than others. How do any of us cope with a parent who seems to want to control us, tell us what to do when 'we' are the professionals? If we can be aware of our own feelings about power and control we can identify when we seem to be getting into a power struggle with parents, other professionals and even the babies themselves.

Parents are sometimes told not to pick up babies when they cry for fear of 'spoiling' them or to maintain a regular, rigid feeding routine, or that a baby will not 'remember' painful medical procedures, a violent incident or emotional upheaval within the family. We know that none of this is actually true and/or beneficial to the baby but there is an elusive quality about caring for infants which seems to bring forth in some people a need to apply rigid routines especially around feeding which seem to arise from a fear that if the baby is not 'controlled' in some way then they will turn into a selfish 'monster'. The idea of the 'evil' baby may seem far-fetched but it is surprising how many parents will attribute quite malevolent feelings to their baby as reasons for quite normal behaviour. Professionals are not immune! It is also sometimes difficult for professionals to separate out their own experiences of being a parent and the routines, regimens, etc. that they followed or are following from those of the parents and infants they are working with. For example, trainers of student nursery nurses can find students who are parents difficult because they want to apply their practices to everyone else and find it very difficult to accept material which contradicts what they are doing or have done in the past. It can be a minefield!

The last question, how does the baby react?, is perhaps the most difficult to answer. Do you want the baby to like you? Of course, for those professionals whose interventions are brief and intermittent this may not seem applicable, but nevertheless even someone carrying out a one-off assessment or development check on a baby may find themselves smiling and cooing in order to get the baby to smile at them as a reward. If we work with a baby or group of babies regularly, we need to think about not only what we bring to the babies via our behaviour but also what we want from them. Do we secretly want to be the favoured carer? Is it a good thing to be surrounded by smiling babies and a failure if a crying baby is not settled straight away? Babies can be perceived by parents as the answer to their hopes and dreams, as a fulfilment of their own emotional needs. Work with babies can also awaken these primary needs in professionals.

The ethos of the work setting

While the personal beliefs and emotional style of any one professional will influence their work with families, unless they are working on their own (e.g. as childminders) they will also be part of a team. Each team will also have a management structure, a professional purpose and an ethos. The latter will be influenced not only by a formally recognized 'mission statement' but also by the beliefs of the manager/senior staff and those of the rest of the team, which may not necessarily coincide.

For example, a day centre for children and families had supporting parents and parenting skills as its main role and function. It was both a therapeutic and an assessment centre and there was much liaison with childcare professionals in health, social services and education. The organization of the playgroup was seen as primarily 'child centred' with a particular emphasis on the importance of play. However, staff members were very varied in their personal interpretations of what 'child centred' and 'play' actually meant. Opportunities for learning through discovery and exploration were therefore not always fulfilled. Sometimes, an individual interpretation of a philosophy can indicate a great deal about the defences and beliefs of the individual concerned. For example, feeding a number of babies at the same time can be rationalized as 'early socialization'. A lack of coherent or regular planning by adults can be rationalized as ensuring that activities are 'child centred'. Such philosophies may be part of a process that enables staff to give some kind of objectivity to their personal defence mechanisms against the children's needs for individual attention, observation and assessment, which may seem overwhelming at times.

The knowledge, attitudes and belief system of one team member can also undermine group knowledge and understanding. For example:

> An adviser visited a preschool setting which accepted children
> from 6 weeks to 4 years of age. She was there to explain the new
> Foundation Stage guidance for 3-year-old children. During her
> visit she was asked by some staff members about what they
> should do with a girl who refused to 'work'. She wanted to play
> all the time, would climb onto furniture, did not want to sit for
> any length of time and was becoming a real nuisance. Initially the
> adviser assumed they were talking about a child of around 4 but
> something in the way they were describing the girl's behaviour
> led her to ask exactly what age was this child. It transpired that
> she was 15 months of age.

Some members of staff were finding the perfectly normal, developmentally appropriate behaviour of this child 'difficult' as it did not fit into their schedule of activities and a stated aim of 'education' within the setting. How had they forgotten all their training? What had led them to set aside what, on an 'academic' level, they 'knew' and to treat this child as a 'problem'? What made the situation more difficult was one member of staff who, during discussion about the situation was very challenging and confrontational about the guidance being offered. Sometimes, a single member of a staff team, who is by no means necessarily the most senior, can influence the atmosphere, approach and behaviour of many others in the team. If this happens, individuals can find themselves behaving in ways that in other circumstances they might question or even condemn, but their own feelings of perceived or actual powerlessness can render them helpless with all that that implies, which leads me to think briefly about the additional pressures that working within an organization may bring.

Professionals often have to carry the needs of parents as well as those of children. Work in 'caring/education' professions often also means long hours, a great deal of paperwork and frequent media attention, so such work has a public as well as a private face. The behaviour of many early years professionals, especially teachers and social workers, is under public scrutiny and mistakes or tragedies can be doubly traumatic because of this attention. Expectations by others of how such professionals should behave and what they should and should not be doing in their day-to-day work add further pressure to already demanding and some-times difficult and/or sensitive work. This can radically affect decisions regarding the type of care and/or education delivered in the setting. For example, the pressure by parents on early years workers in day settings for 'formal education' can sometimes lead to inappropriate tasks/activities being promoted which are neither developmentally appropriate for many of the children nor satisfying for those delivering the 'curriculum'. Babies do not escape, as the monitoring of their develop-ment can lead to an overemphasis on cognitive achievements which may be poorly understood by some inexperienced and/or untrained members of staff.

Blackmore (1978) quoted in Doctor *et al.* (1994) identified four types of stress relating to policing which could easily be extrapolated into early years work:

- external stress related to negative public attitudes;
- organizational stress such as low pay;
- performance-related stress such as work schedules;
- personal stress such as marital problems.

Obholzer (undated) stresses that psychoanalysts firmly believe in mental pain and that most of us spend a great deal of time and energy avoiding it, most commonly by denial (i.e. pretending that what is painful or worrying does not exist). He goes further by stressing that mental pain does not *only* exist in the mind of the individual but can also take the form of 'institutional pain arising from the nature of the work of the organization' (pp. 4–5). He talks about the different responses of organ-izations who acknowledge difficulties arising from the work of their staff and support the individuals concerned and those organizations who at-tempt to behave as if the reality of the stresses and strains does not exist or is of no importance. The defences that organizations unconsciously use are those embedded in their structure: the delegation of power, the use of authority and attention to task and performance. It is clear that both organizational stress and personal stress can influence the profes-sional practice of the individual. An example of how demands for 'deliv-ery' of service can affect staff behaviour is a situation where a class of 42 3- and 4-year-olds were being offered the full Literacy Hour in a setting. These children were obviously not very receptive and the staff were desperately trying to keep order. They started to shout at the children to make them 'behave', sit and listen. In this instance, there were wider problems with complex reasons as to why this curriculum requirement for older children was being offered but nevertheless it does reflect how the pressures of performing can also chase good practice out of the door.

Summary

Early years work brings with it two distinct patterns of stress, one overt and the other covert. The overt stress is a requirement for competent, sensitive people able to work with children at a 'grass roots' level. Early years workers in whatever profession and/or setting are often the child's first confidant. The responsibility and sense of ethical duty is counter-acted by a society which gives low status (and frequently low pay!) to early years work and does not appear to appreciate the reality of how adults affect the day-to-day lives of children, especially those that are working with infants and very young children.

In order for professionals to work effectively with babies, young children and their parents, their first duty is to recognize themselves for who they are, what they believe and why. The emotions we see in infants and young children do not only belong to them, they belong to us. We have all been helpless infants, we all carry with us our history including that of being parented and therefore, consciously or unconsciously, we know what children are going through at any particular time. When we watch a small child enter the nursery school gates for the first time, we may suddenly be transported back to our own first days at school. When we see a baby we may feel delight but we may also feel some fear or trepidation as to how to care for and provide this infant with what they need. It may be easier for us to concentrate on the feeding and bathing of infants and not perhaps to consider what multiple carers, frequent staff changes and lack of individual attention might mean to their developing minds and bodies.

In the next chapter we consider loss in the particular context of babies with special needs.

9 WHEN DREAMS GO AWRY

In this penultimate chapter, I will consider aspects of grief and loss in the context of the birth of, or subsequent diagnosis of, children with special needs. In essence, the fundamental grieving or mourning process can be extrapolated to all situations of loss. It is only the intensity, duration and progress of each stage that will change depending on the individual and the context of the loss situation. In my view, loss and sadness lie at the heart of much unwanted behaviour in both children and adults, although the sadness and grief that may be felt is often subsumed by other emotions such as anger, anxiety or fearfulness depending on the timing and duration of the loss experience and the way in which individuals address their innermost feelings, framed by their temperament.

The dream for all babies is that they achieve their potential whatever that may be. While the dream of what the child will be may go awry for the parents of children with special needs, there is still the hope that the child will be loved and accepted for who they are and achieve what is within their gift. Perhaps the greater tragedy is when we adults take away the unformed dreams of a baby through the manner in which we model behaviours to, care for and teach that child.

In Chapter 3 we considered the potential emotional context in which children are born: already loved and anticipated or dreaded, already invested with a personality or denied one, carrying the baggage of their parents' own dreams for themselves or their baby. Happily, for most babies, the welcome they receive at birth is one of love and joy. However, there is one question that is still asked of midwives at birth and one wish expressed to them before birth: 'Is the baby all right?' and 'Will my baby be all right?' The fundamental hope that the baby will be physically and mentally healthy is powerful and on this foundation lies parental expectations, hopes and dreams. When it turns out that the baby is not 'all right', this 'loss' can be traumatic. Some parents may already know, through antenatal tests, that their child may need special attention and care. The process of their coming to terms with this change in their anticipated future may already have begun, although, as with nearly all parents, especially with a first baby, the reality may be different to that imagined.

With some babies it is only at the birth that a 'difference' is to be found and with others there is a slow realization that 'something is not quite right'. One parent has provided a moving description of the fundamental changes involved in coming to terms with an unlooked-for reality and has been courageous enough to share this on the internet (see: www.nas.com/downsyn/holland.html):

I am often asked to describe the experience of raising a child with a disability – to try to help people who have not shared that unique experience to understand it, to imagine how it would feel. It's like this . . .

When you are going to have a baby, it's like planning a fabulous vacation – to Italy. You buy a bunch of guidebooks and make your wonderful plans. The Colosseum, the Michelangelo David, the gondolas in Venice. You may learn some handy phrases in Italian. It's all very exciting.

After months of eager anticipation, the day finally arrives. You pack your bags and off you go. Several hours later, the plane lands, the stewardess comes in and says, 'Welcome to Holland'.

'Holland?', you say, 'What do you mean, Holland? I signed up for Italy! I'm supposed to be in Italy! All my life I've dreamed of going to Italy!'

But there's been a change in the flight plan. They've landed in Holland and there you must stay.

The important thing is that they haven't taken you to a horrible, disgusting, filthy place full of pestilence, famine and disease.

It's just a different place.

So you must go out and buy new guidebooks. And you must learn a whole new language. And you will meet a whole new group of people you would never have met.

It's just a different place. It's slower paced than Italy, less flashy than Italy. But after you've been there for a while and you catch your breath, you look around and you begin to notice that Holland has windmills, Holland has tulips. Holland even has Rembrandts.

But everyone you know is busy coming and going from Italy . . . and they're all bragging about what a wonderful time they had there. And for the rest of your life, you will say, 'Yes, that's where I was supposed to go. That's what I had planned.'

And the pain of that will never, ever, ever, ever go away . . . because the loss of that dream is a very, very significant loss.

But if you spend your life mourning the fact that you didn't get to Italy, you may never be free to enjoy the very special, the very lovely things about Holland.

There are two things to which I would like to draw your attention. First, that in some versions of this I have seen, the sentence about pain and loss is not there. Second, this parent's approach is ultimately *positive*, even though she acknowledges grief, loss and some anger. What she implies is that there is a process of coming to terms with the loss of 'going to Italy' and then discovering that 'being in Holland' can also bring joys. Parents of children who require additional support in their daily living and learning will, to different degrees, go through this process too, and what is important for professionals to think about is that each parent will approach the process in a different way, depending on their attitudes, beliefs and values. In addition, parents may be at different stages of this process when professionals meet them. As with the grieving process following bereavement, individuals can get 'stuck' in a particular part of the process and can remain there for years in some cases, without their condition being recognized by the person and/or help being sought. The other side of the coin is that professionals, be they health visitors, social workers, special needs teachers, nursery nurses or childminders who come into contact with special needs children will have beliefs about and towards them, whether physical, social or emotional, and their own experiences of loss and grief.

Such beliefs will encompass learning opportunities, 'behaviour management', the level of emotional understanding and so on. Beliefs will also reflect personal prejudices and/or needs. Parents and workers are also members of 'the public' and the public have a very mixed attitude to people with additional requirements, especially if those people look 'normal', such as children with autism or severe emotional disturbance: a child with autism panicking desperately over a change in the vehicle that has come to collect him could be interpreted as being 'a spoilt child, out of control' by someone observing from across the road.

There are generalized assumptions about the behaviour or aptitude of those who have lost some physical ability. The Radio 4 programme *Does He Take Sugar?* identifies the invisibility felt by those in wheelchairs, for example, and the assumption that such a person cannot think for themselves. The high profile of someone like Stephen Hawking, who has profound loss of physical ability and yet an intelligence which goes far beyond that of most of us, is a good example of the mistaken nature of this particular generalized assumption.

As I said earlier, one of the realities we have to face is that when working with babies and their families we must deal with the parents' attitudes *and* our own. We are not automatically accepting, tolerant or non-judgemental of people who behave differently to ourselves. If we meet someone who appears to reject their baby because of some disability, or conversely cares for the baby to the exclusion of other children and their partner, we may experience a wide range of emotions which will influence our behaviour towards the parent and the type and quality of the advice we give. We may also have our own experiences to contend with. For example, a professional may have a child who has some kind of emotional/behavioural and/or physical disability. How does such a person prevent overidentification with a parent ('I know how you feel') or feel challenged in their care of their own child by the apparent absolute dedication of the other parent? As already indicated, many professionals will have their own experiences of loss and grief and just as with parents who are working through this change in their hopes and dreams about their child, so the professional may be at a certain stage in their own 'working through' of their particular issues, and each party in this scenario may be at different points in the management of their emotions and their ability to self-reflect.

An additional point when working with children with special needs is that in some circumstances the conditions which result in disability may also imply a shortened lifespan for the child, resulting in a double loss for the parents. The fate of children is to endure the death of their parents – parents are not generally expected to witness the death of their children. This is, however, a relatively recent state of affairs in western society, as not so long ago children frequently died of conditions such as smallpox, measles, polio, tuberculosis, etc., most of which are now successfully controlled by immunization or antibiotics. Although obviously everybody dies, nevertheless death rates are falling with people living longer and generally healthier lives. The death of a child has become a thankfully rare occurrence and this means that life threatening illnesses or disabling conditions are 'unusual' and therefore the social support systems in society are perhaps not so prevalent. At a time when almost everything is openly discussed, death itself remains somewhat of a taboo and the striving of society for youth, beauty and perfection means that the child who has a deformity of some sort has an uphill struggle to be seen for the person rather than the outer appearance. Self-esteem and self-worth appear to be overly tied up with how one appears to others and so parents and those working with children who do not match the supposed ideal have to face all these issues including perhaps their own unwanted negative feelings.

Another note of caution for professionals is that they must be careful not to make assumptions about what either or both parents might feel about the child or what their attitudes might be. It may be automatically assumed for example that the mother will be totally accepting of the baby or that partners, siblings, relatives and friends will only feel positively towards the new baby. Feelings of shame and guilt around possible negative feelings may be transformed into superhuman efforts of care or into confrontational approaches with medical, social, education or health care staff. As professionals we need to heed our own insights and concerns into the behaviour of parents. We must also be careful of our expectations of how people should react and not be dismissive of the parent, for example, if such expectations are not met.

The process of loss

Bryner (2001) describes Elizabeth Kubler Ross' stages of grieving for patients with terminal illness that have been found to hold validity for those suffering any kind of loss. These are: denial, anger, bargaining, depression and acceptance. Bowlby (1980) also describes similar stages of mourning. These are numbing, disbelief, anger, disorganization and reorganization. The latter two broadly equating with depression and acceptance. Adults and children go through these phases with varying intensities, durations and perspectives. The stages may exist for all, but the expression of them depends in part on the accompanying context of age, cognitive and emotional development. Bryner uses the grieving 'stages' to describe what children might go through when parents are separating/divorcing and again, these insights can usefully be considered when thinking about how children may perceive the grief of their parents. It is important that professionals who are working with parents whose child has been recently 'diagnosed' as having special needs or whose baby has special needs, that any siblings are aware of the emotional atmosphere in the home and its aftermath. Even babies and very young children may suffer from the decreased interaction that might occur when the primary caregiver is immersed in the care of the 'special' child. An older child may interpret the parental preoccupation with the new baby as evidence of their own 'badness' and work very hard through a variety of means to re-establish their 'position' in the family. Sensitive professionals need to be alert to this and also be sensitive to any situations which may be mirroring their own past or current experiences.

Professionals may also find that any sense of loss at the birth of a child with special needs is 'downplayed' or denied by the parents. A parent may be seen to be 'wonderful', apparently fully accepting the situation and this may indeed be the case. However, because negative emotions are not 'permitted' in such circumstances, or thoughts such as 'how can I resume my interesting career when my child needs such care?' may feel too awful/selfish to be expressed, such worries, doubts and fears are secreted away. In spite of the increasing openness and sensitivity of midwives, doctors, health visitors and so on and the opportunities for discussion provided, parents may simply feel that what they are thinking/feeling is just too 'bad' and that professionals will think ill of them. This may be an unwarranted assumption but it is often a real fear, nonetheless. If a parent harbours a secret hope that their child could have become the doctor, pilot or environmental activist that they wanted to be but circumstances have prevented them, how do they deal with their lost dreams? Bowlby felt that unrecognized or unacknowledged loss could lead to both physical and psychological illness. Leading on from this, Fraley and Shaver (1999) describe individually meaningful but apparently unconnected or even seemingly trivial situations, such as attending another child's sports day, invoking episodes of one of the grieving stages.

As we know, both children and adults have an emotional inner world and develop a range of strategies to cope with strong emotion. Those adults whose strategy has been 'dismissing' may 'play down' their feelings but may also have actual 'blunting' of their general emotional states – in other words, they may not feel that much. This does *not* mean that such people are uncaring, it is just that they have adopted a way of coping which is rather like a dog shaking water off its coat – they shake off the pain and get on with things. It is important to recognize that, as Fraley and Shaver (1999) point out, some research indicates there is a difference between 'truly low anxiety' individuals and 'repressors'. Professionals in their day-to-day life may not have the time, resources or training to consider individual parental attitudes, temperament and so on. However, if working to support families with special needs children, parental behaviour should be considered in the light of what they might potentially be going through during their adjustment to 'living in Holland'.

Summary

Grief and loss experienced in the particular context of a baby with special needs resonates with the experience of other forms of loss. When working with children and parents we need to be acutely aware of the many different kinds of loss that must be endured and acknowledge that all of us face loss with a myriad of individual variations. What is important for us too, is to remember that situations of loss and grief may resonate in us and activate memories or reawaken feelings we may not have been fully aware we had. As professionals we are not immune from the pain of others nor our own pain, and either or both can act like filters for our thinking – not allowing us to reflect on the whole situation or see the actual reality, but a mirror image of something we ourselves might have suffered.

10 THE YEAR OF OPPORTUNITY

This book has stressed throughout that babies are emotional beings and that their earliest experiences are of paramount importance. It is therefore puzzling to me, in the light of not only the research but also the individual stories of many people, that the power of early experience still seems to be denied or played down by some corners of society. The sticking point seems to be that if we acknowledge what research and experience consistently tell us, we have to ask ourselves some very hard questions. What makes these questions even harder (and the asking of them even less likely) is that as a society we seem to be moving towards more group care for our children. More and more children at younger and younger ages are being placed in day care for longer and longer periods of time. While day care in many circumstances is beneficial to the child and supportive to parents, the decisive factor is the *quality* of such care and the availability of skilled, experienced, caring and nurturing adults to provide the highest quality of care at this vulnerable time. However, we are sadly reluctant to pay realistic wages to such people and, even more sadly, may pay less attention to the attributes of day care personnel than to the attributes of the car we want to buy.

What we are actually talking about when we talk of the care of babies and very young children is the support and promotion of the future well-being of each of these vulnerable individuals whose futures are in our hands. Somehow the importance of bringing up children has been lost in issues such as women's equality in the workplace and the importance placed on material success. We seem to have forgotten the old adage 'the hand that rocks the cradle rules the world', but it nevertheless remains the case that it is through our principles, boundaries and moralities that the ethos of the coming generation is formed.

A teacher colleague who teaches 15- and 16-year-olds talked of her growing despair at the progressive isolation she has witnessed over the past years. These teenagers are essentially 'bringing themselves up'. Their parents are busy working and do not have time to interact with their children. The children find that they are simply left to their own devices, often alone in their rooms watching TV, videos or playing on the computer. Strong anecdotal evidence from early years staff including nursery nurses and teachers also indicates that some children in both preschool and Reception classes are unused to any kind of social group activity such as eating together, and recent polls indicate that regular family meals are becoming a 'thing of the past' as is, unhappily, the reading of stories at bedtime.

This situation is not the case in most homes, but it certainly exists in a significant proportion of them. What must it be like for a 4-year-old who does not know what it is to have regular access to their parents or to have a routine which underpins the events of the day? What safety and emotional security can this child have gained from their day-to-day existence? Why is it that such markers, which so many adults remember even if their home life was turbulent, gave such comfort and still do so? This is not to promote some over-romanticized view of family life but to highlight that routine, familiarity and the presence of caring adults gives sanctuary to a child. This is also not to deny that for many children family life is far from a sanctuary, but an impoverished background with a worn-out mother and a drunken father can still contain moments of cherished. What counts is feeling loved and valued even in the middle of apparent hopelessness and despair. Babies cling like limpets to any sign of love and care they may encounter and such is the driving force of this need they (or rather we) squirrel away such experiences into the fabric of our emotional being. An emotionally impoverished environment however will create fundamental difficulties in babies' lives.

As adults we have enormous responsibilities. If we show no respect for our institutions, our teachers, our authority figures, then our children will show no respect either. If we continue to downgrade the importance of childrearing then we will continue to recruit staff who vary widely in quality, commitment and motivation. If we only stress academic qualifications and do not accept the wide variation in skills, aptitudes and talents in human beings and value those equally then society as a whole misses out. If we continue to say that all adult behaviours are acceptable 'if it feels good and hurts no one' then we cannot expect children to learn about care and respect for the feelings of others. If we are so busy as adults that we cannot take time to listen to our children, read to them, eat with them, talk to them, then we will produce adults who will have lost the power to empathize with others. Such human qualities as courage, loyalty, respect, trust, honesty, integrity and tolerance do not simply 'happen'. We are born with the innate *capacity* for them but it is our experiences which shape whether these qualities come to the fore or whether they remain buried in a neural and emotional graveyard of lost opportunities. We learn to love from infancy but we can also learn to hate, to mistrust others, to despise and ridicule them, to treat the hearts of others with the disdain with which our own hearts were broken.

Frankl (1987) describes his experiences in a concentration camp, and notes that it took a relatively short time for people to become apathetic towards the cruelty and injustice around them and be unmoved by the suffering of someone else. Think about the sensitivity of the developing brain and consider the baby who grows up in an environment of neglect and/or apathy: how can such a child believe in a world of hope? In the concentration camps, people clung to their previous experiences of warmth and love, of people who cared, of happier times. What if a child's main experiences are of shifting relationships with little or no routine or comfort? What might a child make of their world and how are they going to learn to deal with it? It is not enough for us to throw up our hands in horror when we hear of a 12-year-old rapist or a 10-year-old murderer. We have to ask *why*, and be honest in our answers, and take *responsibility* as a society.

Frankl goes on movingly to describe how those who were able to tap into their 'internal resources' were able to survive the unimaginable hardships they endured and seemed to survive longer than those who were more physically robust. For him, the knowledge of his love for his wife and hers for him was his saviour. He describes love as being the ultimate saviour of the human psyche. However, he means 'love' as something which has a deep, almost spiritual dimension and I would maintain that it is only through having experienced as an infant the undemanding love of the parent which is tuned-in to the baby, is responsive and sensitive and all enveloping (that multi-modal experience) that we, as humans, can then go on to be able to give love and be loveable. Thankfully, most of us do, but there are significant numbers of infants who do not. The use of our imaginations, for example, as Frankl and others who have had similar experiences movingly describe, can take us away from our real circumstances and allow us to take up images of safety and trust – but how can a troubled child who is unable to move from the 'concrete' (i.e. the real and seen) develop the resources to cope with future adversities?

A final point I wish to draw from Frankl's experiences is his description of suffering as behaving like a gas:

> If a certain quantity of gas is pumped into an empty chamber, it will fill the chamber completely and evenly, no matter how big the

chamber. Thus suffering completely fills the human soul and conscious mind, no matter whether the suffering is great or little. Therefore the 'size' of human suffering is absolutely relative.

(Frankl 1987: 43)

This is important to remember as there should be no 'league table' for judging how 'bad' an experience might be for an infant or very young child. We cannot say, for example, that for a baby to be sexually abused is 'worse' than being chronically neglected. The baby perceives its experiences as they occur – and what the baby experiences will be personal to itself. An example is how an adult may describe an incident from their childhood to a sibling or parent and be met with astonishment because the incident 'was not like that at all'. The parent may retrospectively rationalize their behaviour by saying 'Well, what I meant was . . .' and so on. This does *not* mean that the adult's perception of their experience was a lie but merely shows how differently we can interpret what happens to us. Babies are 'empty chambers' as far as experience goes and the 'gas' of what they experience will influence their ultimate sense of who they are. If we neglect children we run the risk of taking away from them one of their options for achieving their potential.

Of course, as previously discussed, development is dynamic and we humans are highly receptive, flexible and adaptable. Different experiences can play a great part in changing the course of a child's life. Early years workers can provide a wonderful opportunity to support and help children. For example, a teacher who senses a child's innate ability in spite of difficult or challenging behaviour may be able to point the child down a different road. A nursery nurse who consistently shows interest in and care of a child who appears withdrawn and sad may encourage and promote positive self-esteem and ultimately a greater ability to learn. A childminder who introduces books to a child who has only ever watched TV opens doors to another world. An adult who is prepared to give a cuddle to a smelly and dirty child, a school that provides breakfast to children in an area where many children may be under- or poorly nourished may make a huge difference to the future lives of those children. Examples of both individual and group positive interventions are endless. Care, compassion and interest from the adults who surround babies and children give momentum to daily acts of kindness which promote children's well-being.

However, as time marches on, most therapists would say that a child's behaviour becomes more difficult to change. It is in our early years that the emotional foundations for our being are laid down, when the capacity for joy, curiosity, laughter, fun and exploration are at their potential peak. We must do what we can for babies: they are the future and how we treat them will affect how they treat us in our old age, and how they will treat their children, their peers, the environment and all that is in it.

In this high-technology world, where communication is instant, where changes in technology mean that we all have access to almost everything, how do we draw boundaries? How do we help children develop their imaginations, their pretend play skills if they see everything on a screen, and how do they develop their coping mechanisms if they watch alone? Technology is wonderful but was never meant to replace humanity, just as knowing about the human genome does not give the whole picture of who a person is, and even more importantly, *why* that person is. It is only the scaffolding.

Perhaps the greatest harm we do to babies and young children is to take away from them their chance to achieve their full potential whatever that may be. We do this through either not providing emotional security in the first place or else presenting them with a negative view of themselves through the many forms of abuse of which we as adults are capable. We then compound the problem by not protecting them, not taking their troubles seriously or by denying their capacity to suffer.

This book has come full circle, from the baby, to the baby in the adult, and now back to considering the future of the baby. We know what babies need and we must be strong enough to provide it. Fortunately, wherever we look there are examples of excellent care and professional practice. As well as those wonderful parents (still the great majority) who love, respect and enjoy their children, there are professionals who care desperately about the babies and young children in their care. They constantly strive to promote children's potential and provide positive nurture and learning opportunities which enhance children's already positive world, or provide troubled children with a positive world view. There is always hope that each baby will find someone who will believe in them and, like the good fairies in the traditional tales, endow them with the capacity to take their rightful place in the world.

BIBLIOGRAPHY

Abrams, S., Field, T., Scafidi, F. and Prodromidis, M. (1995) Newborns of depressed mothers, *Infant Mental Health Journal*, 16: 233–9.

Ainsworth, M.D. (1985) Patterns of infant/mother attachments, *Bulletin of the New York Academy of Medicine*, 61(9).

Ames, E.W. (1997) *The Development of Romanian Orphanage Children Adopted to Canada: Final Report to the National Welfare Grants Program*. Burnaby, British Columbia: Simon Fraser University.

Atchley, R.A. and Atchley, P. (1998) Hemispheric specialization in the detection of subjective objects, *Neuropsychologia*, 36(12): 1373–86.

Atkinson, L. and Zucker, K.J. (eds) (1997) *Attachment and Psychopathology*. New York: Guilford Press.

Azar, S.T., Povilaitis, T.Y., Lauretti, A.F. and Pouquette, C.L. (1998) The current status of etiological theories in intrafamilial child treatment, in J.R. Lutzker (ed.) *Handbook of Child Abuse Research and Treatment*. New York: Plenum Press.

Baillargeon, R. (1987a) Object permanence in 3.5–4.5m old infants, *Developmental Psychology*, 23: 655–64.

Baillargeon, R. (1987b) Young infants' reasoning about the physical and spatial properties of a hidden object, *Cognitive Development*, 2: 179–200.

Baillargeon, R. (1994) How do infants learn about the physical world? *Current Directions in Psychological Science*, 3: 133–40.

Baillargeon, R. (1998) Infants' understanding of the physical world, in M. Soubarin, F. Craik and M. Robert (eds) *Advances in Psychological Science*, vol. 2, pp. 503–29. Hove: Psychology Press.

Baillargeon, R., Kotovsky, L. and Needham, A. (1995) The acquisition of physical knowledge in infancy, in D. Sperber, D. Premack and A.J. Premack (eds) *Casual Cognition: A Multidisciplinary Debate*. New York: Oxford University Press.

Beebe, B. and Lachmann, F.M. (1994) Representation and internalization in infancy: three principles of salience, *Psychoanalytic Psychology*, 11(2): 127–65.

Benoit, D., Parker, K.C.H. and Zeanah, C.H. (1997) Mothers' representations of their infants assessed prenatally: stability and association with infants' attachment classifications, *Journal of Child Psychology & Psychiatry*, 38: 307–13.

Birnholz, J.C. (1981) The development of human fetal eye movement patterns, *Science*, 213: 679–81.

Blackmore, J. (1978) Are police allowed to have problems of their own?, *Police Magazine*, 1(3): 47–55.

Blair, R.J., Morris, J.S., Frith, C.D., Perrett, D.I. and Dolan, R.J. (1999) Dissociable neural responses to facial expressions of sadness and anger, *Brain*, 122: 883–93.

Blomhoff, S. *et al.* (2000) Emotional responses' impact on intestinal reactivity, *Journal of Digestive Diseases and Sciences*, 45(June): 1153–65.

Boris, N.W. and Zeanah, C.H. (eds) (1999) Disturbances and disorders of attachment, *Infant Mental Health Journal*, 20(1).

Bowlby, J. (1944) Forty-four juvenile thieves: their characters and home life, *International Journal of Psycho-Analysis*, 25: 10–52.

Bowlby, J. ([1969] 1991) *Attachment and Loss*, vol. 1 *Attachment*. London: Penguin.

Bowlby, J. ([1973] 1991) *Attachment and Loss*, vol. 2 *Separation*. London: Penguin.

Bowlby, J. ([1980] 1991) *Attachment and Loss*, vol. 3 *Loss*. London: Penguin.

Bowlby, J. (1988) *A Secure Base*. London: Routledge.

Brozgold, A., Martin, C., Pick, L., Alpert, M. and Welkowitz, J. (1998) Social functioning and facial emotional expression, *Neurological and Psychiatric Disorders in Applied Neuropsychology*, 5(1): 15–23.

Bryner, C.L. (2001) Children of divorce, *Journal of the American Board of Family Practitioners*, 14(3): 178–83.

Butterworth, B. (1999) *The Mathematical Brain*. London: Macmillan.

Calder, A.J., Young, A.W. and Perrett *et al.* (1996) Categorical perception of morphed facial expressions, *Visual Cognition*, 3(2): 81–117.

Calder, A.J., Rowland, D. and Young, A. *et al.* (2000) Caricaturing facial expressions, *Cognition*, 76: 105–46.

Cantalupo, C. and Hopkins, W. (2001) Asymmetric Broca's areas in great apes, *Nature*, November.

Capps, L., Sigman, M. and Mundy, P. (1994) Attachment security in children with autism, *Development and Psychopathology*, 6: 249–61.

Cassidy, J. and Shaver, P.R. (eds) (1999) *Handbook of Attachment: Theory, Research and Clinical Application*. New York: The Guilford Press.

Child Maltreatment (1999) Reports to the National Child Abuse and Neglect Data System (see www.acf.dhhs.gov/progams/cb/publications/cm99/index.htm).

Chiron, C., Jambaque, I., Nabbout, R., Lounes, R., Syrota, A. and Dulac, O. (1996) The right brain hemisphere is dominant in human infants, *Brain*, 119(5): 1617–25.

Chisholm, K., Carter, M.C., Ames, E.W. and Morison, S.J. (1995) Attachment security and indiscriminately friendly behaviour in children adopted from Romanian orphanages, *Development and Psychopathology*, 7: 283–94.

Clancier, A. and Kalmanovitch, J. (1987) *Winnicott and Paradox*. London: Tavistock.

Coplan, J.D., Trost, R.C., Owens, M.J. *et al.* (1998) Cerebrospinal fluid concentrations of somatostatin and biogenic amines in grown primates reared by mothers exposed to manipulated foraging conditions, *Archives of General Psychiatry*, 55: 473–7.

Courchesne, E., Chism, H. and Townsend, J. (1994) Neural activity: dependent brain changes in development – implications for psychopathology, *Development and Psychopathology*, 6: 697–72.

Cox, M.W. and Howarth, C. (1989) The human figure drawings of normal children and those with severe learning difficulties, *British Journal of Developmental Psychology*, 7: 333–9.

Crandell, L., Fitzgerald, H. and Whipple, H. (1997) Dyadic synchrony in parent-child interactions: a link with maternal representations of attachment relationships, *Infant Mental Health Journal*, 18(3): 247–64.

Crawford, N. (1986) *Power and Powerlessness in Organizations*, Tavistock Clinic Paper No. 52. London: Tavistock Clinic.

Crittenden, P. (1997) Toward an integrative theory of trauma: a dynamic-maturation approach, in D. Cicchetti and S. Toth (eds) *The Rochester Symposium on Developmental Psychopathology*, vol. 10, pp. 34–84. Rochester, NY: University of Rochester Press.

Crittenden, P. (2000) Dispositional representations of violence. Paper presented at the 'Actualities and Representations of Violence' symposium, 43rd Congress of the Swiss Infant and Adolescent Psychiatry and Psychotherapy Society, Laussane, Switzerland, April.

Crockenberg, S.B. and Smith, P. (1982) Antecedents of mother-infant interaction and infant irritability in the first three months of life, *Infant Behaviour and Development*, 5: 105–19.

Dale, P., Green, R. and Fellows, R. (2002) *What Really Happened? Child Protection Case Management of Infants with Serious Injuries and Discrepant Parental Explanations*. London: NSPCC.

Damasio, A.R. (1994) *Descarte's Error*. London: PaperMac.

Damasio, A.R. (1998) Emotion in the perspective of an integrated nervous system, *Brain Research Reviews*, 26: 83–6.

Damasio, A.R., Grabowski, B., Damasio, H. *et al.* (2000) Subcortical and cortical brain activity during the feeling of self-generated emotions, *Nature Neuroscience*, 3(10): 1049–56.

Dawson, G. (1991) A psychobiological perspective on the early socioemotional development of children with autism, in D. Cicchetti and S. Toth (eds) *Models and Integration*, pp. 207–34. Rochester, NY: University of Rochester Press.

DeMause, L. (1982) *Foundations of Psychohistory*. New York: Creative Roots.

Demetriou, A. (ed.) (1998) Cognitive development: steps en route to developmental cognitive science, *Learning and Instruction: The Journal of the European Association for Research in Learning and Instruction* (special issue), 8(4).

Department of Health (DoH) (1999) *Working Together to Safeguard Children*. London: HMSO (see also www.doh.gov.uk/quality5.htm).

Diamond, A. (1985) Development of the ability to use recall to guide action as indicated by infants' performance on AB, *Child Development*, 44: 28–33.

Diego, M.D., Field, T., Hermandez-Reif, M. (2001) BIS/BAS scores are correlated with frontal EEG asymmetry in intrusive and withdrawn depressed mothers, *Infant Mental Health Journal*, 22(6).

Doctor, R.S., Curtis, D. and Isaacs, G. (1994) Psychiatric morbidity in policemen and the effect of brief psychotherapeutic intervention: a pilot study, *Stress Medicine*, 10: 151–7.

Edhborg, M., Seimyr, L., Lundh, W. and Widstrom, A-M. (2000) Fussy child, difficult parenthood? Comparisons between families with a 'depressed' mother and a non-depressed mother 2 months post-partum, *Journal of Reproductive and Infant Psychology*, 18(3): 225–38.

Eisenbruch, M. (2000) Concepts of perinatal mental disorder, in V. Skultans and J. Cox (eds) *Anthropological Approaches to Psychological Medicine*. London: Jessica Kingsley.

Ekman, P. (1992) Facial expressions of emotion: an old controversy and new findings, *Philosophical Transactions of the Royal Society*, B335: 63–9.

Ekman, P. (1994) Strong evidence for universals in facial expressions, *Psychological Bulletin*, 115: 268–87.

Emde, R. (1985) Assessment of infancy disorders, in M. Rutter and L. Hersov (eds) *Child and Adolescent Psychiatry*. Oxford: Blackwell.

Farroni, T., Johnson, M., Brockbank, M. and Simion, F. (2000) Infants' use of gaze direction to cue attention: the importance of perceived motion, *Visual Cognition*, 7(6): 705–18.

Feldman, R., Greenbaum, C., Yirmiya, N. and Mayes, L.C. (1996) Relations between cyclicity and regulation in mother-infant interaction at 3 and 9 months, and cognition at 2 years, *Journal of Applied Developmental Psychology*, 17: 347–65.

Feldman, R., Greenbaum, C. and Yirmiya, N. (1999) Mother-infant affect synchrony as an antecedent of the emergence of self-control, *Developmental Psychology*, 35(1): 223–31.

Field, T. (1998) Maternal depression effects on infants and early interventions, *Preventative Medicine*, 27: 200–3.

Field, T., Fox, N.A., Pickens, J. and Nawrocki, T. (1995) Right frontal EEG activation in 3–6 month old infants of depressed mothers, *Developmental Psychology*, 31: 358–63.

Fischer, K.W. and Rose, S.P. (1994) Dynamic development of coordination of components in brain and behavior, in K.W. Fischer and G. Dawson (eds) *Human Behavior and the Developing Brain*. New York: Guilford Press.

Fitzgerald, H.E. and Field, T.F. (eds) (1997) Depression, *Infant Mental Health Journal*, 18(4).

Fletcher, P.C. *et al.* (2001) *Responses of Human Frontal Cortex to Surprising Events are Predicted by Formal Associative Learning Theory*. www.neurosci.nature.com.

Fonagy, P. (2000) Plenary address to the International Association of adolescent Psychiatry, San Francisco, January.

Fonagy, P., Steele, M., Steele, H. *et al.* (1991) The capacity for understanding mental states: the reflective self in parent and child and its significance for security of attachment, *Infant Mental Health Journal*, 12: 201–18.

Fonagy, P., Steele, M., Steele, H., Higgitt, A. and Target, M. (1994) Theory and practice of resilience, *Journal of Child Psychology and Psychiatry*, 35: 231–57.

Forde, E.M.E. and Humphreys, G.W. (2000) The role of semantic knowledge and working memory in everyday tasks, *Brain and Cognition*, 44(2): 214–52.

Fox, N., Calkin, S.D. and Bell, M.A. (1994) *Neural Plasticity and Development in the First Two Years of Life: Evidence from Cognitive and Socioemotional Domains of Research*. New York: Cambridge University Press.

Fraiberg, S., Adelson, E. and Shapiro, V. (1975) Ghosts in the nursery: a psychoanalytic approach to the problems of impaired infant-mother relationships, in S. Fraiberg (ed.) *Clinical Studies in Infant Mental Health*. London: Tavistock.

Fraley, C.R. and Shaver, P.R. (1999) Loss and bereavement: attachment theory and recent controversies concerning 'grief work' and the nature of detachment, in P.R. Shaver and J. Cassidy (eds) *Handbook of Attachment: Theory, Research and Clinical Applications*. New York: The Guilford Press.

Frankl, V.E. (1987) *Man's Search for Meaning*. London: Hodder & Stoughton.

Freudigman, K.A. and Thoman, E.B. (1993) Infant sleep during the first post natal day: an opportunity for assessment of vulnerability, *Pediatrics*, 92(3): 373–9.

Frick, J. and Richards, J.E. (2001) Individual differences in infants' recognition of briefly presented visual stimuli, *Infancy*, 2(3): 331–52.

Frost, J.A., Binder, J.R., Springer, J.A. *et al.* (1999) Language processing is strongly left lateralized in both sexes, *Brain*, 122(2): 199–208.

Galvin, M.R., Stilwell, B., Adinamis, A. and Kohn, A. (2001) Conscience sensitive, psychiatric diagnosis of maltreated children and adolescents, *Conscience Works: Theory and Research*, 1: 1–81.

Glaser, D. (2000) Child abuse and neglect and the brain – a review, *Journal of Child Psychology and Psychiatry*, 41(1): 97–116.

Goldschmied, E. and Jackson, S. (1994) *People Under Three – Young Children in Day Care*. London: Routledge (training video also available).

Goleman, D. (1996) *Emotional Intelligence*. London: Bloomsbury.

Goodlin-Jones, B.L., Burnham, M.M., Gaylor, E.E. and Anders, T.F. (2001) Nightwalking, sleep-wake organization and self-soothing in the first year of life, *Journal of Developmental and Bahavioral Pediatrics*, 22: 226–33.

Gopnik, A., Meltzoff, A. and Kuhl, P. (1999) *How Babies Think*. London: Weidenfeld & Nicolson.

Gowen, J.W. (1995) The early development of symbolic play: young children, *Journal of the National Association for the Education of Young Children*, March: 75–84.

Graham, G. (1999) Self-consciousness, psychopathology and realism about self, *Anthropology and Philosophy*, 2(2).

Green, A.H., Voeller, K., Gaines, R. and Kubie, J. (1981) Neurological impairment in maltreated children, *Child Abuse and Neglect*, 5: 129–34.

Greenough, W.T. and Black, J.E. (1992) Induction of brain structure by experience: substrates for cognitive development, in M.R. Gunnar and C.A. Nelson (eds) *Developmental Behaviour Neuroscience*. Hillsdale, NJ: Lawrence Erlbaum.

Guedeney, A. (1997) From early withdrawal reaction to infant depression: a baby alone does not exist, *Infant Mental Health Journal*, 18(4): 329–49.

Harkness, S., Keefer, C.H. and Super, C.M. (1999) Culture and ethnicity, in M. Levine, W. Carey and A. Crocker (eds) *Developmental-Behavioral Pediatrics*, 3rd edn. Philadelphia, PA: W.B. Saunders & Co.

Harris, L.J., Almerigi, J.G. and Kirsch, E.A. (2000) Side preference in adults for holding infants: contributions of sex and handedness in a test of imagination, *Brain and Cognition*, 43: 246–52.

Harris, P.L. (1989) Object permanence in infancy, in A. Slater and J.G. Bremner (eds) *Infant Development*. Hove: Lawrence Erlbaum.

Hart, B. and Risley, T.R. (1995) *Meaningful Experiences in the Everyday Experiences of Young American Children*. Baltimore, MD: Paul H. Brooks.

Hart, S., Field, T. and Roitfarb, M. (1999) Depressed mothers' assessments of their neonates' behaviours, *Infant Mental Health Journal*, 20(2): 200–10.

Heller, S.S. and Zeanah, C.H. (1999) Attachment disturbances in infants born subsequent to perinatal loss: a pilot study, *Infant Mental Health Journal*, 20(2): 188–99.

Hepper, P.G. and Shahidullah, S. (1992) Habituation in normal and Down's syndrome fetuses, *The Quarterly Journal of Experimental Psychology*, 44B(3/3): 305–17.

Hernandez-Reif, M., Field, T., Del Pino, N. and Diego, M. (2000) Less exploring by mouth occurs in newborns of depressed mothers, *Infant Mental Health Journal*, 2(3): 203–10.

Hertenstein, M.J. and Campos, J.J. (2001) Emotion regulation via maternal touch, *Infancy*, 2(4): 549–66.

Hesse, E. (1999) The adult attachment interview, historical and current perspectives, in J. Cassidy and P.R. Shaver (eds) *Handbook of Attachment*. New York: Guilford Press.

Hiscock, H. and Wake, M. (2001) Infant sleep problems and postnatal depressed mothers: a community-based study, *Paediatrics*, 6: 1317–22.

Hoff-Ginsberg, E. (1991) Mother-child conversation in different social classes and communicative settings, *Child Development*, 62: 782–96.

Humphreys, G. (2000) The role of semantic knowledge and working memory in everyday tasks, *Brain and Cognition*, 44: 214–52.

Ito, Y., Teicher, M.H., Glod, C.A. *et al.* (1993) Increased prevalence of electrophysiological abnormalities in children with psychological, physical and sexual abuse, *Journal of Neuropsychiatry and Clinical Neurosciences*, 5: 401–8.

Izard, C.E., Kagan, J. and Zajonc, R. (eds) (1984) *Emotion, Cognition and Behaviour*. Cambridge: Cambridge University Press.

Johnson, S. (2001) Visual development in human infants: Binding features, surfaces and objects, *Visual Cognition*, 8(3/4/5): 565–78.

Johnson, S., Slaughter, V. and Carey, S. (1998) Whose gaze will infants follow? The elicitation of gaze-following in 12-month-olds, *Developmental Science*, 1(2): 233–8.

Jones, N.A., Field, T., Fox, N.A., Davalos, M. and Gomez, C. (2001) EEG during different emotions in 10-month-old infants of depressed mothers, *Journal of Reproductive and Infant Psychology*, 19(4): 294–312.

Kamel, H. and Dockrell, J.E. (2000) Divergent perspectives, multiple meanings: a comparison of caregivers' and observers' interpretations of infant behaviour, *Journal of Reproductive and Infant Psychology*, 18(1): 41–60.

Karen, R. (1998) *Becoming Attached*. Oxford: Oxford University Press.

Kawashima, R., Sugiura, M., Kato, T. *et al.* (1999) The human amygdala plays an important role in gaze monitoring, *Brain*, 122(4): 779–83.

Kihlstrom, J.F., Marchese-Foster, L.A. and Klein, S.B. (1997) Situating the self in interpersonal space, in U. Neisser and D.A. Jopling (eds) *The Conceptual Self in Context*. Cambridge: Cambridge University Press.

Kim, J.J. *et al.* (1999) Direct comparison of the neural substrates of recognition memory for words and faces, *Brain*, 122(6): 1069–83.

Kingstone, A., Kelland Friesen, C. and Gazzaniga, M.S. (2000) Reflexive joint attention depends on lateralized cortical connections, *Psychological Science*, 11(2).

Komada, Y., Yamamoto, Y., Shirakawa, S. and Yamazaki, K. (2001) Is the sleep initiating process affected by psychological factors? *Psychiatry and Clinical Neurosciences*, 55: 177–8.

Korn, M.L. (2001) New findings in molecular biology and memory: the work of Eric Kandel. Paper presented at the American Psychiatric Association Annual Meeting.

Laevers, F. (1996) *A Process Oriented Monitoring System for Young Children*. Leuven: Centre for Experiential Education.

Langridge, D., Connolly, K.J. and Sheeran, P. (2000) Reasons for wanting a child, *Journal of Reproductive and Infant Psychology*, 18(4): 321–38.

LeDoux, J. (1998) *The Emotional Brain*. New York: Simon & Schuster.

Levine, M.D., Carey, W.B. and Crocker, A.C. (1999) *Developmental-Behavioral Pediatrics*, 3rd edn. Philadelphia, PA: W.B. Saunders.

Lis, A. and Zennaro, A. (1997) A semi-structured interview with parents to be during pregnancy, *Infant Mental Health Journal*, 18(3).

Loughlin, B. (1992) Supervision in the face of no cure: working on the edge of the boundary, *Journal of Social Work Science*, 6(2).

Lundy, B., Field, T. and Pickens, J. (1996) Newborns of mothers with depressive symptoms are less expressive, *Infant Behaviour and Development*, 19: 419–24.

Lyons-Ruth, K. (1996) Attachment relationships among children with aggressive behavior problems: the role of disorganized early attachment patterns, *Journal of Consulting and Clinical Psychology*, 64: 32–40.

McCraty, R., Atkinson, M., Tomasino, D. and Tiller, W.I. (1997) The electricity of touch: detection of measurement of cardiac energy exchange between people, in K.H. Pibram and J.S. King (eds) *Brain and Values*. Hillsdale, NJ: Lawrence Erlbaum.

McIntyre, J., Zago, M. and Lacquaniti, F. (2001) Does the brain follow Newton's laws? *Nature Neuroscience*, 4(July): 693–4.

Maclean, L., McDermott, M.R. and May, C.P. (2000) Method of delivery and subjective distress: women's emotional responses to childbirth practices, *Journal of Reproductive and Infant Psychology*, 18(2): 153–62.

MacLean, P. (1990) *The Triune Brain in Evolution*. New York: Plenum Press.

Magnusson, D. (1999) Holistic interactionism: a perspective for research on personality development, in L. Pervin and P.J. Oliver (eds) *Handbook of Personality Theory and Research*, 2nd edn. New York: The Guilford Press.

Main, M. and Kaplan, G.C. (1991) The adult attachment classification system, version 5. Unpublished manuscript, Department of Psychology, University of California.

Marianne, S. De Wolff and Marinus, H. van IJzendoorn (1997) Sensitivity and attachment: a meta-analysis on parental antecedents of infant attachment, *Child Development*, 68(4): 571–91.

Marvin, R.S. and Britner, P.A. (1999) Normative development, in J. Cassidy and P.R. Shaver (eds) *Handbook of Attachment*. New York: The Guilford Press.

Marrone, M. (1998) *Attachment and Interaction*. London: Jessica Kingsley.

Menzies Lyth, I. (1988) The function of social systems as a defence against anxiety, in I. Menzies Lyth (ed.) *Containing Anxiety in Institutions*. London: Free Association Press.

Merzenich, M.M., Recanzone, E.G., Jenkins, W.M., Allart, T.T. and Budo, R.J. (1988) Cortical representational plasticity, in P. Rakic and W. Singer (eds) *Neurobiology of Neocortex*, pp. 41–67. New York: Wiley.

Mesulam, M.M. (1998) From sensation to cognition, *Brain*, 121(6): 1013–52.

Montagu, A. (1994) Interview, *Touch the Future*, Spring.

Moore, M.S. (1990) Understanding children's drawings: developmental and emotional indicators in children's human figure drawings, *Journal of Educational Therapy*, 3(2).

Morris, J.S., Friston, K.J. and Buchel, C. *et al.* (1998) A neuromodulatory role for the human amygdala in processing emotional facial expressions, *Brain*, 121: 47–57.

Muller, H.J., Elliott, M.A., Herrmann, C.S. and Hecklinger, A. (2001) Neural binding of space and time: an introduction, *Journal of Visual Cognition*, 8(3/4/5): 273–85.

Murray, L., Fiori-Cowley, A. Hooper, R. and Cooper, P. (1996) The impact of postnatal depression and associated adversity on early mother-infant interactions and later infant outcomes, *Child Development*, 67(5): 2512–26.

Murray-Parkes, C., Stevenson-Hinde, J. and Marris, P. (1991) *Attachment Across the Life Cycle*. London: Routledge.

NCANDS (National Child Abuse and Neglect Data System) (2000) www.calib.com/nccanch/pubs/factsheets/canstats.cfm.

Neisser, U. and Jopling, D. (eds) (1997) *The Conceptual Self in Context*. Cambridge: Cambridge University Press.

Neville, H.J., Bavelier, D., Corina, D. *et al.* (1998) Cerebral organization of language in deaf and hearing subjects: biological constraints and effects of experience, *Proceedings of the National Academy of Science*, 95: 922–9.

Nichols, M.J. and Newsome, W.T. (1999) The neurobiology of cognition, *Nature*, 402(December).

Norton, K. and Dolan, B. (1995) Acting out the institutional response, *The Journal of Forensic Psychiatry*, 6(2): 317–32.

Nutbrown, C. (1999) *Threads of Thinking*. London: Paul Chapman.

Oates, J. (ed.) (1994) *The Foundations of Child Development*. Buckingham: Open University Press.

O'Hara, M.W. and Swain, A.M. (1996) Rates and risk of postpartum depression, a meta-analysis, *International Review of Psychiatry*, 8: 37–54.

Obholzer, A. (undated) *Institutions: Planning and Reality*, Tavistock Clinic Paper No. 120. London: Tavistock Clinic.

Ornstein, R. (1997) *The Right Mind*. San Diego, CA: Harcourt Brace.

Panksepp, J. (1998) *Affective Neuroscience: The Foundations of Human and Animal Emotions*. New York: Oxford University Press.

Panksepp, J. (2001) The long-term psychobiological consequences of infant emotions: prescriptions for the twenty-first century, *Infant Mental Health Journal*, 22(1–2): 132–73.

Pederson, C. (2001) Posting on www.psychoanalysis.net/JAPA.

Penrose, R. (1990) *The Emperor's New Mind*. London: Vintage.

Perlow, M. (1995) *Understanding Mental Objects*. London: Routledge.

Perry, B. (1994) Sequelae of childhood trauma: post-traumatic stress disorders in children, in M. Murberg (ed.) *Catecholamine Function in Post-Traumatic Stress Disorder: Emerging Concepts*, pp. 253–76. Washington: American Psychiatric Press.

Perry, B. (1999) Memories of fear, in J. Goodwin and R. Attias (eds) *Images of the Body in Trauma*. New York: Basic Books.

Perry, B. (1998) Neuropsychological aspects of anxiety disorders in children, in C.E. Coffey and R.A. Brumback (eds) *Textbook of Pediatric Neuropsychology*. Washington, DC: Psychiatric Press.

Perry, B. (2001) *The Developmental Hot Zone*. www.teacher.scholastic.com/professional/bruceperry/hot_zone.htm.

Perry, B. and Pollard, R. (1998) Homeostasis, stress, trauma and adaptation: a neurodevelopmental view of childhood trauma, *Child and Adolescent Psychiatric Clinics of North America*, 7(1): 35–51.

Perry, B., Pollard, R., Blakley, T., Baker, W. and Vigilante, D. (1995) Childhood trauma, the neurobiology of adaptation and 'use dependent' development of the brain: how states become traits, *Infant Mental Health Journal*, 16(4): 271–91.

Pervin, L.A. and Oliver, P.J. (1999) *Handbook of Personality*. New York: The Guilford Press.

Pianta, R. *et al.* (1989) Results of the mother-child interaction research project, in D. Cicchetti and V. Carlson (eds) *Child Maltreatment*. Cambridge: Cambridge University Press.

Pinker, S. (1998) *How the Mind Works*. London: Penguin.

Pollock, J.J. (1992) Predictors and long-term associations of reported sleeping difficulties in infancy, *Journal of Reproductive and Infant Psychology*, 10: 151–68.

Raths, J. (2001) Teachers' beliefs and teaching beliefs, *Early Childhood Research and Practice*, 3(1).

Reder, P., Duncan, S. and Gray, M. (1993) *Beyond Blame*. London: Routledge.

Rolls, E.T. (2000) Precis of the brain and emotion, *Behavioural and Brain Sciences*, 23: 177–234.

Rose, S., Futerweit, L. and Jankowski, J. (1999) How affect might influence attention, *Child Development*, 70.

Rosenblum, O., Mazet, P. and Benony, H. (1997) Mother and infant affective involvement states and maternal depression, *Infant Mental Health Journal*, 18(4): 350–63.

Rutter, M. and Hersov, L. (eds) (1994) Assessment of infancy disorders, in M. Rutter, E. Taylor and L. Hersov (eds) *Child and Adolescent Psychiatry: Modern Approaches*. Oxford: Blackwell.

Sadeh, A., Dark, I. and Vohr, B.R. (1996) Newborns' sleep wake patterns: the role of maternal, delivery and infant factors, *Early Human Development*, 44: 113–26.

Sam, M., Vora, S. and Malnic, B. *et al.* (2001) Odorants may arouse instinctive behaviours, *Nature*, 12(July).

Sameroff, A.J. (2000) *Study Guide for ED209 Course: Child Development*. Milton Keynes: Open University.

Schiffer, F. (2000) Hemispheres and distinct personalities, *Journal of Trauma and Dissociation*, 1: 83–104.

Schneider-Rosen, K. (1990) The development and reorganisation of attachment relationships, in M. Greenberg, D. Cicchetti and M.E. Cummings (eds) *Attachment in the Preschool Years*. Chicago: University of Chicago Press.

Schonkoff, J.P. and Phillips, D.A. (eds) (2000) *From Neurons to Neighborhoods: The Science of Early Child Development*. Washington: National Academy Press.

Schore, A.N. (2000) Attachment and the regulation of the right brain, *Attachment and Human Development*, 2(1).

Schore, A.N. (2001) The effects of a secure attachment relationship on right brain development, affect regulation and infant mental health, *Infant Mental Health Journal*, 22(1–2).

Schuetze, P. and Zeskind, P.S. (2001) Relations between women's depressive symptoms and perceptions of infant distress signals varying in pitch, *Infancy*, 2(4): 483–99.

Schwarz, E.D. and Perry, B.D. (1994) The post-traumatic response in children and adolescents, *Psychiatric Clinics of North America*, 17(2): 311–26.

Schwartz, G.E. and Russek, L.G. (1997) Do all dynamical systems have memory? Implications of the systemic memory hypothesis for science and society, in K.H. Pibram and J.S. King (eds) *Brain and Values*. Hillsdale, NJ: Lawrence Erlbaum.

Seeley, Murray and Cooper (1996) The Cambridge case notes study, *The Health Visitor*, 69: 129–38.

Shahidullah and Hepper (1992) Hearing in the fetus: prenatal detection of deafness, *International Journal of Prenatal and Perinatal Studies*, 4(3&4): 235–40.

Shammi, P. and Stuss, D.T. (1999) Humour appreciation: a role of the right frontal lobe, *Brain*, 122(4): 657–66.

Shaw, D.S. and Vondra, J.I. (1995) Infant attachment security and maternal predictors of early behavior problems: a longitudinal study of low-income families, *Journal of Abnormal Child Psychology*, 23: 335–57.

Shaw, D.S., Owns, E.B., Vondra, J.I. *et al.* (1997) Early risk factors and pathways in the development of early disruptive behavior problems, *Development and Psychopathology*, 8: 679–700.

Shaywitz, B.A., Shaywitz, S.E., Pugh, K.R. *et al.* (1995) Sex differences in the functional organization of the brain for language, *Nature*, 373: 607–9.

Siddiqui, A., Hagglof, B. and Eisemann, M. (2000) Own memories of upbringing as a determinant of prenatal attachment in expectant women, *Journal of Reproductive and Infant Psychology*, 18(1): 67–74.

Sigman, M., Cohen, S.E. and Beckwith, L. (1997) Why does infant attention predict adolescent intelligence? *Infant Behaviour and Development*, 20: 133–40.

Singer, J.L. (1994) Imaginative play and adaptive development, in J. Goldsein (ed.) *Toys, Play and Child Development*. New York: Cambridge University Press.

Slade, A. (1999) Individual psychotherapy: an attachment perspective, in J. Cassidy and P.R. Shaver (eds) *The Handbook of Attachment*. New York: The Guilford Press.

Slater, A. and Kirby, R. (1998) Innate and learned perceptual abilities in the newborn infant, *Experimental Brain Research* (abstract), 123(1/2): 90–4.

Sorce, C., Emde, R.N., Campos, J. and Klinnert, M.D. (1983) Maternal emotional signalling: its effect on the visual cliff behaviour of 1-year-olds, *Developmental Psychology*, 23: 195–200.

St George, M., Kutas, M., Martinez, A. and Sereno, M.I. (1999) Semantic integration in reading: engagement of the right hemisphere during discourse processing, *Brain*, 122(7): 1317–25.

Stapp, H.P. (1998) Pragmatic approach to consciousness, in K.H. Pibram (ed.) *Brain and Values*. London: Lawrence Erlbaum.

Stein, T. (1999) Common issues in feeding, in M.D. Levine, W.B. Carey and A.C. Crocker (eds) *Developmental-Behavioural Paediatrics*, 3rd edn. Philadelphia, PA: W.B. Saunders.

Stern, D.N. (1985) *The Interpersonal World of the Infant*. New York: Basic Books.

Strathearn, L., Gray, P.H., O'Callaghan, M.J. and Wood, D.O. (2001) Childhood neglect and cognitive development in extremely low birth weight infants: a prospective study, *Pediatrics*, 108(1): 143–51.

Stroufe, L.A. (1981) *Infant Caregiver Attachment and Patterns of Adaptations in Preschool: The Roots of Maladaptation and Competence*. London: Tavistock.

Stroufe, L.A. (1997) *Emotional Development*. Cambridge: Cambridge University Press.

Tronick, E. and Cohn, J. (1989) Infant-mother face-to-face interaction: age and gender differences in coordination and mis-coordination, *Child Development*, 59: 85–92.

Troutman, B. and Cutrona, C. (1990) Nonpsychotic postpartum depression among adolescent mothers, *Journal of Abnormal Psychology*, 99: 69–78.

Trowell, J. and Bower, M. (1995) *The Emotional Needs of Children and Young Families*. London: Routledge.

van der Kolk, B.A. (1994) The body keeps the score: memory and the emerging psychobiology of post-traumatic stress, *Harvard Review of Psychiatry*, 7: 253–65.

Veddovi, M., Kenny, D.T., Gibson, F., Bowen, J. and Starte, D. (2001) The relationship between depressive symptoms following premature birth: mothers' coping style and knowledge of infant development, *Journal of Reproductive and Infant Psychology*, 19(4): 313–23.

Verrier, N.N. (1993) *The Primal Wound*. Ringoes, NJ: Tapestry Books.

Ward, M.J. and Carlson, E.A. (1995) Associations among adult attachment representations, maternal sensitivity and infant-mother attachment in a sample of adolescent mothers, *Child Development*, 66: 69–79.

Weiss, R.S. (1991) The attachment bond in childhood and adulthood, in C. Murray-parkes, J. Stevenson-Hinde and P. Marris (eds) *Attachment Across the Life Cycle*. London: Routledge.

Wessel, M. (1963) The prenatal pediatric visit, *Paediatrics*, November.

Wessel, M. (1987) *Parents' Book for Raising a Healthy Child*. New York: Ballantine Books.

Wessel, M. (1989) Men's symptoms during pregnancy, *New York Times*, 23 July.

Wessel, M., Cobb, J.C., Jackson, E.G. *et al.* (1954) Paroxysmal fussing in infancy, sometimes called 'colic', *Pediatrics*, 14: 421–34.

Whiffen, V. and Gottlib, I. (1989) Infants of postpartum depressed mothers: temperament and cognitive status, *Journal of Abnormal Psychology*, 98: 274–79.

Winnicott, D.W. (1957) *Mother and Child: A Primer of First Relationships*. New York: Basic Books.

Winnicott, D.W. (1963) The development of the capacity for concern, *Bulletin of the Meninger Clinic*, 27: 167–76.

Winnicott, D.W. (1964) *The Child, the Family and the Outside World*. Harmondsworth: Penguin.

Winnicott, D.W. (1965) *Maturational Processes and the Facilitating Environment*. New York: International Universities Press.

Winston, J.S., Strange, B.A., O'Doherty, J. and Dolan, R.J. (2002) Automatic and intentional brain responses during evaluation of trustworthiness of faces, *Nature Neuroscience*, 5(3): 277–83.

Wolke, D. (2000) Disturbed attachment, behavioural strategies, breastfeeding and sleeping difficulties, *AIMH Newsletter*, 2(1).

Yufik, Y.M. (1998) Virtual associative networks, in K.H. Probram (ed.) *Brain and Values*. London: Lawrence Erlbaum.

Zafrana, M. (2000) *Preschool Education: The Golden Age of Humanity*. Thessaloniki: University of Thessaloniki.

Zelkowitz, P. and Milet, T.H. (1997) Stress and support as related to postpartum paternal mental health and perceptions of the infant, *Infant Mental Health Journal*, 18(4): 424–35.

Zuckerman, B., Als, H., Bauchner, H., Parker, S. and Cabral, H. (1990) Maternal depressive symptoms during pregnancy and newborn irritability, *Developmental and Behavioural Pediatrics*, 11: 190–4.

Zuravin, S.J. (1999) Child neglect: a review of definitions and measurement research, in H. Dubowitz (ed.) *Neglected Children: Research, Practice and Policy*. Thousands Oaks, CA: Sage.

INDEX